▼▼▼▼▼▼▼▼▼▼▼▼▼▼▼▼

TEACHING

Your College Experience

CONCISE EDITION
by Jewler and Gardner
with McCarthy

A GUIDE FOR INSTRUCTORS

ARTHUR J. ACTON
Vice President, Academic Affairs
Chatham College

WILLIAM C. HARTEL
Professor of History
Marietta College

STEPHEN W. SCHWARTZ
Dean, McDonough Center for
Leadership and Business
Marietta College

Wadsworth Publishing Company
Belmont, California
A Division of Wadsworth, Inc.

To Mary Ann, Barbara, and Beverly
for their patience and support
in our efforts

The Freshman Year Experience is a servicemark of the University of South Carolina. A license may be granted upon written request to use the term The Freshman Year Experience in association with educational programmatic approaches to enhance the freshman year. This license is not transferable and does not apply to the use of the servicemark in any other programs or on any other literature without the written approval of the University of South Carolina.

The Mini-College activity on pp. 29–31 is adapted from J. William Pfeiffer and John E. Jones (Eds.), A Handbook of Structured Experiences for Human Relations Training, Vol. II (San Diego, CA: Pfeiffer & Company, 1974). Used with permission.

Printed in the United States of America

1 2 3 4 5 6 7 8 9 10—97 96 95 94 93

ISBN 0-534-19964-X

▼▼▼▼▼▼▼▼▼▼▼▼▼▼▼▼▼▼▼▼▼▼▼▼▼

Contents

PART

1

▼▼▼▼▼▼▼▼▼▼▼▼▼▼▼▼

Planning and Teaching a Successful First-Year Experience Seminar

CHAPTER 1 ▼▼▼▼▼▼▼▼▼▼▼▼▼▼▼▼▼▼▼▼▼▼▼

Introduction

HOW TO USE THIS MANUAL

This manual is divided into three major parts and offers something for every instructor. How much you use each part will depend in large measure on you—who you are, what you need from an instructor's manual, and where you and your institution are in the process of creating, implementing, or modifying a first-year experience seminar.

Differences in the Concise Edition

This instructor's manual, designed specifically for instructors using *Your College Experience: Concise Edition,* is very similar to the original *Guide for Instructors* that accompanied the original text. It has been modified to incorporate the changes in chapter structure that occur in the concise edition; to make allowance for instructors who want additional readings for their course; and to serve those who want to address an audience made up of nontraditional students.

Instructors who plan a traditional three-credit course will find that the shorter version of the text and manual opens up a number of options. They can choose to cover the material more slowly and spend more time on each subject; they can spend more time on experiential activities and exercises (which involve students more but tend to require more time); or they can choose to expand the special topic or theme and include some supplemental readings or text. A frequent theme in first-year experience courses is "coming of age" or "life transitions." Many autobiographies lend themselves to reflective discussions on the transition to adulthood, for traditional students, or on the return or entry into college, for nontraditional students. Books that can be successfully used to develop this theme include Russell Baker's *Growing Up,* Maya Angelou's *I Know Why the Caged Bird Sings,* and Jill Kerr Conway's *The Road from Coorain.*

Using Different Parts of the Manual

If you are a seasoned instructor or administrator of a first-year experience course, you will find much in this introduction that is familiar to you, and you may wish to only skim Part 1. You should find Part 2 of more immediate and pragmatic benefit. It examines the student text chapter by chapter, providing you with general suggestions on how to teach each chapter. The relationship of the specific chapter to the rest of the text is explained, and chapter instructional goals, a detailed elaboration of the teaching objectives, a list of questions students typically ask, and some tips on teaching the chapter are provided. Part 3 offers useful supplemental resources and support services that even the most experienced instructor should find helpful.

If you are a first-time instructor in an established program, the manual will serve you well as an introduction and as a support as you proceed through the course. Part 1 provides you with background on the history and scope of the national Freshman Year Experience$_{SM}$ movement. It also helps you understand why certain elements are included in your program and enables you to ask thoughtful questions of the other instructors and your program coordinators. Part 1 also provides suggestions for the organization, content, and instruction of your class. The degree to which you implement these suggestions will depend on the latitude you have to personalize the content or delivery of your class.

Part 1 provides an overview of the whole course and the basic details of design and implementation, including (a) four different detailed syllabi, (b) descriptions of the features of successful seminars, (c) tips on getting started, (d) specific suggestions on how to use the textbook, and (e) strategies for building support for your program. Parts 2 and 3, as we've mentioned, give you the practical detail and the additional resources you will need to run your course.

If you are just starting or are about to start a first-year experience seminar, this manual should provide all you need to begin. It is designed to guide you step by step through the process of creating a first-year seminar. Whether you are planning your program as an individual or as a group, the manual provides you with a variety of organizational models from which to choose and a myriad of specific suggestions for using the text. If you need more information, you'll find the additional references and readings provided in the bibliography in Part 3 to be especially valuable. Finally, personalized assistance is as near as your phone. You may contact any one of us directly: Art Acton, Chatham College, Pittsburgh, PA, (412) 365-1155; Bill Hartel, Marietta College, Marietta, Ohio, (614) 374-4798; and Steve Schwartz, Marietta College, Marietta, Ohio, (614) 374-4760. We are all experienced teachers of the first-year experience seminar and will be happy to provide any advice you need.

GOALS OF THE PROGRAM

The fact that you have picked up this manual and have read this far indicates that you have at least a passing interest in a course specifically designed for first-year students. You and your institution already may be wrestling with a number of issues that can be directly related to the first-year experience, such as retention, new student orientation, and study skills instruction. The reasons for establishing a course for entering students are as varied as the institutions that have established them, but generally the factors at the root of the movement were identified in 1986 by John Gardner of the University of South Carolina (and are adapted here):

1. **Altruism:** There are still many in academe who *genuinely* care for first-year students.

2. **Financial pressures:** Declining enrollments of traditional-age students, increasing competition for the available pool of students, and concerns for job security have produced an environment in which leaders and institutions must learn to care more about entering students if they are to survive.

3. **Educational deficiencies:** Many high school graduates are poorly prepared to meet the challenges of college; hence, there is an increasing need to remedy these deficiencies in the freshman year. The President's National Commission on Excellence in Education in 1983–1984 was particularly successful in focusing attention on this issue.

4. **Aging faculty:** Because the professorate in American higher education is aging, there is increasing need for development of new faculty. Many of The Freshman Year Experience_SM enhancement programs have strong faculty development components. Because faculty are now advancing in years, more are tenured and full professors who politically can afford to focus more on freshman issues without the fear that to do so will impede their career advancement.

5. **Declining enrollments:** The decline of enrollment in the liberal arts and education has had particular impact on faculty in those areas, who, if they are to keep their jobs, must find new markets, ventures, and enrollments, such as those found in first-year experience seminars.

6. **Consumer rights:** Across the country, greater attention is being paid to the rights of consumers, who must learn their options, rights, obligations, privileges, and responsibilities in an increasingly complex marketplace (if only to prevent institutions from being sued themselves for failing to meet the rights of their own consumers). The first-year experience seminar is a natural vehicle for this kind of instruction.

7. **First-year experience seminar revival:** A revival of first-year experience seminars is taking place, spurred by the efforts of some scholarly academic revivalists, such as Lee Noel, formerly of The American College Testing Service; John Whiteley, University of California at Irvine; Alexander Astin, University of California at Los Angeles; and John Gardner, University of South Carolina.

8. **Competition:** Because the competition for students has been increasing, more attention and focus has been directed toward their needs. There is now more study of students and more efforts to understand them better.

9. **Declining revenues:** Declining revenues have led some institutions to reduce freshman enrollment by raising standards; therefore, the overall quality of the freshman class at many institutions has increased. Recruiting such students is expensive; thus institutions are highly motivated to keep these freshmen they have worked so hard to recruit.

10. **Compliance agreements:** A number of states are legally required under federal desegregation compliance agreements to see that their states' institutions of higher learning recruit and retain certain types of students. Some of these students may not come with all the necessary

skills to succeed in college. The first-year experience seminar is one way to teach them those skills.

11. **The "new" freshman:** There has been a dramatic change in the profile of a first-year student. More are nontraditional, older, wiser, working, married, assertive, part-time, demanding, and less like their instructors were when they were first-year students (Gardner, 1986).

Among the eleven factors listed above, you will probably find all or most of those that motivate your interest in establishing or considering the establishment of a first-year student program. The factors you identified as the motivation for your course should determine the goals for the course. Similarly, the goals, content, outcomes, and evaluation of the course should all be related.

If you have clearly identified why you are interested in creating a first-year experience seminar, you are well on your way to defining the specific goals for your program. Sometimes you may have one major goal, such as increasing retention, but other positive results may occur as a fortuitous by-product. University 101 at the University of South Carolina identified fifteen additional by-products of the seminar that also could be defined as specific goals for your program (Gardner, 1986):

1. Providing an extended orientation—what colleges and universities call "continuing orientation."
2. Introducing students to higher education as a discipline per se.
3. Teaching academic survival skills.
4. Improving attitudes toward faculty and the teaching/learning process.
5. Providing a support group and a sense of community.
6. Providing a mentor or significant other.
7. Teaching and requiring the use of the institution's support services.
8. Making friends.
9. Providing career counseling and assistance in making decisions about majors, especially for undecided students.
10. Getting involved in the life at the school outside the classroom.
11. Improving compliance with desegregation mandates by promoting persistence of minority students.
12. Making first-year students feel significant.
13. Generating enthusiasm for the institution.
14. Exploring the cultural life of the school.
15. Making students more informed consumers of the opportunities and requirements of their education in their institution.

A BRIEF HISTORY OF FIRST-YEAR EXPERIENCE SEMINARS AND THE FRESHMAN YEAR EXPERIENCE_SM MOVEMENT

The Origins of the Movement, 1900–1960

The first-year experience course concept dates from the nineteenth century. In 1888 Boston University established the first freshman orientation course. Reed College in Portland, Oregon, offered the first orientation course for credit in 1911 (Fitts & Swift, 1924, in Gordon, 1989). By 1926 eighty-two colleges or universities offered first-year experience courses for credit (Brubacher & Rudy, 1958, in Gordon, 1989).

Credit and noncredit orientation courses for entering students proliferated in the years between the wars. The courses of that period were surprisingly similar in form and content to the seminars of today. Among the most frequent topics included were study skills; the history and tradition of the college; life and activities at college; the curriculum; religion, ethics, and morals; use of the library; the college administration; time management; college problems in general; and the purpose of a college education (Gordon, 1989).

The Revival of First-Year Experience Programs

Entering student orientation programs declined after World War II, and it could be claimed that by the mid-1960s the orientation course was nearly obsolete (Gordon, 1989). The 1970s saw the revival of the first-year experience course in response to a generation of "new students"—older adults, first-generation students, and less academically prepared students (Cross, 1971, in Gordon, 1989). The University of South Carolina and other institutions founded their programs in reaction to the student unrest that disrupted campus life. The University of South Carolina's seminar, University 101, was established to create a more positive attitude among the students toward the university and to improve student retention (Gardner, 1986).

This revival, begun in the early 1970s, has become an international movement. By the 1980s concern about what happens in the first year had risen to prominence in the eyes of American educators. The American Council on Education report, *Campus Trends, 1988*, indicated that nine out of ten colleges and universities had recently completed or were in the midst of curriculum change. Among the major changes, 59 percent of the institutions indicated they were putting a greater emphasis on the first year. This reiterated the findings of the National Institute of Education 1984 report, *Involvement in Learning*, which stated that six of ten institutions reported a greater emphasis on the first year.

That educators are concerned is also evidenced by the response to the national conferences on The Freshman Year Experience$_{SM}$ hosted by the University of South Carolina. What began in February 1982—when fewer than 200 people attended the first conference in Columbia, South Carolina—has grown dramatically. In 1989–1990 more than 2,200 educators attended six national, regional, and international meetings on The Freshman Year Experience$_{SM}$.

Planning Your Course: Asking the Questions

As you contemplate establishing a first-year experience seminar, you will quickly become aware of a number of basic questions you must answer almost immediately. These are the questions that every instructor or program director before you has had to answer, and they have been around as long as there have been first-year programs.

The first questions to be answered are:

1. How long should the course be?
2. Should the course be for credit and, if so, how many credits?
3. Should the course be letter graded or pass/fail?
4. Should the course be required of all entering students?
5. Should a separate seminar be designed for students who are non-traditional and/or commuter students?
6. What should the course be called?
7. Who should be in charge of the course?
8. Where should the course be housed?
9. Who should teach the course?
10. How should teachers be prepared?
11. How closely should multiple sections be coordinated?
12. How can you use other students to work with freshmen?

There are no simple answers to these questions. Many different models of first-year orientation seminars have been developed, and almost everything has been tried somewhere. We can recommend some approaches, however, as likely to work best.

Designing a Course

As early as 1924, Fitts and Swift outlined some of the basic issues associated with designing a course. They identified the following questions (Gordon, 1989):

► What constitutes a fitting title or name?

► In which department should such a course be taught?

► Who should direct the course?

► Which methods of instruction should be used?

► What instructional personnel should assist with the course?

► What is the place of an orientation course in the college curriculum?

► What textbooks, syllabi, and supplementary reading should be used?

QUESTIONS AND ANSWERS

Q: How long should the course be?
A: A full term.

A seminar course for the full length of the term provides a wide range of topics and enables instructors to discuss those topics at the times in the term when they are most needed. The material thus will be more immediately relevant to the students.

A full-term course also provides students with continuing support throughout the term. This reduces the risk of attrition—not only in the early critical weeks but also during other stressful times, like midterm.

A term-long course also strengthens the student–faculty relationship. The instructor can monitor the student's progress during the entire term. The extended relationship also increases the probability of the student and the faculty member developing a mentoring relationship in which the instructor becomes that "adult significant other" so critical in improving student retention.

A term course incorporating group-building strategies creates a sense of belonging to a group—and hence to the institution—for the student. This "peer bonding" aids in the adjustment process and also contributes to retention (Cuseo, 1991). (For further discussion of group building see Chapter 3.)

Q: Should the course be for credit?
A: Yes!

Academic credit makes students take the course seriously; it is the ultimate motivator and legitimizer. "Without such official recognition by the institution," according to Gordon and Grites (1984), "neither the student nor the instructor can maintain the levels of motivation and interest necessary for the course to achieve its intended outcomes." Gardner (1986) adds, "Academic credit is a necessity for the ultimate institutionalization of these courses because credit is the grand legitimizer in American higher education." Awarding credit also reduces student perception that the course is primarily remedial (Cuseo, 1991).

Q: How many credits should the course be?
A: Three.
The first-year experience seminar should be the same number of credits as other typical first-year courses, such as English composition, history, or psychology. At most institutions this means 3 credits. To give the course fewer credits reduces its significance to the student and the instructor. A 1 credit course, for instance, has less impact on the student's GPA and on the instructor's teaching load, demands less time of the student and the instructor, and overall is taken less seriously. If credit is the grand legitimizer, equal credit gives equal legitimacy.

Q: Should the course be letter graded or pass/fail?
A: Graded.
Graded seminars are more likely to be taken seriously by the student. First-year experience seminars, however, are offered both for grades and for pass/fail credit, and each alternative has its advocates.

Those who support the pass/fail format believe it is more compatible with the course objectives of helping students in their transition to college life. It strengthens the socialization aspects of the course and puts the focus on the student rather than on what the student produces. A pass/fail system creates an environment that is nonthreatening and noncompetitive and enables students to get what they want out of the course. If the course is not required, a nonthreatening environment will also encourage weaker students who most need the course to enroll in it. And a pass/fail system facilitates an easier, more relaxed relationship between the student and the instructor/mentor than does a graded course (*Transitions*, 1991).

Those who support a letter-graded course contend that letter grading makes students and faculty take the course more seriously. Competition, these advocates argue, enhances rather than detracts from the course and encourages both students and faculty to perform better.

Both groups acknowledge that a first-year seminar taught as a pass/fail course runs the risk of being perceived as an easy, or a "blow-off," class, although supporters deny that it has to be that way (*Transitions*, 1991).

Q: Should the course be required?
A: No.
Requiring the course for all entering students can diminish the course's effectiveness. Although it can be argued that all students might benefit from a first-year seminar, the course is probably much more useful for some students than for others. In addition, requiring any specific course can modify the student attitude toward the course significantly. Students who self-select the course are more likely to be interested in or value the class and less likely to demonstrate the hostility and resentment that is sometimes evidenced when students are required to take a course. Requiring the course for all students will necessitate a larger number of sections and may overtax your ability to recruit instructional faculty committed to the course.

Even if the course is not a specific college requirement, it ideally should be set up to meet a general education or distribution requirement of some sort rather than being purely elective. This will reinforce its value to students and enable them to include it on their list of completed requirements. Because of the substantial writing component of the first-year seminar, some schools have agreed to count it as a writing course, which is a graduation requirement.

Alternative models have included requiring the course for special populations, such as provisionally admitted students, undecided students, or even leadership students. Sometimes, counseling students at registration encourages particular groups to enroll. Alternatively, if the course is not required, a first-year registration system can be designed that attracts or persuades special categories of students to sign up for the seminar. This is discussed in Chapter 8 of this manual.

A case also can be made for making the course a requirement. In a sense, one function of a first-year seminar is to "naturalize" the students to a new educational culture. If the course familiarizes students with the new environment, provides the tools needed to survive in and contribute to the environment, and asserts the dominant values of that environment, then a significant case can be made for the required course.

The final decision, then, depends on the nature of the course and the institutional resources for offering the course.

Q: Should nontraditional students and/or commuting students be mixed with traditional resident students?
A: It depends.
The answer depends in part upon the objectives of the course and the composition of your student body. Including nontraditional and traditional students in the same seminar can help both groups develop an appreciation for the other's situation and generate stimulating classroom dialogue.

On the other hand, each group has very different needs as first-year students. Creating a peer support network for nontraditional students and a sense of belonging for traditional students may be more important and easier to achieve if classes are formed exclusively from the discrete groups. In general, few problems should result from mixing commuter and resident students in the same seminar except for occasional logistical problems regarding out-of-class group meetings. Commuting students' connections to the institution may be enhanced if they develop close relationships with resident students that will help keep them on campus.

Q: What should the course be called?
A: This varies.
First-year experience seminars have had a wide variety of titles—University 101, College 101, [Name of the College] 101, Freshman Seminar 101, Introduction to Liberal Studies, Introduction to College Life, Psychology of College Adjustment, Becoming a Master Student, the College Experience Seminar, and so on. The title can, of course, create an image and set the tone for the course. The name of any course typically indicates something of its content and, frequently, which office or department is responsible for the course. Titles that are too generic or that imply a nonsubstantive course may reinforce the image in the minds of both students and faculty that it is an easy, or "blow-off," course. Conversely, a title that conveys too pedantic an image or focus may turn students off. Titles are obviously more important if the course is elective and must be "marketed" to students.

Q: Who should be in charge of the course?
A: The faculty.

The faculty must have ultimate ownership of the first-year seminar, but partnerships with Student Affairs colleagues are essential. As Boyer (1987) has noted, active faculty participation as developers and instructors of the orientation seminar is critical for its success and for the success of the first-year experience (Cuseo, 1991).

First-year seminars evoke various reactions from the faculty. Initially, faculty are frequently reluctant converts and tend to be skeptical of courses that originate from student affairs or that emphasize affective experiences and have too little "content." It is, therefore, usually wiser to build the course program from the faculty. This gives the course more academic credibility and more support from the faculty for the program. However, orientation seminars must have the commitment and support of the Student Affairs office. Student Affairs professionals are usually enthusiastic proponents of first-year seminars. Their support should be encouraged from the beginning, and their participation as instructors should be solicited as the program gets going. A faculty–Student Affairs partnership is critical for the success of the course because Student Affairs professionals frequently will be needed to handle certain topics not in the natural domain of faculty, such as sexually transmitted diseases.

Q: Where should the course be housed?
A: With the academic dean.

Colleges and universities are organized by departments and disciplines. Because first-year courses have no specific discipline base, they must find a home and champions outside the traditional structure of the departments. For long-term success the first-year program needs both faculty and administrative leadership and support. Ideally, one or more senior and respected faculty members should play a leadership role in developing and directing the program. In addition, it is important, if not imperative, that a senior-level academic administrator be an enthusiastic supporter of first-year programming if the program is to succeed.

Without a departmental base the program, at the outset, lacks a budget and, more important, staff. Staff must be recruited from the departments. This requires the support of the chief academic officer.

Q: Who should teach the course?
A: Faculty and staff.

Staffing a first-year program can be a challenge. To retain academic credibility, it should initially be created and staffed by the faculty in partnership with Student Affairs professionals. As the program grows, other staff, particularly from Student Affairs, should also be encouraged to teach the course. Staffing the first-year course with the best possible teaching faculty should also contribute significantly to student retention (Cuseo, 1991; National Institute of Education, 1985; Noel et al., 1985). It also can have an important faculty and administrative development effect. For the faculty, it can "increase their sensitivity to the significant personal adjustments which adolescents (and returning adult students) must make upon entering college" (Gordon, 1989). It introduces faculty to alternative teaching strategies and revives enthusiasm for teaching. It can provide development for administrators as well. Many deans, both academic deans and Student Affairs deans, teach this course. It gives Student Affairs administrators a unique opportunity to relate to students in a different way, and it gives them credibility with the faculty as teachers. It also affords Student Affairs staff the chance to learn that faculty are not impersonal ogres. Finally, putting administrators in the classroom again renews their understanding of the faculty members' task.

Q: How should the teachers be prepared?
A: Through a teacher training program.

Faculty training was among the important characteristics of the new generation of first-year seminar courses identified at the 1984 National Conference on The Freshman Year Experience$_{SM}$ (Gordon, 1989). For many programs, including South Carolina's University 101, a faculty training seminar is required. Training seminars are offered regularly at the University of South Carolina as well as at a number of other colleges and universities. Some universities find it more convenient to bring in a consultant or facilitator to run a training seminar for a group of faculty on their own campus. A number of consultants are available through The Freshman Year Experience$_{SM}$ network (see Part 3).

Teacher training is critical for a successful seminar. Most traditionally educated faculty are unfamiliar and uncomfortable with the objectives and strategies of first-year experience seminars. A training seminar informs them of the goals and objectives of a first-year program, provides them with a smorgasbord of ideas to employ in their classes, builds a support network of other faculty and program administrators on and off their campus, and, we hope, makes them converts to and proselytizers for the first-year experience movement.

Q: How closely should multiple sections be coordinated?
A: It depends.

Among first-year seminar organizers there is divergence over whether the seminar should follow a general model but be individualized by the instructor or whether it should be uniform from section to section and instructor to instructor. The arguments for each system can be summarized briefly.

If each instructor is allowed to teach an individually designed course under general guidelines, the result is more variety, greater faculty interest, and more flexibility. Faculty are individualists, and many faculty feel strongly that a course is their own property and should reflect their own interests and talents. They resent lock-step course administration and content. It is, therefore, easier to recruit enthusiastic faculty to teach in the program if they are allowed a wider latitude to design and implement their individual section of the course. Allowing faculty individual autonomy enables them to draw on their own expertise and incorporate it into their course. This gives greater variety for students and permits the course to be designed for special populations. Some experts, in fact, believe that there are significant advantages to designing first-year seminars for specific groups, such as returning adult students, commuters, student athletes, honors students, residence hall students, high-risk students, handicapped students, students in certain majors, undecided students, and even parents of entering students (Gordon, 1989).

Conversely, having all sections follow essentially the same syllabus and do essentially the same activities at the same time has other advantages. From the student point of view, students are more comfortable knowing that demands on each student are the same in every section regardless of the instructor. There is a strong perception of fairness and equity when the number of papers to write, the number of pages to read, and the number of

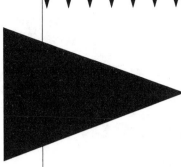

Paraprofessional Teachers

The use of peers as paraprofessional teachers in the classroom has the following advantages:

► Peers may elicit involvement of first-year students more effectively because they are not perceived as intimidating authority figures.

► The peer teachers' involvement (and retention) at the college will be enhanced because of increased contact with a faculty member.

► Peer teachers can be expected to develop higher-level cognitive skills as a result of the teaching experience (Whitman, 1988).

► Peer teachers are a very cost-effective form of student support (Cuseo, 1991).

events to attend are the same for everyone. For the instructor, concurrent assignments and activities facilitate coordination and strengthen mutual support. If, for example, all classes are making a trip to the learning assistance center in the second week, the first-year program director can coordinate arrangements with the director of the center to schedule all the classes. Sometimes multiple sections can be placed in the class schedule at the same time to enable two or more sections to meet together for a special speaker or event. Teachers who are following a coordinated syllabus can meet together regularly to exchange information on the effectiveness of activities and help each other with planning and idea sharing.

Q: How can you use upper-class students to work with freshmen?
A: As peer advisors.
Advanced students are used in several programs in the role of peer counselors, mentors, or advisors. For traditional-aged first-year students in particular, peers can have an important influence. Peer counseling can be arranged in a number of different ways. You can have one or two upper-class "counselors" for the class. Ideally, they should be students who are familiar with the course and perhaps are sitting in on part or all of the class sessions. They should be given credit or recognition of some sort, perhaps on a co-curricular transcript (Cuseo, 1991). A ready-made group of peer advisors can be found in the Residence Assistance staff. Not only can they help in class, but they are also available out of class. If the number of upper-class students is large relative to the number of first-year students, they could even be assigned one on one to entering students. In any event, the upper-class peers should have some training and a clear understanding of their role.

Incorporating the Features of Successful Seminars

GROUP BUILDING

Purpose

The most important first activity for your first-year experience class is becoming a group. Research on student retention clearly indicates that among the most important factors in student persistence is whether students establish a relationship with the institution or, more important, with people at the institution; that is, it is important that they feel like they belong. Among the most important relationships for students are those with their peers. Many students form these relationships quickly through clubs, teams, groups on their dorm floor, or other organizations, but some do not. The first-year course is a structured way for your students to form these relationships—for some of them it will be their first "belonging place." The first step in establishing that sense of belonging is group building—getting them to know each other as individuals and to become comfortable with talking and working with each other, that is, forming a solid, caring group. Creating a sense of belonging on campus can be particularly difficult for nontraditional and commuter students. Assignments that build subgroups and networks outside of the classroom can help strengthen their sense of belonging.

Group building facilitates the functioning of the rest of the term's work. After the students get to know and are comfortable with each other, the discussion and activities inside and outside of class work more effectively. Students are more at ease in expressing their opinions, and the interchange can become much more lively. When students are asked to work together on out-of-class assignments, they will work more effectively with people they are comfortable with.

Group building is not, however, without its dangers, and one of the most perilous occurs when the group—either consciously or unconsciously—decides to freeze a student out of the group. As instructors, we must be on guard and proactive at all times, and if we see someone being excluded, we must take appropriate measures. We must clarify for the entire class—and also for ourselves—the view that group membership does not mean we all like each other. What is important, of course, is that the members recognize themselves as a group and treat each other with respect.

Process

Many activities are available to serve as "ice breakers" to begin building the group. Three commonly used activities are the "Name Chain," the "Ball of String," and the "Interview and Introduction." Do one of these on the first day of class. You may wish to do a second on the second day as well.

Name Chain. The Name Chain is a simple activity in which the students tell something about themselves. The Name Chain works best if the students are formed in a circle so that they can all see each other. The procedure, which you should explain as you begin, is simple. Each person will introduce himself or herself and share some personal information. He or she will then reintroduce the previous two individuals who have spoken and repeat some things about them that he or she remembers.

To begin, explain the rules of the Name Chain and then model the introduction by introducing yourself. Make your introduction reasonably long so that the students find some things with which to identify. This will help them decide what to say about themselves.

You may find that students are very reticent to talk about themselves. Most will probably say only one or two sentences about themselves. You may need to prompt the first two or three students to make sure that they understand what they are to do. Occasionally you may have to intervene to help people with names and to keep the activity on track.

There are numerous variations on this activity. You can simplify it by asking only that they repeat the first name of the previous two individuals, or you can make it more difficult by asking them to repeat the first names of all the people before them. This latter variation will help everyone learn everyone else's first name quickly. When the last student is done, the groups will probably insist that you complete the circle by taking another turn. Be prepared!

If you have about twenty students in your class, this activity should take from 20 to 50 minutes, depending on the volubility of the group.

Ball of String. The Ball of String activity is a variation of the Name Chain. Follow the procedure described for the Name Chain with the entire group sitting or standing in a circle. Instead of going around the circle in order, the instructor introduces himself or herself to the class and then throws a very large ball of yarn or string to someone else in the circle while holding the end of the string. The person who catches the ball introduces himself or herself and tosses the ball to someone else while holding onto the string. When the exercise is completed, you should have a net of string connecting everyone in the class. This is a good opportunity to talk about forming connections with people and a "network" of friends. The rest of the exercise is run the same as the Name Chain and takes about the same amount of time.

Interview and Introduction. The Interview and Introduction activity differs in that it pairs students with each other. Each student interviews his or her partner and prepares to introduce that student to the class. (If you have an odd number of students in the class, put three people in one group.) You can suggest the kinds of questions to ask each other. Where are they from? Why did they come to this school? What do they expect to major in? Do they expect to be in any sports or activities? What did they do in high school? How many brothers and sisters do they have? What is their favorite TV show? What books are they currently reading or have they recently completed? Allow 5 to 7 minutes for them to interview each other. Then call on them in pairs to introduce each other to the class. This activity takes between 30 and 50 minutes.

Reflections on Group Building

Many of the activities you do in a first-year experience class will require the students to work together in groups. As the term progresses, you will discover that they have come to know each other well. They will not all become good friends, but most will have one or two close friends from the class. You may see them together on campus or read about them in their journals; this will tell you that your group building has been successful.

Moreover, the group can take on a dynamic quality of its own. Because the students are comfortable talking openly with each other, they may become louder and seemingly more tumultuous than other, more formal, classes. Resist the temptation to try to control their exuberance.

THE JOURNAL

Purpose

*Your College Experience: Strategies for Success, Concise Edition,** includes a journal writing assignment at the end of each chapter or unit within chapters. These assignments help students to develop their writing skills and improve organizational thinking. They also establish rapport and communication with the instructor, provide an outlet to work through feelings and experiences, and serve as a record of the first-term college experience.

Writing. Writing is like riding a bicycle: the more you do, the better you get at it. The more students write, the better they will get at it and the more at ease they will become. For first-year students who frequently have very little to say, the idea is to get them to say something—almost anything. A relatively nonthreatening, nonjudgmental writing activity like journal keeping emphasizes putting words down on paper without fear of being criticized for style, grammar, and other constructs of formal writing. The objective is to unblock and let writing flow. More suggestions on writing are provided in Chapter 5.

Organized Thinking. Putting thoughts down on paper begins the process of organizing thought. As students distill their thoughts into written words, they practice the skill of transforming ideas into written expression. This organizational skill is further developed as students examine what they have written and use it as the basis for additional writing assignments.

Communication. The journal can be the most important mechanism for establishing a connection between the instructor and the student. Among the goals of the first-year experience course is building a relationship between

*From now on abbreviated *YCE.*

Journal: A Personal Record

If you found your home on fire, what's the one item you would carry out to safety? I wouldn't have to think twice. At the bottom of my shirt drawer . . . is a spiral-bound book with a cover of imitation black leather. Embossed on the cover, in faded gold ink, is "1964."

. . .

I feel funny committing this to print now; but there seems no other way to convey how much the book labeled "1964" means to a man now thirty-four. It was half my life ago, and yet because of the book I am there again. When you are seventeen you are too new at things to edit yourself; you put it down as it happened, and let it go at that. Some nights I feel the book is burning itself up in that dresser drawer. My guess is that a grown man could not keep a journal like the one kept by a seventeen-year-old boy. By the time we are adults, we censor ourselves even in our thought processes. In the diary, if something bad happened in my life, I could write: "And the all-time loser loses again," and I would mean it. The next day I would write of cruising along with my friends, and there would not be a hint of despair.

Bob Greene, "American Beat." *Esquire* (November 1981).

the instructor and the student. For success, students need a network of friends and support, including peers and faculty or administrators, that is, a caring adult.

In the journal students can open up to instructors, sharing their past, present, and future. They frequently reveal very personal information that some faculty are uncomfortable with but that can bond the students with their instructor. It is frequently easier for students, in the quiet isolation of their rooms, to put down on paper feelings, thoughts, and opinions they would feel uncomfortable sharing with instructors in the classroom or face to face in the office. Responding to their students' journals gives instructors a chance to reveal themselves as individuals—with likes, dislikes, and interests that humanize them and make them more approachable. In short, the journal can break down the formal barriers that inhibit communication.

An Outlet. For students the journal can be an important outlet to record their thoughts and feelings. For some it replaces the daily diary they have been keeping for years. For others it is a substitute for the conversation after school with Mom, when they unloaded the burdens of the day. For still others it is just an occasion or a mechanism to sit back and reflect on all the strange and wonderful things they are experiencing.

A Personal Record. Although students may find journal writing something of a chore, they will often come to value the product. It becomes a record of

Journal: A Personal Record

When I got up this morning, I started to think about change. We talked in College 101 about how old boyfriend–girlfriend relationships end a lot of the time when one of the persons goes to college. I know it's true, and I thought I accepted the change, but it just occurred to me this morning how much I have changed. That's what is happening to me and Frank. I have changed so much in four months that it's almost scary. In four short months I went from wanting to quit college before I even started, wanting to marry Frank and have his children, to loving college and my independence; wanting to date other guys and go out, and wanting to put my career above all other things; wanting to achieve great success. Maybe this isn't all good, but it can't be all bad either. Life never stops changing. We can't take a break and stop living for even one day. This change isn't always good or for the best, but it is relevant to life.

From a first-year student journal, Marietta College (with permission of the author).

one of the most significant times in their lives and has value as a personal history. The more seriously they take the assignment and the more they put into it, the more they will value the end result. Many students comment months or years later on the pleasure they get from rereading their journal and seeing themselves again as first-year students.

Process

It is important that students take journal assignments seriously. Collect the journals regularly, read them, comment on them, and count them as a significant part of the course grade.

Regularity. Collect the journals reasonably frequently. Once a week is probably optimal. If you collect them more frequently, it becomes an administrative nuisance; if you collect them less frequently, the students will be tempted to write most of the entries at one sitting. Weekly collections also establish a regular dialogue between the student and the instructor. After you collect the journals, don't keep them for long. Return them quickly and regularly. A plan that works well is to collect the journals on Thursday (in Tuesday/Thursday classes) or Friday (in Monday/Wednesday/Friday classes) and return them on the following Monday or Tuesday. This gives you the weekend to read them, and you are still giving prompt feedback.

Format. The most useful format is to require all students to write on the same size 8½" x 11" three-hole punched paper. They should turn in only the days they have just written, not the whole journal. To avoid losing loose sheets of paper, keep an envelope for each student with his or her name clearly marked on the envelope.

Journal: A Personal Record

I went almost alone . . . knowing hardly a soul . . . for the first three months it seemed to me, going around to lectures and meetings as if everyone . . . had friends but me. I was . . . thrilled but desperately lonely. I didn't know which way to turn, how to meet people.

John Reed, class of 1910, on his arrival at Harvard (cited in Goodwin, 1987).

Comments. Try to read all the journals completely. Remember, this is personal writing and open communication. Your comments should be nonjudgmental. No matter how horrible the spelling, punctuation, or grammar, resist the temptation to mark the mechanical errors. That will only stifle the willingness to write.

Also resist the temptation to preach on issues of morality or behavior. For example, if the student writes about a drunken binge and how he or she was sick as a dog afterward, avoid moralizing about the "evils" of drink. You might ask the student if he or she learned anything from the experience. Or perhaps you could relate something about an experience of your own that helps the student see that you can sympathize. Revealing yourself—likes and dislikes, experiences and values—can help establish a personal relationship with the student. One technique that can work well is to ask questions like, How did you feel about that? What did your friends say about your doing that? Asking questions is a particularly good way to get students to write back in the next week's journal and to get a dialogue going.

The journal is a personal communication between you and the student. As such it is built on trust. That trust can only be achieved through a commitment to keep everything that is written in the journal confidential. Students consider the confidentiality of this communication very important. Don't breach that trust. There are exceptions, however, that you should warn them about as you explain the journal to them. If they reveal information about themselves or others that you think may put them or someone else at risk of serious harm, you should make it clear that you will inform whoever is necessary to prevent that from happening.

Beginning the Journal

First Assignment. On the first day of class explain the journal and your expectations as part of the explanation of the class syllabus. For the first week ask your students to write about themselves; they may want to write something about their families, their hobbies, their likes and dislikes, and so on. Journal Entry 1 on p. 20 invites students to tell about themselves.

(text continues on p. 21)

Journal Entry 1
Getting to Know You

Please complete the following:

1. Birthdate.
2. Write ten sentences that best describe you.
3. Write ten sentences that best describe your family.
4. What do you see yourself doing 5 years from now? 10 years?
5. Of all the things you do in your free time, which do you like most? Least?
6. Without mentioning specific names, what are the qualities of people you respect and admire most? Least?
7. What do you and your friends have in common?
8. What are your favorite sports, hobbies, or crafts, if any?
9. What is your favorite TV show? Why?
10. What is the most recent book you read for fun, and what did you like or dislike about it?
11. What is there about you that makes your friends like you?
12. What one thing do you want your instructor to know about you? Why?

Final Journal Paper

The first-year seminar journal comments on the entering student's various relationships at school:

1. Academic
2. Domestic
3. Interpersonal
4. Economic
5. Recreational
6. Historical

In a 2,500-word paper in which you make specific reference to your journal entries, explain and evaluate these relationships, paying particular attention to the transitions you have experienced. In doing so, you might want to take the following into consideration:

► Were the relationships good or bad, beneficial or harmful?
► Were they static and unchanging or dynamic and continuously developing?
► Did they satisfy your expectations, or did they fall short?
► Are you better or worse because of them?
► If they could be improved, how would you want to improve them?
► What part did you play in shaping these relationships? Were you active or passive; did you direct, or were you directed?

In light of this evaluation, write a statement about what you would like these relationships to be a year from now. What specific measures can you take to bring about positive changes to make your college experience more personally rewarding?

Journal: A Personal Record

Thursday is my second day of classes I had on Tuesday so I wasn't as nervous as I was on Tuesday. I knew where my classrooms would be and a couple of people in them. . . . I still feel very new, almost as new as my first day on campus. I still feel shy and quiet. Sometimes unable to talk to people in my classes. . . . I hope I will be able to overcome my shyness.

From a first-year student journal, Waynesburg College (with permission of the author).

Tell your first-year students to plan a time each day to sit down and spend a few minutes recording the events of the day and their reactions to them. Warn them that trying to cram a week's journal writing into one night defeats the purpose of the journal and is usually readily apparent to the instructor.

Be sure to remind your students of the specific journal assignment from the text that they should write on each week. A good time to do that is at the beginning or end of each class meeting when you remind them of their other assignments, or when you collect or return the journals for the week.

Final Journal Paper. An effective summary exercise for the journal is a journal paper that is assigned at the beginning of the term and submitted near the end. The students use their journal as a primary source for this paper. This writing activity encourages them to take the journal writing seriously because they will be using the information later, and a superficial journal is a poor basis for writing a paper. Second, the final paper provides an occasion at the end of the term for them to reflect on all that has happened during the first term. Finally, it asks them to transform their informal journal writing into the formal writing of a term paper, which allows them to practice editing and rewriting skills. A sample of a final journal paper assignment appears on p. 20.

Admittedly, the journal does not "work" for every student. It is only one tool to achieve the course's objectives. Some students remain reticent. Their journals are little more than a litany of the day's events: "I got up; I went to breakfast; I went to history; it was boring; I ate dinner; I went to bed." For others the journal becomes an important part of the first-year experience, a bridge to a new friend—their instructor—and a record of one of the most important periods of their lives.

First-year student journals always have a timeless quality. Each new class records anxiety, excitement, uncertainty, and wonder at their new experiences. Journals provide for the instructor a unique window on the first-year experience, an otherwise unobtainable perspective on what students are thinking and doing. Reading journals reminds instructors that a lot more is going on in student lives than studying for the classes that we faculty think are so important. Old relationships are ending and new ones are being created—with both the opposite sex and the same sex. New involvements are challenging them—sports, fraternities, sororities, and a myriad of activities. Meanwhile, families and friends back home are changing as they try to define this new relationship.

Students should be urged to keep their journals for enjoyment and perspective in future years. Journals will also provide faculty readers with countless valuable insights into students and will be an important faculty/staff development aid.

VALUES CLARIFICATION

Purpose

Virtually all college and university mission statements assert the commitment to help students clarify their personal values. The first-year experience seminar can directly serve that mission. Our society is one of tremendous diversity, and, even in the most homogeneous student body, students bring with them a wide variety of values and perspectives. For first-year students the revelation that their values are not fully shared by everyone else may be eye opening or even shocking. The purpose of values clarification activities is to help the students understand and be able to articulate their own personal values and to learn to tolerate the value differences of others.

Process

Use the values clarification activities provided in this chapter—the Drawbridge exercise and the Kidney Transplant Problem and "Who Stays?" exercises—to help students understand their personal values. Each activity takes about 40 minutes.

Drawbridge Exercise. Begin the activity by dividing the class into small groups. Ask the students to read the story (on p. 23) and individually rank each character's responsibility for the baroness's death. Allow 5 to 7 minutes for this part of the exercise.

Then ask them to get together as a group and reach a group consensus on the characters' responsibility. One person for the group should be designated as a "recorder/reporter." Allow 10 to 15 minutes for this part of the exercise.

Ask each group to report their conclusions and record them in front of the class on the blackboard or a large tablet. From this point you can lead a discussion about the results, keeping in mind that there is no right answer. Many issues will arise for discussion.

Perhaps some groups failed to reach agreement. This can lead to a discussion of group process or decision making. Did some people concede just to reach agreement? Did they decide by voting? Were decisions different because the gender mix of the groups was different?

Did the group make assumptions about the characters that were not specified in the story? Are judgments often made based on unverified assumptions about people? Is the historical context meaningful? Were values different then, and should these characters be judged by a different standard? Can you reach a consensus as a group? Is that important, or can you agree to disagree?

(text continues on p. 27)

Drawbridge Exercise

Read the story below; then follow the instructions at the end of the story.

As he left for a visit to his outlying districts, the jealous baron warned his pretty wife: "Do not leave the castle while I am gone, or I will punish you severely when I return!"

But as the hours passed, the young baroness grew lonely, and despite her husband's warning, decided to visit her lover, who lived in the country-side nearby.

The castle was located on an island in a wide, fast-flowing river, with a drawbridge linking the island and the land at the narrowest point in the river.

"Surely my husband will not return before dawn," she thought, and she ordered her servants to lower the drawbridge and leave it down until she returned.

After spending several pleasant hours with her lover, the baroness returned to the drawbridge, only to find it blocked by a madman wildly waving a long, cruel knife. "Do not attempt to cross this bridge, baroness, or I will kill you," he raved.

Fearing for her life, the baroness returned to her lover and asked him to help.

"Our relationship is only a romantic one," he said. "I will not help."

The baroness then sought out a boatman on the river, explained her plight to him, and asked him to take her across the river in his boat.

"I will do it, but only if you can pay my fee of five marks."

"But I have no money with me!" the baroness protested.

"That is too bad. No money, no ride," the boatman said flatly.

Her fears growing, the baroness ran crying to the home of a friend, and after again explaining the situation, she begged for enough money to pay the boatman his fee.

"If you had not disobeyed your husband, this would not have happened," the friend said. "I will give you no money."

With dawn approaching, and her last resource exhausted, the baroness returned to the bridge in desperation, attempted to cross to the castle, and was slain by the madman.

Directions: In the preceding story, there are six characters. They are (in alphabetical order):

The Baron _____   The Friend _____

The Baroness _____   The Lover _____

The Boatman _____   The Madman _____

Using the list above, rank each character according to how responsible he or she was for the baroness's death. Rank the characters from 1 to 6, with 1 being the most responsible and 6 being the least responsible. Now, work with the other members of your group, and decide as a group on a rank order for the six characters.

Kidney Transplant Problem

Tonight, the Laymen's Board of Review of General Hospital meets to consider applicants for kidney transplants. Each of the patients described below has been evaluated by the medical staff, and it has been determined that each patient will probably die in 3 to 6 weeks without a transplant. The best statistical estimates are that only about five donors will be available during that period. The board must establish a priority list of who will get the kidneys by ranking in order the nine applicants.

1. John Hallbright. Age 41. Married. Two children, a son 12 and a daughter 4. College graduate. Works as an officer in a bank. Wife also employed as an elementary school teacher.

2. Marie Villareal. Age 39. Unmarried. College graduate; holds a Master's in physical therapy. Employed at VA hospital 14 years; is head of Physical and Occupational Therapy treatment center.

3. Pamela Watson. Age 23. Married, no children. College graduate. Teaches social studies and is cheerleader advisor in junior high school. Husband is a teacher in the high school. Medical diagnosis indicates a heart condition that may cause complications in a transplant operation.

4. Avery Smith. Age 51. Married. Three children, daughter 19, sons 17 and 15. High school graduate. Owner and operator of Smith Industries, Inc., a machine shop that employs 150. City councilman for 12 years; member of library board of directors for 6 years.

5. William Work. Age 11. One of seven children of Mr. and Mrs. Ralph Work. Has received a kidney transplant that failed.

6. Walker Red Cloud. Age 22. Ojibwa Indian. At least four children by two wives. Fourth grade education. No occupation.

7. Nancy Adams. Age 34. Divorced. Three children, daughter 7, twin sons 6, all in her custody. Employed as a secretary in a real estate office. Receives no child support from her ex-husband, whose whereabouts are unknown.

8. Mary Parenti. Age 12. IQ 87. Teachers describe her as shy, withdrawn, and inhibited. Family immigrated to New York the year she was born. Family owns restaurant where both parents work.

9. Juan Gonzalez. Age 32. Married, eight children. Migrant worker. Wife and three oldest children also work as migrant workers.

Who Stays?

The Problem

Enrollment has been cut back at this college. As a member of the board, it is your responsibility to rank the students according to who deserves to remain in this college, *number 1* being the most deserving. Each of these students has been enrolled for about 7 weeks. Descriptions of their precollege situations and performances, as well as the circumstances of their college career thus far, are listed.

Factors to Keep in Mind

1. The person's potential, abilities, or capabilities
2. The person's motivation to perform
3. The degree of difficulty in conquering the problems of each individual
4. Whether services are available to help the student overcome his or her problems
5. The outcome of his or her education; how badly each wants to achieve
6. The probability of successful completion of a college education

The Students

Angela: Extremely intelligent; senior class valedictorian; has won awards in the National Science Fair for exhibits; received a full scholarship from a national company to the college of her choice; has much difficulty relating to others on a social basis; has definite plans to major in chemistry; an out-of-state student; is having great difficulties adjusting to dorm life; is homesick.

Albert: An All-State quarterback in high school; plans to play college football on a full scholarship; scored extremely poorly on the college admittance tests although his high school scores were average; has no major; plans to become a coach; poor classroom attendance.

Jill: Ranked in the middle of her graduating class; did fair in high school math; did poorly in high school science; parents pushed her toward her declared major in biology; doing poorly in these college subjects; has good study habits; has high capabilities in English; lives at home; family problems are developing.

Carolyn: A divorced mother with two children; 24 years old; has returned to college to continue her college education after dropping out 6 years earlier; is working and raising her family; commutes; major is a 2-year degree in secretarial sciences; receives financial aid.

Dominique: An exchange student from Venezuela; lives in a men's dorm; visiting our college for one semester; has already earned a degree in his own country; doing very well academically; involved in several campus organizations; self-supported; here to experience our lifestyle; not working toward any particular major.

(continued)

Thomas: Outgoing and well-liked among his peers; poor grades; studied little in high school and has few study skills; undecided major; his parents pay for his education; an in-state student; lives on campus; enjoys the college party life most of all.

Howard: Ranked in the top 5 percent of his graduating class; out-of-state student; lives on campus; came from an influential family in a small town; was "Mr. Popular" in high school; is having a terrible time adjusting to college life; very homesick; grades are dropping as time passes; uninvolved in campus life; has much potential that could be used.

Gina: An accounting major; dropped all but 9 hours of classes; very poor classroom attendance; extremely active in her sorority; poor grades; parents pay for everything; in-town student; lives on campus; her parents donate a scholarship to our college.

Evelyn: She is 63 years old; worked in a day-care center for the past 15 years; prior to that, she was a housewife and mother; is working toward a degree in child psychology; receiving financial aid for returning students over 60; doing well academically.

Karl: Average grades; commutes; works 20 hours a week to pay for his education; is aiming for a degree in engineering; would like to get more involved in activities on campus but does not have the time; high potential in math; a hard worker.

ONLY THE TOP FIVE STUDENTS WILL BE ALLOWED TO REMAIN IN SCHOOL!

Kidney Transplant and Who Stays? Exercises. Begin the activity by dividing the class into small groups. Ask the students to read either the Kidney Transplant story (on p. 24) or the Who Stays story (on pp. 25–26) and individually rank each character according to who gets the transplant or who stays. Allow 5 to 7 minutes for this part of the exercise.

Bring the students together as a group to reach a consensus on their list. One person for the group should be designated as a "recorder/reporter." Allow 10 to 15 minutes for this part of the exercise.

Ask each group to report their conclusions and record them in front of the class on the blackboard or a large tablet. From this point you can lead a discussion about the results, keeping in mind that there is no right answer. Both of these exercises are about making "win–lose" decisions. In the Who Stays exercise, some students will be allowed to stay and some will not; in the other exercise, some will receive a transplant and will probably live, and some will not receive a transplant and will probably die.

You can talk about the process of making decisions. Did the groups establish criteria in advance for making decisions? Can they specify what the criteria are? Help the students to see if there are any identifiable criteria for their choices. Again, how did they reach a consensus? Is it important in this case? Did they make assumptions that were unspecified, assumptions that were perhaps based on stereotyping or generalized entirely from their own experiences?

Reflections on Values Clarification

Although values clarification is an important part of the institution's mission, instructors must walk a fine line between *clarifying* values and *advocating* a position or foisting one on students, especially where controversial issues such as abortion or the death penalty are concerned. The goal should be to help students develop their *own* positions and values, not to have them take on the values and positions of others. America is a complex and diverse society, one in which we all must learn to understand and respect the values and traditions of others.

MAKING CONNECTIONS OUTSIDE THE CLASSROOM

Purpose

Making students more aware of the resources and opportunities that their institution provides and broadening their intellectual and academic experiences are two of the primary objectives of first-year experience courses. These objectives can frequently be met through organized activities that take students beyond the regular framework of the classroom.

Process

Institutional resources can frequently be experienced better than they can be described. Finding places and things, even on a small campus, often can be confusing or intimidating. You can acquaint your students with the resources of your institution in two ways. You can plan a class activity, during class time, that will literally take the students out of the classroom to explore the campus. You could, for example, arrange to take the students on a tour of offices or program areas. On a small campus you could visit the dean of admissions, the registrar, the dean of students, the academic dean, or maybe even the president. At a large university you might want to tour the student center and introduce the people and facilities that are available. An alternate approach is to set up a scavenger hunt that requires them, as teams, to visit various offices to acquire some piece of information and report back to the class.

You can also plan visits to the theater, where a staff member will introduce your class to the theater—stage, props, makeup room, and so on—and provide an introduction to a play. Then you can plan to have the class attend the play. A similar approach can be used for almost any other program, such as music concerts, speakers series, and public forums.

Many first-year seminar programs incorporate a special academic theme —for example, the nature of civic responsibility—that is highlighted through a series of public programs (such as a speakers series) required of all students in the first-year seminar. Either the instructional team or an individual instructor can plan such a program or take advantage of existing ones. Make attendance at some of these events a requirement, and discuss them in class afterward or ask students to write about them in their journals.

A first-year student speakers series can give your program considerable visibility. Funding for such programs is frequently available from outside sources, either public agencies or private donors. A speakers series can also enhance the academic credibility of the seminar. As discussed in Chapter 8 of this manual, the administration appreciates recruitment of an audience for public programs.

Reflections on Out-of-Class Activities

A student once expressed regret about not taking our first-year experience course. "Why?" we asked. "Because they got to go to all those lecture programs," she replied. "But they were open to everyone," we pointed out. "Yes," she admitted, "but they were *required* to go." This exchange illustrates what we in higher education know to be true. When students have requirements, they frequently later recognize that the requirements were "good for them." In some cases a requirement may even change their lives. Some students who had never been to a play before actually became active theatergoers after being required to go.

GETTING STUDENTS INVOLVED

Purpose

Attendance at out-of-classroom activities is one step in getting students involved in the life of the college. Retention literature shows clearly that students who have a sense of being a part of the community or of having some "belonging place" are much more likely to persist. It is possible to help students achieve a sense of belonging by structuring requirements and activities. This requirement can be particularly important for commuter students, who are less likely to feel integrated into the campus community than are residential students. Nontraditional students and students with jobs off campus may have more difficulty with this requirement. But it may be particularly important to find ways to get them involved.

Research has shown that a substantial commitment of time by students to nonacademic activities—even 20 to 30 hours a week—does not adversely affect their grades. These commitments do, however, increase the students' satisfaction with college life. *"More involvement is strongly correlated with higher satisfaction"* (Light, 1990).

Many instructors of first-year seminars believe the easiest way to structure involvement is to require it. They require students to join an organization and attend a specified number of campus events, and they award them points for doing so. If you are averse to mandating group involvement, perhaps you could make it optional for extra credit. In the main text, Chapter 11, *Yourself and Others*, provides exercises and activities to encourage student involvement. You can help by providing information and encouragement. You might take time in class periodically to ask one or more students which organizations they have joined and what they have been doing. Or have them write about their campus involvements for 5 minutes one day.

You should decide in advance what you are going to count as an activity of involvement and be prepared to answer a number of questions about your requirement. Do varsity sports count? Do fraternities? Is there a date by which students must have joined their organizations and attended a specified number of events?

"Making the connections outside the classroom" and "Getting students involved" can be combined by requiring students to attend a number of mixed events: one male and one female athletic event; one student music event; one student government meeting; and so on.

Reflections on Getting Students Involved

Suggesting, encouraging, or requiring involvement not only aids retention but also provides rewards for active students. Giving students credit for involvement conveys the idea that co-curricular activities (for which we do not normally give credit) provide an important form of learning.

Suggesting, encouraging, or requiring attendance at nonacademic events sends the same message and reinforces the idea that being an active member of a community is more than just going to class. Knowing that their classmates are attending an activity and seeing them perform—on the stage, on the playing field, or in the concert hall—also is a positive reinforcer to those who have joined a team or performing group.

THE MINI-COLLEGE

Purpose

A frequently used activity in first-year seminars is the Mini-College. The objective of the activity is for students to create a "mini-college" by preparing course descriptions, selecting the curriculum of the college, and scheduling and offering the courses.

The Mini-College is designed for several purposes: to introduce students to the concept and process of the college curriculum, to have students practice skills in organization and presentation, and to have students demonstrate their expertise in something.

Process

Preparation. The Mini-College has two parts and needs to be performed over several class periods. In Part 1 students create the course descriptions and choose the curriculum. In Part 2 they present their mini-classes. A few days in advance of the Mini-College, the students should prepare course descriptions for 5- to 7-minute "courses" they are able to teach. These descriptions should be similar to ones found in a college catalog. On the day the curriculum committee (made up of selected students in your class) meets, students should submit their course descriptions on 3 × 5 cards. The curriculum committee then meets and selects a number of courses from those cards.

A few days later, Part 2 begins. You will need to decide in advance how many "classes" to schedule. You can usually schedule as many as five or six in a 50-minute class period. If there is a vacant classroom nearby, you might even set up two classes at once so that there is a "schedule" of classes from which students can choose. Most instructors plan on having six to eight students—or about one-third of the class—make presentations. You will have to decide how you will evaluate the student "teachers."

The Curriculum Committee. On the day set for the curriculum activity, select a "curriculum committee" of about five students. (One way to do this in a class of twenty is to count off by fours and take all the number threes.) Arrange a circle of chairs in the middle of the room for the committee. Arrange the rest of the students in a larger circle around the committee. Give the committee the stack of cards with the course descriptions on them, and ask them to select the "curriculum" for the "college." Tell them how many classes you want them to select, but otherwise give them relatively little direction. They may talk among themselves or speak to or ask questions of the rest of the class, but the students in the outer circle may not initiate questions or discussion with the committee. Give the committee about 15 minutes to do their task. Immediately afterward, process the curriculum committee activity, and allow students 2 or 3 days to prepare their classes.

Presentation of Courses. On the day appointed for the Mini-College, the student "teachers" whose courses were selected make their presentations. The topics on which they can present a course should be drawn from the students' interests and need not be academic. Mini-courses have been presented on such varied subjects as fly fishing, drawing the human figure, and fortune telling. They might also be more academic if students choose subjects such as the anatomy of the knee, exercises to strengthen the back, or the periodic table. Inform your students that the subjects they plan to teach must be suited to the classroom environment. That is, they should not plan to teach a unit on "rushing the net" in tennis. They must also be prepared to provide their own props and supplies.

The rest of the students in the seminar are the "students" who attend the Mini-College. If you set up the college with two classes at once, you can have students select a schedule and change classes between periods.

Reflections on the Mini-College

The Mini-College enables the instructor to discuss a variety of subjects. Processing the curriculum committee activity can focus on group decision making—how did the committee members make their decisions, and how do other committees or groups make decisions? Did they establish logical criteria for their selection? Or did they pick and choose the courses arbitrarily? Did you hear comments like, "I like the sound of this course" or "I don't want to teach anything"? In most cases the committee chooses the courses without asking the students in the outer circle anything. Processing can open a discussion on why they didn't solicit information from the prospective "students" or from the "instructors" of the classes. These discussions lead logically to a discussion about your college or university. How did its curriculum get created? How are courses approved? Do students have any input into the decisions? Should they? Do instructors? This can also lead to a more general discussion of the curriculum, the liberal arts, and the goals of higher education.

The Mini-College is usually great fun for the students. The "teachers" enjoy parading their expertise, and the students enjoy the classes. The "teachers" can get a brief perspective on what being on the other side of the desk is like, and the students in the classes can get a new perspective on some of their classmates.

There are many variations on this basic Mini-College format. Some instructors skip the curriculum committee and personally select the students to give the classes; some require all the students to do a class; some require all the students to come *prepared* to give a class; some do the curriculum committee and the Mini-College on the same day. Try different ideas and see which one works with your students.

EVALUATION

Purpose

Program evaluation can serve several purposes. Most commonly it provides the instructor, the instructional team, or the program director with diagnostic feedback on what works and what doesn't. This data can help you to determine how to modify the course. Second, evaluation provides information for institutional decision making. At some institutions first-year seminars can prove controversial or may not be highly valued. In such situations course evaluation or related institutional research can be important to build institutional support for continuance of the course.

Process

Regardless of whether you have a common syllabus or a series of sections taught differently by different instructors, a simple instrument may provide all the information you will need. A sample evaluation instrument is provided on p. 32.

You can modify the evaluation to list the specific activities that you included in your course. After you have administered the evaluation, tabulate the results for all the classes and draw some generalizations for future modifications and planning.

End-of-term evaluations, however, cannot help in the middle of the semester. They will not help you decide what to do next week. "Many faculty members point out that feedback *during* a course when immediate changes and midcourse corrections are still possible, is even more valuable" (Light, 1990). One widely used technique is the 1-minute paper. At the end of a class session take a minute or two and have the students write about the class.

Another means of midcourse evaluation is the journal itself. Ask students to comment on the usefulness of specific classes and on other matters pertaining to the class. Remember, the journal is a major form of feedback.

(text continues on p. 33)

Evaluation

A. 1. What did you understand to be the purpose of the seminar?

   2. Did it achieve its purpose?

B. 1. What do you understand to be the purpose of the journal?

   2. Was keeping a journal of value to you?

C. Did this course help you improve your

   1. Writing skills?

   2. Speaking skills?

D. Listed below are the major activities of the seminar. If you did not attend the activity, write "absent" and go on to the next item. If you did attend, indicate with a "yes" or "no" whether you found the activity beneficial, and explain in what way the activity was or was not beneficial.

   1. Exercises designed to introduce members of the group

   2. Drawbridge exercise

   3. Symposiums

   4. Papers on assigned readings

   5. Presentations on taking essay exams, reading a book, and note taking

   6. Mini-College

   7. Presentation on the Myers-Briggs Type Indicator

   8. Movie "You Pack Your Own Chute"

E. Did you find the college activities you attended (art exhibit, play, and so on) beneficial? If so, in what way?

F. Did the course neglect to cover something you thought was important? If so, what?

The 1-Minute Paper

Patricia Cross, now at the University of California at Berkeley, suggests a simple device called the 1-minute paper. The idea is to conclude a regular class lecture or discussion a minute or two before the end of class time. Then, ask each student to take out a sheet of paper and write down brief answers to two questions:

1. What is the big point you learned today?
2. What is the main unanswered question you leave class with today?

A box is placed on a table near the classroom door, and students simply drop their papers in the box as they leave. The papers are written anonymously for the professor to read after class (Light, 1990).

For the broader objective of institutional effectiveness, you will want to plan a strategy with your director of institutional research. Numerous studies of first-year programs have tested the seminar's impact on retention/persistence, campus involvement, academic success, and so on. The National Resource Center for The Freshman Year Experience$_{SM}$ at the University of South Carolina can provide you with some assistance on how to plan an assessment of the effectiveness of your first-year program.

Reflections on Evaluation

An evaluation research project should be part of your first-year course plan from the beginning. First-year program enthusiasts know the program's positive effect on entering students, have directly seen and experienced its value, and can support their views with a myriad of anecdotal reports. The persuasive function of research, however, is without equal in convincing faculty and administrators of the value of a first-year program. At some colleges the first-year seminar has received more scrutiny and examination than any other program, and the positive results of planned research have enabled it to survive.

CHAPTER 4

Creating the Course

BUILDING A TEAM

First-year experience seminars can be developed and taught by individuals alone. But many successful programs employ some sort of team support system for course development and implementation. Under such a system, a team, composed, for example, of faculty, academic, and student affairs administrators, takes joint responsibility for developing and implementing the course.

A team is particularly helpful for course development. Ideally a first-year program should have someone designated as the director or team leader to call the team together, facilitate discussion, and coordinate services. The team should meet as often as necessary to design the course. Throughout the early discussions, the team should answer any of the unanswered questions from Chapter 2. If the sections are to be closely coordinated, course creation should be the responsibility of the team. If not, the team approach is still beneficial in generating and sharing ideas.

Teamwork should also extend into the term. In some programs the instructors meet as often as once a week to coordinate their efforts and to provide a support system. During these meetings the director can distribute materials, and the instructors can exchange experiences and ideas, coordinate use of campus resources, and modify and amend elements in the syllabus. The director, for example, could distribute copies of the exercises that are going to be used that week and review them. The next week the group could analyze the effectiveness of the exercises, identify any problems, share creative approaches, decide if such exercises should be used in the future, and plan possible improvements. A brief record of the conclusions of these discussions can make the planning for future years much easier.

Finally, the team should meet at the end of the term to evaluate the seminar and do preliminary planning for the next year. Even during the "off season" an instructional team might meet to identify future instructors and plan for the next year's implementation.

A seminar can, of course, literally be team taught. A team, composed of one experienced and one inexperienced instructor, provides an excellent means of "training" a new instructor, particularly if a training program is not available for new faculty. The first-year experience seminar lends itself to a team format. You can enliven the class and keep students' attention by alternating instructors during the class period as you shift topics and activities.

Even if you are designing and teaching your course alone, you can still take advantage of informal "teams." If the course has been offered on campus, start by spending some time talking with instructors who have taught it in the past. Find out what worked for them and what did not, and ask if they will work with you throughout the semester. Ask the program director if he or she is willing to provide you with feedback on your class and to suggest ideas you might try. Plan a support group of new instructors. If you attended a training workshop, get together with a few of the "graduates." You can also build a team of off-campus supporters and experts. Contact the National Resource Center for The Freshman Year Experience_{SM} for the names of faculty with whom you might consult.

DEFINING THE CONTENT

You have your team and are ready to design your course. You have made the major decisions addressed in Chapter 2: Your course has a title; you know how many credits the course is; you know who is teaching the course; and so on. You also have defined, at least to yourself, the main objectives of the course and the principle topics you want to cover. You have read about some elements of successful programs, and you have examined the main text.

Next you must address the specific components you wish to include in your course and methods for evaluating student performance. The type and number of components will be determined by the number of class sessions and the objectives of the course. If you plan a heavy emphasis on study skills and your class meets only ten times in the semester, you will have little time to explore any topics other than study skills. If you wish to address broader issues of values, diversity, and a wide range of student transition experiences, you will have to increase the number of class meetings to accommodate additional activities.

To determine topics, begin with a brainstorming activity in which you list the topics and ideas you would like to cover in the course, for example, test-taking skills, relationships, wellness, or minorities. Prepare another list of the activities you would like to do, for example, visit the library, go to a play, or have a pizza party. Prepare a third list of the required student activities and projects you will use for formal evaluation. Reexamine the text and the syllabi provided in this chapter for ideas.

Use the information provided in Part 2 of this manual to calculate approximately how much class time each topic, exercise, or activity will take. Write the time beside the item on your list. Arrange the topics in the order in which you anticipate teaching them. You can follow the order of the text, or you can arrange them to meet specific needs. Start with enough topics to fill about two-thirds of the class meetings; you can always add more content if there are gaps in your syllabus.

Two notes of advice for your planning: (1) you will probably not be able to cover as much as you anticipate, and (2) your plan should have some flexibility built into it. Things always seem to take longer than you anticipate.

If a class discussion is going well, you will not want to cut it off prematurely. You need to be able to shift topics to other days or possibly even cut sections from the syllabus. The best plan is to build in one or two periods to catch up or have activities planned that you can easily omit if you are running behind. In fairness to your students, try to stick closely to the syllabus for assignments you expect them to complete, but, remember, this is one course in which process is more important than content. There is nothing that absolutely must be covered.

Conversely, always come prepared with an idea and materials for an extra activity in case one you planned fails or takes only a fraction of the time you expected. The times you estimate for exercises in the text may vary considerably, depending on class size, on how talkative the students are, and on the time of day. Any number of things may influence how long students will take to complete an exercise. An extra activity will fill in the gap if you are unexpectedly left with 20 spare minutes.

When you prepare the list of the elements you will use to evaluate the students, you will need to assign each of the activities a weighted value. To do this, you will need to answer several questions: How many and what kinds of writing assignments will you require? Are you going to require the oral presentation described in Chapter 8 of the main text? Will you require attendance at outside events or participation or membership in some campus organization? Consider including the features of successful seminars described in Chapter 3 of this manual. The box on p. 37 lists some elements you might want to incorporate. A table on how you might weight the elements is also shown.

PUTTING IT ALL TOGETHER

Take your lists and work them together to create your syllabus. Alternate heavier "academic" days with more informal exercises; for example, note-taking exercises might be followed by a campus tour. Allow one or more class periods for student oral reports (see Chapter 8 of the main text), most of one class period for peer review of each formal paper and one or more days for the Mini-College (*IM,* * Chapter 3).

As you construct your syllabus, calculate assignments and timing of due dates carefully. You may want to cover Chapter 8 in the main text—the library assignment/oral reports—relatively early to get the groups organized and started on their projects. You will need to decide if you want the reports to be given several days in succession or scattered throughout the semester.

Remember, a syllabus is a critical document for any course; it is a road map, a planning calendar, even a contract. Moreover, a comprehensive syllabus can provide comfort for those students and faculty who need structure. You should consider, in fact, two syllabi: a general one for the students and one with more detail for yourself or the faculty instructional team. Even if you intend to allow a great deal of individual freedom of instruction, you may wish to reach agreement on some basic components like the journal; the number of papers, quizzes, or other graded activities; and the weights you will assign them.

---

* *IM* indicates that the cross-referenced material appears in this manual.

Sample Evaluation Components List

Writing assignments (3 at 3–5 pages each)
Group oral report (5 minutes per person)
Out-of-class exercises (5)
Co-curricular events (attend 4)
Journal
Attendance and class participation

Weighted Value for Grading

Book papers (10% each)	30%
Oral presentation	10%
Exercises	5%
Co-curricular events	10%
Journals	25%
Number (5%)	
Content (10%)	
Final Paper (10%)	
Attendance and class participation	20%
TOTAL	100%

A SAMPLE STUDENT SYLLABUS

This syllabus assumes the following content and course requirements.

1. **Writing**: Three formal papers 3–4 pages in length and a final journal paper 5–7 pages long. Three class periods set aside for peer review of formal papers (*IM*, Chapter 5).

2. **Theme**: A theme or topic (for example, The Individual and the Community) to explore through selected readings. This topic should be integrated into class activities (*IM*, Chapter 5).

3. **Oral presentation** (*YCE*, Chapter 8): A class of twenty divided into four groups of five; four class periods assigned for student reports.

4. **Co-curricular events**: Required attendance at four outside events and subsequent discussion in class (*IM*, Chapter 3).

Purpose/Rationale

First-year students will probably be more unclear about the goals of this seminar than about the goals of most of their other courses. Therefore, it is critical that you state the goals clearly and concisely.

This course is designed to introduce the first-year student to the possibilities for personal growth provided by a liberal arts education. To accomplish this goal, the students and their peers will engage in a series of in-class and out-of-class activities that encourage the students to recognize their own individual contribution to the group learning experience.

Personal

Next, you should include the basic information the student will need to know about you:

Instructor: Donald Adam
Telephone: 1155
Office: Coolidge 131
Office Hours: Monday, Wednesday, Friday: 9:00–10:00, 2:00–4:00
Tuesday, Thursday: 10:00–12:00, 1:00–3:00
Class Days: Monday, Wednesday, Friday
Time: 1:00 p.m.
Room and Building: Falk Hall 220

Explicit Goals

Again, because the content of this course is unfamiliar, state clearly what things you intend to happen. You may wish to add to, change, or delete goals from the following list.

1. **Adjustment to college:** The first year in college is a time of major transition for students. This course provides a means of examining transitions and developing strategies to cope with those transitions. In doing so, it defines the values of [name of school] as an academic [and residential] institution so that students have a clearer sense of the adjustments they must make.

2. **Group building:** This takes the form of special exercises in order to "build the group." The purpose is both the development of the individual and the development of relationships. The course intends to create a "belonging place" for new students.

3. **Introduction to college life:** The students are exposed to guest speakers, are asked to participate in college events, and are directed to certain key support services and college resource facilities.

4. **Values clarification:** The students are encouraged to explore and define their personal values through special values clarification exercises; through journal writing, with periodic specific assignments; and through participation in a number of other in-class activities.

Instructor's Expectations of the Students

It is equally important to define the behaviors you expect of your students.

1. **Perfect attendance:** If students must be absent, we expect them to let us know beforehand. In-class experiences are difficult to duplicate.

2. **Willingness to participate in class and small-group discussions:** Involvement is imperative and required.

3. **Preparation for class:** When work has been assigned for class, we expect that it be done and that it be completed by the due date.

4. **Mature, polite behavior:** In our class meetings we will frequently discuss controversial issues; therefore, politeness and respect for the opinion of others is a must. The same polite behavior is expected at all co-curricular events (for example, forums, convocations, plays, field trips, and sporting events).

5. **Participation in group activities:** Several times during the semester, students will be divided into groups that will meet outside of class. Each group will choose a leader who will be responsible for scheduling group meetings well in advance. We expect all members of the group to participate equally.

Work to Be Done

Students have a legitimate right to know exactly what specific assignments they can expect and how the assignments will be evaluated.

1. **Reading**
   Jewler, Gardner, and McCarthy, eds., *Your College Experience: Strategies for Success,* Concise Edition

2. **Papers**
   a. Three formal papers (typed), topics to be supplied, minimum 3 pages
   b. Final journal analysis paper, minimum 5 pages

3. **Journal**
   First-year seminar students keep a daily journal that they submit to their instructors on the last class meeting of each week. The instructor will return these journals the following week. These journals are intended to be a record of the students' college experience as well as a place to respond to specific journal assignments or class and reading notes. Journals should also be used to record observations about the transition to college, about life in general, about performance in classes or as members of a group, or about other matters of interest.

   The journal can be considered one end of a written conversation with the instructor. **It is kept confidential.** It is a place to make comments or ask questions. The journal will be the basis for the final writing assignment.

4. **Oral presentations**
   For these discussions, the class will be divided into four groups of five students. Each student group will be responsible for leading one class discussion. Once the groups are formed, each group will choose a group leader, who will be responsible for calling meetings and

assigning roles. Your instructor will give you details concerning the oral presentations.

5. **Co-curricular events**

   In addition to in-class activities, first-year seminar students are required to attend the following co-curricular events:

   a. One female athletic event

   b. One male athletic event

   c. One fall play production

   d. Two all-campus lectures

   e. One campus music event

   Instructors will monitor the attendance for these events.

6. **Mini-College**

   All students will participate in this activity. Your instructor will give you details concerning the Mini-College.

Grading

Activities will each be assigned a weighted value for grading. The values are as follows:

Book papers (10% each)	30%
Oral presentation	10%
Exercises	5%
Journals	25%
Number (5%)	
Content (10%)	
Final paper (10%)	
Co-curricular events	10%
Attendance and class participation	20%
TOTAL	**100%**

The Weekly Schedule

The student syllabus should include a list of topics and assignments. The example below is built from the Instructor Syllabus provided for a 14 week, 3 credit, 3 sessions per week course on pp. 45–51. Others can be constructed from the other sample instructor syllabi provided.

Week 1

Day 1
Topic: Introduction to the course, group building
Reading assignment for Day 2: YCE, Chapter 1, *Keys to Success*
Out-of-class activity: Exercise 1.1

Day 2
Topic: Group building, setting goals, understanding the journal
Reading assignment for Day 3: None
Out-of-class activity: Exercise 1.5

Day 3
Topic: Group building, student self-examination of college goals
Reading assignment for Week 2, Day 1: None
Out-of-class activity: Attend all-campus speakers' program

Week 2

Day 1
Topic: Prepare for formal writing
Reading assignment for Day 2: Theme reading [article chosen by instructor]
Out-of-class activity: Exercise 1.7

Day 2
Topic: Integration of writing and theme
Reading assignment for Day 3: *YCE*, Chapter 2, *Time Management: The Foundation of Academic Success*
Out-of-class activity: Exercises 2.1, 2.2, 2.3, 2.4 (2.6)

Day 3
Topic: Discussion and planning of time management
Reading assignment for Week 3, Day 1: *YCE*, Chapter 9, *Finding Answers: Your College Catalog and Academic Advisor or Counselor*, pp. 150–153; history section of college catalog
Out-of-class activity: Exercises 2.5, 2.8
Bring to next class: College catalog

Week 3

Day 1
Topic: Continue discussion of time management; discuss catalog
Reading assignment for Day 3: *YCE*, Chapter 8, *An Information Age Introduction to the Library*
Out-of-class activity: None

Day 2
Topic: Continue discussion of time management and introduce library assignments
Reading assignment for Day 3: *YCE*, Chapter 3, *Learning Styles*
Out-of-class activity: Exercises 3.1, 3.2

Day 3
Topic: Discussion of learning styles
Reading assignment for Week 4, Day 1: None
Out-of-class activity: Exercise 3.5
Assignment Due Next Class Meeting: First Draft of First Paper

Week 4

Day 1
Topic: Critique drafts of papers
Reading assignment for Day 2: *YCE*, Chapter 4, *Listening and Learning in the Classroom*
Out-of-class activity: Exercises 4.1, 4.2

Day 2
Topic: Practice note-taking
Reading assignment for Day 3: None
Out-of-class activity: None
Assignment Due Next Class Meeting: Final Draft of First Paper

Day 3
Topic: Introduction to campus
Reading assignment for Week 5, Day 1: None
Out-of-class activity: None

Week 5

Day 1
Topic: Student group 1 presentation
Reading assignment for Day 2: *YCE*, Chapter 5, *A Sound Approach to Textbooks*
Out-of-class activity: Exercises 5.1, 5.2
Bring a textbook to next class

Day 2
Topic: Learn to read a textbook
Reading assignment for Day 3: Article for précis on theme [instructor's choice]
Out-of-class activity: Attend all-campus speakers' program

Day 3
Topic: Learning to write a précis
Reading assignment for Week 3, Day 1: *YCE*, Chapter 6, *Making the Grade*
Out-of-class activity: None

Week 6

Day 1
Topic: Introduction to examination strategies
Reading assignment for Day 3: None
Out-of-class activity: None

Day 2
Topic: Introduction to the arts
Reading assignment for Day 3: None
Out-of-class activity: Attend play
Assignment Due Next Class Meeting: First Draft of Second Paper

Day 3
Topic: Critique of drafts of papers
Reading assignment for Week 7, Day 1: *YCE*, Chapter 7, *Teacher and Student: Partners in Learning*
Out-of-class activity: Exercises 7.1, 7.2

Week 7

Day 1
Topic: Identify qualities of a good teacher
Reading assignment for Day 3: Theme essay
Out-of-class activity: None
Assignment Due Next Class Meeting: Final Draft of Second Paper

Day 2
Topic: Exploration of theme
Reading assignment for Day 3: None
Out-of-class activity: None

Day 3
Topic: Student group 2 presentation
Reading assignment for Week 8, Day 1: *YCE*, Chapter 9, pp. 154–159
Out-of-class activity: Exercises 9.4, 9.5, attend all-campus speakers' program

Week 8

Day 1
Topic: Learn about the role of the academic advisor
Reading assignment for Day 2: None
Out-of-class activity: None

Day 2
Topic: PIZZA PARTY! [cancel regular class; schedule party for evening]
Reading assignment for Day 3: None
Out-of-class activity: None

Day 3
Topic: Examine career values
Reading assignment for Week 9, Day 1: *YCE*, Chapter 10, *Major, Career, and Transfer Planning*
Out-of-class activity: Exercises 10.1, 10.2, 10.4

Week 9

Day 1
Topic: Career exploration
Reading assignment for Day 2: None
Out-of-class activity: Exercises 10.5, 10.6, 10.7, 10.8

Day 2
Topic: Presentation of career options
Reading assignment for Day 3: None
Out-of-class activity: None

Day 3
Topic: Discussion of transfer planning or financial aid
Reading assignment for Week 10, Day 1: *YCE*, Appendix A, *How to Manage Your Money and Obtain Financial Aid*
Out-of-class activity: None

Week 10

Day 1
Topic: How to manage your money
Reading assignment for Day 2: theme reading
Out-of-class activity: Attend all-campus speakers' program

Day 2
Topic: Discussion of semester theme topic
Reading assignment for Day 3: *YCE*, Chapter 11, *Yourself and Others*
Out-of-class activity: Exercise 11.2

Day 3
Topic: Discussion of relationships
Reading assignment for Week 11, Day 1: None
Out-of-class activity: None
Assignment Due Next Class Meeting: First Draft of Third Paper

Week 11
Day 1
Topic: Critique drafts of papers
Reading assignment for Day 2: None
Out-of-class activity: Exercise 11.5

Day 2
Topic: Discussion of assertiveness
Reading assignment for Day 3: None
Out-of-class activity: Exercise 11.7
Assignment Due Next Class Meeting: Final Draft of Third Paper

Day 3
Topic: Discussion of getting involved
Reading assignment for Week 12, Day 1: None
Out-of-class activity: None

Week 12
Day 1
Topic: Student group 3 presentation
Reading assignment for Day 2: YCE, Chapter 12, *Healthy Decisions: Sexuality, Drugs, and Stress*
Out-of-class activity: Exercise 12.1

Day 2
Topic: Discussion of sexuality
Reading assignment for Day 3: None
Out-of-class activity: Exercise 12.2

Day 3
Topic: Discussion of alcohol and drugs
Reading assignment for Week 13, Day 1: None
Out-of-class activity: None

Week 13
Day 1
Topic: Presentation of Mini-College
Reading assignment for Day 2: Theme paper
Out-of-class activity: None

Day 2
Topic: Discussion of semester theme topic
Reading assignment for Day 3: None
Out-of-class activity: Exercise 12.4

Day 3
Topic: Discussion of stress management
Reading assignment for Week 14, Day 1: None
Out-of-class activity: None

Week 14
Day 1
Topic: Student group 4 presentation
Reading assignment for Day 2: None
Out-of-class activity: None

Day 2
Topic: College outcomes
Reading assignment for Day 3: None
Out-of-class activity: None
Assignment Due Last Day of Class: Final Draft of Journal Paper

Day 3
Topic: Class evaluation

SAMPLE INSTRUCTOR SYLLABI

The sample syllabi below do not assign all the exercises. About half have been chosen, some for the students to do on their own and some to do in class. You can easily substitute exercises from this Instructor's Manual or use your own. There are plenty here from which to choose. Be sure to assign exercises in advance of their due date. Note that some exercises require as much as a week; so be sure to allow enough time to complete them. Collect some of the exercises you assign to assure that they are being done and to give credit for them; record them and return them. Some exercises are for different types of students; analyze your class (older students, commuters, minorities, etc.) and choose the most appropriate exercises.

Organization

As indicated previously, you don't have to teach the chapters in the text in the order they are written. The syllabi shown here arrange them in a different order. The instructor's syllabi also give some suggestions on the order in which to do the activities during the class period. Four model syllabi are provided on the pages that follow: 3 credits, 3 sessions/week (14 weeks); 1 credit, 1 session/week (14 weeks); 3 credits, 3 sessions/week (10 weeks); 1 credit, 1 session/week (10 weeks).

14 WEEK MODELS

3 Credits, 3 Sessions/Week

This sample syllabus is based upon the assumptions and requirements described earlier in this chapter.

Week 1

Day 1
Objectives: Introduction to the course, group building
Activities: 1. Give a general introduction to and description of the course
2. Distribute and discuss syllabi, course expectations, etc.
3. In-class exercise: Name Chain [*IM*, Chapter 3]
4. Discuss beginning of the semester [*IM*, Chapter 6]
Reading assignment for Day 2: *YCE*, Chapter 1, *Keys to Success*
Out-of-class activity: Exercise 1.1

Day 2
Objectives: Group building, setting goals, understanding journal
Activities: 1. In-class exercise: Paired Introductions [*IM*, Chapter 3]
2. Discuss Chapter 1 (*YCE*), *Keys to Success*
3. Process Exercise 1.1
4. Write Exercise 1.2 (5 minutes)
5. Review and expand upon discussion of journal
6. Introduction to the course theme
Reading assignment for Day 3: None
Out-of-class activity: Exercise 1.5

Day 3
Objectives: Group building, student self-examination of college goals
Activities: 1. Collect journals
2. Process Exerise 1.5

      3. In-class exercise: Drawbridge [*IM*, Chapter 3]

      4. Write Exercise 1.7 (5 minutes)

Reading assignment for Week 2, Day 1: None

Out-of-class activity: Attend all-campus speakers' program

Week 2

Day 1

Objective: Prepare for formal writing

Activities: 1. Return journals

          2. Discuss all-campus speaker

          3. Discuss "How was the first weekend?"

          4. Discuss formal writing assignments

          5. In-class role-playing: Exercise 1.8 (10 minutes)

Reading assignment for Day 2: Theme reading [article chosen by instructor]

Out-of-class activity: Exercise 1.7

Day 2

Objective: Integration of writing and theme

Activities: 1. Theme discussion/presentation

          2. Write reaction paper on theme

          3. Quick introduction to time management

Reading assignment for Day 3: *YCE*, Chapter 2, *Time Management: The Foundation of Academic Success*

Out-of-class activity: Exercises 2.1, 2.2, 2.3, 2.4 (2.6)

Day 3

Objective: Discussion and planning of time management

Activities: 1. Collect journals*

          2. Small group discussion of "Joe, Sheila, and Carmen"

          3. Collect Exercise 2.4

          4. Write on "Why Carmen Succeeds" (5 minutes)

Reading assignment for Week 3, Day 1: *YCE*, Chapter 9, *Finding Answers: Your College Catalog and Academic Advisor or Counselor*, pp. 150–153; history section of college catalog

Out-of-class activity: Exercises 2.5, 2.8

Bring to next class: College catalog

Week 3

Day 1

Objectives: Continue discussion of time management; discuss catalog

Activities: 1. Return journals*

          2. Return Exercise 2.4

          3. Instructor review of the catalog

          4. Group activity: Review Academic Calendar with Exercise 2.4

          5. Discuss formal college rules and expectations (pre-registration, how to drop a course, etc.)

          6. Write on "What makes this college different?" (5 minutes)

Reading assignment for Day 3: *YCE*, Chapter 8, *An Information Age Introduction to the Library*

Out-of-class activity: None

*This entry will not be repeated in the syllabus; however, it is assumed that you will collect the journals the third session of each week and return them the first session of the following week.

Day 2
Objectives: Continue discussion of time management and introduce library assignments
Activities: 1. Group discussion of Exercise 2.1B
2. Collect Exercise 2.1B
3. Review oral presentation assignments (Chapter 8); assign groups
4. Quick introduction of learning styles
Reading assignment for Day 3: *YCE*, Chapter 3, *Learning Styles*
Out-of-class activity: Exercises 3.1, 3.2

Day 3
Objective: Discussion of learning styles
Activities: 1. Collect Exercise 3.2
2. Return Exercise 2.1B
3. Expert presentation on MBTI/learning styles
4. In-class exercise: Exercise 3.3 or 3.4
Reading Assignment for Week 4, Day 1: None
Out-of-class activity: Exercise 3.5
Assignment Due Next Class Meeting: First Draft of First Paper

Week 4
Day 1
Objective: Critique drafts of papers
Activity: Peer review
Reading assignment for Day 2: *YCE*, Chapter 4, *Listening and Learning in the Classroom*
Out-of-class activity: Exercises 4.1, 4.2

Day 2
Objective: Practice note-taking
Activities: 1. Faculty lecture half period on theme
2. In-class exercise: Exercise 4.3
3. Collect Exercises 4.1, 4.2
Reading assignment for Day 3: None
Out-of-class activity: None
Assignment Due Next Class Meeting: Final Draft of First Paper

Day 3
Objective: Introduction to campus
Activity: Campus tour
Reading assignment for Week 5, Day 1: None
Out-of-class activity: None

Week 5
Day 1
Objective: Student group 1 presentation
Activities: 1. Student presentation
2. Critique evaluation
3. Evaluation checklist
In-class exercise: Evaluation checklist
Reading assignment for Day 2: *YCE*, Chapter 5, *A Sound Approach to Textbooks*
Out-of-class activity: Exercises 5.1, 5.2
Bring a textbook to next class

Day 2
Objective: Learn to read a textbook
Activities: 1. Collect Exercises 5.1, 5.2
          2. Read from textbook and take notes
In-class exercise: Exercise 5.3
Reading assignment for Day 3: Article for précis on theme [instructor's choice]
Out-of-class activity: Attend all-campus speakers' program

Day 3
Objective: Learning to write a précis
Activities: 1. Discuss all-campus speaker
          2. Return Exercises 5.1, 5.2
          3. Write précis
          4. Peer review
Reading assignment for Week 3, Day 1: *YCE,* Chapter 6, *Making the Grade*
Out-of-class activity: None

Week 6
Day 1
Objective: Introduction to examination strategies
Activities: 1. Design exam questions (Exercises 6.1, 6.2) based on class theme and lecture
          2. Take exam
          3. Peer review of exam
Reading assignment for Day 3: None
Out-of-class activity: None

Day 2
Objective: Introduction to the arts
Activity: Visiting expert (e.g., theater director)
Reading assignment for Day 3: None
Out-of-class activity: Attend play
Assignment Due Next Class Meeting: First Draft of Second Paper

Day 3
Objective: Critique of drafts of papers
Activity: Peer review of papers
Reading assignment for Week 7, Day 1: *YCE,* Chapter 7, *Teacher and Student: Partners in Learning*
Out-of-class activity: Exercises 7.1, 7.2

Week 7
Day 1
Objective: Identify qualities of a good teacher
Activities: Exercises 7.1, 7.2; discussion of what is a good teacher
Reading assignment for Day 3: Theme essay
Out-of-class activity: None
Assignment Due Next Class Meeting: Final Draft of Second Paper

Day 2
Objective: Exploration of theme
Activity: Instructor-designed activity
Reading assignment for Day 3: None
Out-of-class activity: None

Day 3
Objective: Student group 2 presentation
Activities: 1. Student presentation
2. Critique evaluation
3. Evaluation checklist
In-class exercise: Evaluation checklist
Reading assignment for Week 8, Day 1: *YCE,* Chapter 9, pp. 154–159
Out-of-class activity: Exercises 9.4, 9.5; attend all-campus speakers' program

Week 8
Day 1
Objective: Learn about the role of the academic advisor
Activities: 1. Discuss all-campus program
2. Collect Exercises 9.4, 9.5
3. In-class exercise: Exercise 9.7 (role-play advisor/student)
Reading assignment for Day 2: None
Out-of-class activity: None

Day 2
Objective: PIZZA PARTY! [cancel regular class; schedule party for evening]
Activity: Watch movie related to theme
Reading assignment for Day 3: None
Out-of-class activity: None

Day 3
Objective: Examine career values
Activity: Values auction [see *IM,* Chapter 3, for more on values]
Reading assignment for Week 9, Day 1: *YCE,* Chapter 10, *Major, Career, and Transfer Planning*
Out-of-class activity: Exercises 10.1, 10.2, 10.4

Week 9
Day 1
Objective: Career exploration
Activity: Holland Hexagon exercise
Reading assignment for Day 2: None
Out-of-class activity: Exercises 10.5, 10.6, 10.7, 10.8

Day 2
Objective: Presentation of career options
Activities: 1. Collect Exercise 10.8
2. Presentation by guest speaker on career options
Reading assignment for Day 3: None
Out-of-class activity: None

Day 3
Objective: Discussion of transfer planning or financial aid
Activity: Presentation by financial aid or transfer counselor
Reading assignment for Week 10, Day 1: *YCE,* Appendix A, *How to Manage Your Money and Obtain Financial Aid*
Out-of-class activity: None

Week 10
Day 1
Objective: How to manage your money
Activity: Discussion: "Planning a Budget"

Reading assignment for Day 2: Theme reading
Out-of-class activity: Attend all-campus speakers' program

Day 2
Objective: Discussion of semester theme topic
Activities: 1.   Discuss all-campus program
              2.   Theme discussion
Reading assignment for Day 3: *YCE*, Chapter 11, *Yourself and Others*
Out-of-class activity: Exercise 11.2

Day 3
Objective: Discussion of relationships
Activities: 1.   Collect Exercise 11.2
              2.   Do and discuss Exercise 11.3
              3.   Debate the question, "Who is more romantic, men or women?" (5 minutes)
Reading assignment for Week 11, Day 1: None
Out-of-class activity: None
Assignment Due Next Class Meeting: First Draft of Third Paper

Week 11
Day 1
Objective: Critique drafts of papers
Activity: Peer review of papers
Reading assignment for Day 2: None
Out-of-class activity: Exercise 11.5

Day 2
Objective: Discussion of assertiveness
Activities: 1.   Collect Exercise 11.5
              2.   Do and discuss Exercise 11.4
              3.   Write an opinion on "That Corner in the Cafeteria" (5 minutes)
Reading assignment for Day 3: None
Out-of-class activity: Exercise 11.7
Assignment Due Next Class Meeting: Final Draft of Third Paper

Day 3
Objective: Discussion of getting involved
Activities: 1.   Class presentation by Student Affairs Office
              2.   Collect Exercise 11.7
Reading assignment for Week 12, Day 1: None
Out-of-class activity: None

Week 12
Day 1
Objective: Student group 3 presentation
Activities: 1.   Student presentation
              2.   Critique evaluation
              3.   Evaluation checklist
In-class exercise: Evaluation checklist
Reading assignment for Day 2: *YCE*, Chapter 12, *Healthy Decisions: Sexuality, Drugs, and Stress*
Out-of-class activity: Exercise 12.1

Day 2
Objective: Discussion of sexuality
Activities: 1. Collect Exercise 12.1
          2. Discussion of date rape
          3. Write an opinion on "Sex – Yes = Rape" (5 minutes)
Reading assignment for Day 3: None
Out-of-class activity: Exercise 12.2

Day 3
Objective: Discussion of alcohol and drugs
Activities: 1. Write an opinion paper on drugs and alcohol (5 minutes)
          2. Mini-College curriculum committee [*IM*, Chapter 3]
Reading assignment for Week 13, Day 1: None
Out-of-class activity: None

Week 13
Day 1
Objective: Presentation of Mini-College
Activity: Mini-College [*IM*, Chapter 3]
Reading assignment for Day 2: Theme paper
Out-of-class activity: None
Discontinue collecting journals for last two weeks

Day 2
Objective: Discussion of semester theme topic
Activity: Theme discussion
Reading assignment for Day 3: None
Out-of-class activity: Exercise 12.4

Day 3
Objective: Discussion of stress management
Activities: 1. Discuss Exercise 12.4
          2. Role-play Exercise 12.5, "Divide and Conquer"
Reading assignment for Week 14, Day 1: None
Out-of-class activity: None

Week 14
Day 1
Objective: Student group 4 presentation
Activities: 1. Student presentation
          2. Critique evaluation
          3. Evaluation checklist
In-class exercise: Evaluation checklist
Reading assignment for Day 2: None
Out-of-class activity: None

Day 2
Objective: College outcomes
Activity: Panel presentation by college alumni
Reading assignment for Day 3: None
Out-of-class activity: None
Assignment Due Last Day of Class: Final Draft of Journal Paper

Day 3
Objective: Class evaluation
Activity: Evaluation

1 Credit, 1 Session/Week

The 1 credit/1 session per week course must, of necessity, be significantly different from a 3 credit class because of the shorter instructional time available and the more limited out-of-class demands that it is reasonable to make upon the students. The instructor needs to decide the primary focus of the course and limit the activities to those areas. The primary purpose, for example, could be skill development, in which case the early chapters of *YCE* would be the principle ones used. Or the course could be more issue-focused, in which case the later chapters would be more appropriate.

The sample syllabus assumes a study skills focus and is based upon the following assumptions and requirements in the course:

► **Writing:** One formal paper 3 to 4 pages in length; one class period set aside for peer review. (*IM*, Chapter 5).

► **Oral presentation** (from *YCE*, Chapter 8): Class of twenty divided into four groups of five; two class periods assigned for student presentations.

► **Co-curricular events:** Attendance is required at two outside events that will be discussed in class (*IM*, Chapter 3).

Week 1
Objectives: Introduction to the course, group building
Activities: 1. Give a general introduction to and description of the course
2. Distribute and discuss syllabi, course expectations, etc.
3. In-class exercise: Name Chain [*IM*, Chapter 3]
4. Discuss beginning of the semester [*IM*, Chapter 6]
Reading assignment for Week 2: *YCE*, Chapter 1, *Keys to Success;* Chapter 2, *Time Management: The Foundation of Academic Success*
Out-of-class activity: Exercises 1.1, 2.1, 2.2, 2.4

Week 2
Objective: Discussion and planning of time management
Activities: 1. Introduction to time management
2. Discuss "How was the first weekend?"
3. Small-group discussion of "Joe, Sheila, and Carmen"
4. Collect Exercise 2.4
5. Write on "Why Carmen Succeeds" (5 minutes)
Reading assignment for Week 3: None
Out-of-class activity: Attend all-campus speakers' program

Week 3
Objective: Prepare for formal writing
Activities: 1. Return Exercise 2.1B
2. Discuss all-campus program
3. Discuss formal writing assignments
Reading assignment for Week 4: *YCE*, Chapter 3, *Learning Styles*
Out-of-class activity: Exercise 3.1, 3.2

Week 4
Objective: Discussion of learning styles
Activities: 1. Presentation on MBTI/learning styles
2. In-class exercise: MBTI exercise
3. Collect Exercise 3.2

Reading assignment for Week 5: *YCE*, Chapter 4, *Listening and Learning in the Classroom*
Out-of-class activity: Exercises 4.1, 4.2

Week 5
Objective: Practice note-taking
Activities: 1. Return Exercise 3.2
2. Faculty lecture half period on theme
3. In-class exercise: Exercise 4.3
4. Collect Exercises 4.1, 4.2
Reading assignment for Week 6: *YCE*, Chapter 5, *A Sound Approach to Textbooks*
Out-of-class activity: Exercises 5.1, 5.2
Bring textbook to next class

Week 6
Objective: Reading a textbook
Activities: 1. Return Exercises 3.2, 4.1, 4.2
2. Collect Exercises 5.1, 5.2
3. Read from textbook and take notes
4. In-class exercise: Exercise 5.3
Reading assignment for Week 7: *YCE*, Chapter 8, *An Information Age Introduction to the Library*
Out-of-class activity: None

Week 7
Objectives: Introduction to oral reports; introduction to campus
Activities: 1. Return Exercises 5.1, 5.2
2. Introduction of oral assignments
3. Campus tour
Reading assignment for Week 8: None
Out-of-class activity: None
Assignment Due Next Class Meeting: First Draft of Paper

Week 8
Objective: Critique drafts of papers
Activity: Peer review
Reading assignment for Week 9: *YCE*, Chapter 9, *Finding Answers: Your College Catalog and Academic Advisor or Counselor*
Out-of-class activity: Exercises 9.4, 9.5
Assignment Due Next Class Meeting: Final Draft of Paper

Week 9
Objective: Learn about the role of the academic advisor
Activity: Academic advising role-playing exercise
Reading assignment for Week 10: *YCE*, Chapter 6, *Making the Grade*
Out-of-class activity: Attend all-campus speakers' program

Week 10
Objective: Prepare for examinations
Activities: 1. Discuss all-campus program
2. Design exam questions (Exercises 6.1, 6.2) based on class theme and lecture

3. Take exam
4. Peer review exam

Reading assignment for Week 11: *YCE*, Chapter 7, *Teacher and Student: Partners in Learning*
Out-of-class activity: Exercises 7.1, 7.2

Week 11

Objective: Career exploration
Activity: Holland Hexagon exercise
Reading assignment for Week 12: *YCE*, Chapter 11, *Yourself and Others*
Out-of-class activity: Exercises 11.2, 11.3

Week 12

Objective: Introduction to campus opportunities
Activity: Guest(s) to talk about campus opportunities
Reading assignment for Week 13: None
Out-of-class activity: None

Week 13

Objective: Student group presentations
Activities: 1. Student presentation
2. Critique evaluation
3. Evaluation checklist
In-class exercise: Evaluation checklist
Reading assignment for Week 14: None
Out-of-class activity: None

Week 14

Objectives: Review the semester; evaluate the course
Activities: 1. Formal evaluation
2. Informal discussion of the semester

10 WEEK MODELS

3 Credits, 3 Sessions/Week

The 10 week, 3 credits/3 sessions per week course is slightly shorter than the 14 week course, but is essentially similar. Any number of variations can be made by excluding elements from the 14 week model. The choice depends on the basic objective the instructor defines for the course.

The sample syllabus is based upon essentially the same assumptions and requirements as the 14 week model, including the following:

► **Writing:** Two formal papers 3 to 4 pages in length; one class period set aside for peer review; a final journal paper.

► **Oral presentation** (from *YCE*, Chapter 8): Class of twenty divided into four groups of five; two class periods assigned for student presentations.

► **Co-curricular events:** Attendance is required at two outside events that will be discussed in class.

Week 1

Day 1

Objectives: Introduction to the course, group building

Activities: 1. Give a general introduction to and description of the course
2. Distribute and discuss syllabi, course expectations, etc.
3. In-class exercise: Name Chain [*IM*, Chapter 3]
4. Discuss beginning of the semester [*IM*, Chapter 6]

Reading assignment for Day 2: *YCE*, Chapter 1, *Keys to Success*

Out-of-class activity: Exercise 1.1

Day 2

Objectives: Group building, setting goals; understanding journal

Activities: 1. In-class exercise: Paired Introductions [*IM*, Chapter 3]
2. Discuss *Keys to Success*
3. Process Exercise 1.1
4. Write Exercise 1.2 (5 minutes)
5. Review and expand upon discussion of journal
6. Introduction to the course theme

Reading assignment for Day 3: None

Out-of-class activity: Exercise 1.5

Day 3

Objectives: Group building; student self-examination of college goals

Activities: 1. Collect journals*
2. Process Exercise 1.5
3. In-class exercise: Drawbridge [*IM*, Chapter 3]
4. Write Exercise 1.7 (5 minutes)

Reading assignment for Week 2, Day 1: None

Out-of-class activity: Attend all-campus speakers' program

Week 2

Day 1

Objective: Prepare for formal writing

Activities: 1. Return journals*
2. Discuss all-campus speaker
3. Discuss "How was the first weekend?"
4. Discuss formal writing assignments
5. In-class role-playing (Exercise 1.8)

Reading assignment for Day 2: *YCE*, Chapter 2, *Time Management: The Foundation of Academic Success*

Out-of-class activity: Exercises 2.1, 2.2, 2.3, 2.4 (2.6)

Day 2

Objective: Discussion and planning of time management

Activities: 1. Small-group discussion of "Joe, Sheila, and Carmen"
2. Collect Exercise 2.4
3. Write on "Why Carmen Succeeds" (5 minutes)

Reading assignment for Day 3: *YCE*, Chapter 8, *An Information Age Introduction to the Library*

Out-of-class activity: None

*This entry will not be repeated in the syllabus; however, it is assumed that you will collect the journals the third session of each week and return them the first session of the following week.

Day 3
Objectives: Continue discussion of time management and introduce library assignments
Activities: 1. Return Exercise 2.4
      2. Group discussion of Exercise 2.1B
      3. Collect Exercise 2.1B
      4. Review oral presentation assignments (Chapter 8); assign groups
      5. Quick introduction of learning styles
Reading assignment for Week 3, Day 1: *YCE*, Chapter 3, *Learning Styles*
Out-of-class activity: Exercises 3.1, 3.2

Week 3
Day 1
Objective: Discussion of learning styles
Activities: 1. Collect Exercise 3.2
      2. Return Exercise 2.1B
      3. Expert presentation on MBTI/learning styles
      4. In-class MBTI exercise
Reading assignment for Day 2: None
Out-of-class activity: None
Assignment Due Next Class Meeting: First Draft of First Paper

Day 2
Objective: Critique drafts of papers
Activity: Peer review
Reading assignment for Day 3: *YCE*, Chapter 4, *Listening and Learning in the Classroom*
Out-of-class activity: Exercises 4.1, 4.2

Day 3
Objective: Practice note-taking
Activities: 1. Collect Exercises 4.1, 4.2
      2. Faculty lecture half period on theme
      3. In-class exercise: Exercise 4.3
Reading assignment for Week 4, Day 2: None
Out-of-class activity: None
Assignment Due Next Class Meeting: Final Draft of First Paper

Week 4
Day 1
Objective: Student group 1 presentation
Activities: 1. Return Exercises 4.1, 4.2
      2. Student presentation
      3. Critique evaluation
      4. Evaluation checklist
In-class exercise: Evaluation checklist
Reading assignment for Day 2: *YCE*, Chapter 5, *A Sound Approach to Textbooks*
Out-of-class activity: Exercises 5.1, 5.2
Bring a textbook to next class

Day 2
Objective: Learn to read a textbook
Activities: 1. Collect Exercises 5.1, 5.2
      2. Read from textbook and take notes

In-class exercise: Exercise 5.3
Reading assignment for Day 3: YCE, Chapter 6, *Making the Grade*
Out-of-class activity: Attend all-campus speakers' program

Day 3
Objective: Introduction to examination strategies
Activities: 1. Return Exercises 5.1, 5.2
2. Discuss all-campus speaker
3. Design exam questions (Exercises 6.1, 6.2) based on class theme and lecture
4. Take exam
5. Peer review exam
Reading assignment for Week 5, Day 1: None
Out-of-class activity: None
Assignment Due Next Class Meeting: First Draft of Second Paper

Week 5
Day 1
Objective: Critique of drafts of papers
Activity: Peer review of papers
Reading assignment for Day 2: Theme essay
Out-of-class activity: None

Day 2
Objective: Exploration of theme
Activity: Instructor-designed activity
Reading assignment for Day 3: None
Out-of-class activity: None
Assignment Due Next Class Meeting: Final Draft of Second Paper

Day 3
Objective: Student group 2 presentation
Activities: 1. Student presentation
2. Critique evaluation
3. Evaluation checklist
In-class exercise: Evaluation checklist
Reading assignment for Week 6, Day 1: YCE, Chapter 7, *Teacher and Student: Partners in Learning*
Out-of-class activity: Exercises 7.1, 7.2; attend all-campus speakers' program

Week 6
Day 1
Objective: Identify qualities of a good teacher
Activities: 1. Discuss all-campus program
2. Review and discuss Exercises 7.1, 7.2
Reading assignment for Day 2: YCE, Chapter 9, *Finding Answers: Your College Catalog and Academic Advisor or Counselor*
Out-of-class activity: Exercises 9.4, 9.5

Day 2
Objective: Learn about the role of the academic advisor
Activities: 1. Collect Exercises 9.4, 9.5
2. Values auction [see *IM*, Chapter 3 for more on values]
3. Academic advising role-playing exercise

Reading assignment for Day 3: *YCE*, Chapter 10, *Major, Career, and Transfer Planning*
Out-of-class activity: Exercises 10.1, 10.2, 10.4

Day 3
Objective: Career exploration
Activity: Holland Hexagon exercise
Reading assignment for Week 7, Day 1: None
Out-of-class activity: None

Week 7
Day 1
Objective: PIZZA PARTY! [Cancel regular class; schedule party for evening]
Activity: Values activity: "Who Stays" [see *IM*, Chapter 3]
Reading assignment for Day 2: None
Out-of-class activity: None

Day 2
Objective: Presentation of career options
Activity: Presentation by guest speaker on career options
Reading assignment for Day 3: *YCE*, Chapter 11, *Yourself and Others*
Out-of-class activity: Attend all-campus speakers' program; Exercise 11.2

Day 3
Objective: Discussion of relationships
Activities: 1. Collect Exercise 11.2
              2. Discuss all-campus program
              3. Do and discuss Exercise 11.3
Reading assignment for Week 8, Day 1: None
Out-of-class activity: Exercise 11.5

Week 8
Day 1
Objective: Discussion of assertiveness
Activities: 1. Collect Exercise 11.5
              2. Do and discuss Exercise 11.4
              3. Write an opinion on "That Corner in the Cafeteria" (5 minutes)
Reading assignment for Day 2: None
Out-of-class activity: None
Assignment Due Next Class Meeting: First Draft of Third Paper

Day 2
Objective: Critique drafts of papers
Activities: 1. Return Exercise 11.5
              2. Peer review of papers
Reading assignment for Day 3: *YCE*, Chapter 12, *Healthy Decisions: Sexuality, Drugs, and Stress*
Out-of-class activity: Exercise 12.1

Day 3
Objective: Discussion of sexuality
Activities: 1. Collect Exercise 12.1
              2. Discussion of date rape
              3. Write an opinion on "Sex – Yes = Rape" (5 minutes)
Reading assignment for Week 9, Day 1: None

Out-of-class activity: None
Assignment Due Next Class Meeting: Final Draft of Third Paper

Week 9
Day 1
Objective: Discussion of getting involved
Activity: Class presentation by Student Affairs Office
Reading assignment for Day 2: None
Out-of-class activity: None

Day 2
Objective: Student group 3 presentation
Activities: 1. Student presentation
2. Critique evaluation
3. Evaluation checklist
In-class exercise: Evaluation checklist
Reading assignment for Day 3: None
Out-of-class activity: Exercise 12.2

Day 3
Objective: Discussion of alcohol and drugs
Activities: 1. Collect Exercise 12.2
2. Write an opinion paper on drugs and alcohol (5 minutes)
Reading assignment for Week 10, Day 1: YCE, Appendix A, *How to Manage Your Money and Obtain Financial Aid*
Out-of-class activity: None

Week 10
Day 1
Objective: How to manage your money
Activities: 1. Discussion of "Planning a Budget"
2. Design a budget
Reading assignment for Day 2: None
Out-of-class activity: None

Day 2
Objective: Student group 4 presentation
Activities: 1. Student presentation
2. Critique evaluation
3. Evaluation checklist
In-class exercise: Evaluation checklist
Reading assignment for Day 3: None
Out-of-class activity: None
Assignment Due Last Day of Class: Final Draft of Journal Paper

Day 3
Objective: Class evaluation
Activity: Evaluation

1 Credit, 1 Session/Week

The 1 credit/1 session per week course must, of necessity, be significantly different from a 3 credit class because of the shorter instructional time available and the more limited out-of-class demands that it is reasonable to make upon the students. The instructor needs to decide the primary focus of the course and limit the activities to those areas.

The sample syllabus assumes a study skills focus and is based upon the following assumptions and requirements in the course:

► **Writing:** One formal paper 3 to 4 pages in length; 1 class period set aside for peer review.

► **Oral presentation** (from *YCE*, Chapter 8): A class of twenty divided into four groups of five; two class periods assigned for student presentations.

► **Co-curricular events:** Attendance is required at two outside events that will be discussed in class (*IM*, Chapter 3)

Week 1
Objectives: Introduction to the course, group building
Activities: 1. Give a general introduction to and description of the course
2. Distribute and discuss syllabi, course expectations, and so on.
3. In-class exercise: Name Chain [*IM*, Chapter 3]
4. Discuss beginning of the semester [*IM*, Chapter 6]
Reading assignment for Week 2: *YCE*, Chapter 1, *Keys to Success*; Chapter 2, *Time Management: The Foundation of Academic Success*
Out-of-class activity: Exercises 1.1, 2.1, 2.2, 2.4

Week 2
Objective: Discussion and planning of time management
Activities: 1. Introduction to time management
2. Discuss "How was the first weekend?"
3. Small-group discussion of "Joe, Sheila, and Carmen"
4. Collect Exercise 2.4
5. Write on "Why Carmen Succeeds" (5 minutes)
Reading assignment for Week 3: None
Out-of-class activity: Attend all-campus speakers' program

Week 3
Objective: Prepare for formal writing
Activities: 1. Return Exercise 2.1B
2. Discuss all-campus program
3. Discuss formal writing assignments
Reading assignment for Week 4: *YCE*, Chapter 4, *Listening and Learning in the Classroom*
Out-of-class activity: Exercises 4.1, 4.2

Week 4
Objective: Practice note-taking
Activities: 1. Faculty lecture half period on theme
2. In-class exercise: Exercise 4.3
3. Collect Exercises 4.1, 4.2
Reading assignment for Week 5: *YCE*, Chapter 5, *A Sound Approach to Textbooks*
Out-of-class activity: Exercises 5.1, 5.2
Bring textbook to next class

Week 5
Objective: Reading a textbook
Activities: 1. Return Exercises 4.1, 4.2
2. Collect Exercises 5.1, 5.2
3. Read from textbook and take notes
4. In-class exercise: Exercise 5.3
Reading assignment for Week 6: *YCE*, Chapter 8, *An Information Age Introduction to the Library*
Out-of-class activity: None

Week 6
Objectives: Introduction to oral reports; introduction to campus
Activities: 1. Return Exercises 5.1, 5.2
2. Introduction of oral assignments
3. Campus tour
Reading assignment for Week 7: None
Out-of-class activity: None
Assignment Due Next Class Meeting: First Draft of Paper

Week 7
Objective: Critique drafts of papers
Activity: Peer review
Reading assignment for Week 8: *YCE*, Chapter 6, *Making the Grade*
Out-of-class activity: Attend all-campus speakers' program
Assignment Due Next Class Meeting: Final Draft of Paper

Week 8
Objective: Prepare for Examinations
Activities: 1. Discuss all-campus program
2. Design exam questions (Exercises 6.1, 6.2) based on class theme and lecture
3. Take exam
4. Peer review exam
Reading assignment for Week 9: None
Out-of-class activity: None

Week 9
Objective: Student group presentations
Activities: 1. Student presentation
2. Critique evaluation
3. Evaluation checklist
In-class exercise: Evaluation checklist
Reading assignment for Week 10: None
Out-of-class activity: None

Week 10
Objectives: Review the semester; evaluate the course
Activities: 1. Formal evaluation
2. Informal discussion of the semester

Creating an Interactive Classroom

THE CLASSROOM ENVIRONMENT

Most college classrooms are very formal and, to first-year students, are sometimes threatening. In the first-year seminar, you should strive to create an environment of purposeful yet unintimidating academic activity. Some students will be uncertain about what to expect from the course but will be prepared to take it seriously. Others may think it a "blow off" course or an easy "A." Your role is to set the tone for the class by the way you model the behavior you expect of the students: interest, involvement, curiosity, and so on. Ultimately your personal motivation and enthusiasm and your appreciation of the students may be the most important ingredients in making the course a success.

DELIVERY METHODS

No one method of delivery is inherently superior to any other. Most freshman seminar teachers use a variety of methods of instruction—lectures, group activities, guest speakers, out-of-class visits, and so on.

Lectures

Lectures are the most common and time-honored method of instruction in higher education and the method faculty are most familiar and comfortable with. In spite of the criticism lectures have come under recently, they do have their place in the classroom and can be employed effectively in a freshman seminar. On the one hand, "the great lecture," as Page Smith (1990) has described it, "is thus a demonstration of something precious and essential in the life of the spirit and the mind and the dramatic power that inheres to that unity." On the other hand, he continues, "the casual, the perfunctory, the oft-repeated, the read lecture, the *dead* lecture is a disservice both to the students and to the ideal of learning that presumably holds the whole venture together."

Although the lecture may be useful to introduce material in the instructor's area of expertise or to teach note-taking, this method of instruction should be used sparingly. In lectures students are passive, and the first-year seminar encourages active learning, aspires to be different from traditional content courses, and has no fixed body of knowledge to "cover."

Group Activities

Group activities are probably the most frequently used method of instruction in first-year seminars. They can form the basis for both in-class and out-of-class learning. Group learning and study can help students significantly in the terms ahead. Recent studies make clear that group work pays off. "The payoff comes in a *modest* way for student achievement, as measured by test scores. It comes in a *far bigger* way on measurements of students' involvement in courses, their enthusiasm, and their pursuit of topics to a more advanced level" (Light, 1990).

In-class group activities and discussions can be done with the class as a whole or in smaller groups. Whole-class activities and discussions enable the instructor to control, direct, and participate in the discussion, sharing his or her experiences and expertise. Whole-class discussions can be used at the end of the period for brief discussions of outside events or other activities to which you do not want to devote a large block of time. A disadvantage of whole-class activities is that the size of the class and the more intimidating nature of large classroom discussions limit the number of students who can, or will, speak.

Small-group discussions work well to get students actively involved in learning. Most of the exercises in *YCE* and in this manual are designed to be completed in small groups.

Groups can be organized in a variety of ways, but the simplest is to decide how many groups you want and to count them off into that number of groups, for example, four groups = 1, 2, 3, 4, 1, 2, 3, 4, and so on. Groups of four to five usually work best. Some of the exercises may require different numbers. Occasionally you will want to structure your groups in some other fashion and may want to continue to use the same groups over again. For example, you may want to set up groups for the oral presentations (*YCE*, Chapter 8) on the basis of a common interest in the topic. Or you may want to balance the groups deliberately on the basis of information you have about the students, for example, by sex, race, age, MBTI type, or leadership qualities.

Before you begin most group activities, remind each group that they should have one person act as a recorder. Whatever the group task, the recorder should be prepared to report the group's findings. During the course of the group exercise or activity, you should walk around the classroom and listen in on the group discussions. Make some mental notes about things that you hear that you will want to use in the discussion that follows.

Small-group work is important for out-of-class activities as well. The oral group report from *YCE*, Chapter 8, for example, is designed primarily as an out-of-class group activity. When you set up groups for out-of-class projects, you may want to organize one or two days of in-class exercises in advance so that they will get comfortable with their groups. Or you may want to begin the group activity during part of a class period. (See Part 2, Chapter 8, of this manual for additional information on group work.)

Small-Group Work

"Students overwhelmingly report one additional benefit of small-group work. They point out that *the process of working in a group*, in a supervised setting, teaches them crucial skills. The skills they learn include how to move a group forward, how to disagree without being destructive or stifling new ideas, and how to include all members in a discussion. Few students, if any, have these skills when they arrive at college." (Light, 1990)

Guest Speakers

You may want to use guest speakers in your class to provide special information or to introduce topics you are unfamiliar or uncomfortable with. Guest speakers provide variety and can make students more specifically aware of campus resources by identifying them with a person. For example, if the director of career planning comes to your class, the students will find a familiar face when they go to the career planning office.

Plan your speakers' appearances well in advance to be sure your schedule will fit with theirs. Give them a clear description of the nature of the course, your class, and how their presentation will fit into your course plan. Make sure they know what is expected of them: where and what time they should arrive, how long they should be prepared to speak, which topics they are to deal with, and the function of those topics in the larger scheme of the course. Tell them how many students are in the class, in case they will be bringing handouts, and find out if they need any resources or assistance that you could provide, such as an overhead projector. Call your speakers a day or two before the class as a reminder, and check to make sure they have no additional unanswered questions about what they are to do.

After the presentation thank your speakers by dropping them a note or giving them a call to tell them how much you appreciated their effort. Pass along some favorable comments from the students if possible. They will enjoy hearing how well their wisdom was received. Remember, you may want to have them back again sometime.

Getting Out of the Classroom

On occasion, you will want to break the routine of the structured classroom by going somewhere else. You can do this during regular class time or at other times during the week.

Touring. Tours are a useful instructional activity. Instead of having experts visit your class, you visit them, for example, in the learning center, the career center, or the registrar's office. Arrange the visits in advance so that the people are prepared to accommodate you. If several sections of the class are doing the same tours, the program director should coordinate the schedule. You may want to arrange a tour of the theater, including a presentation by a theater faculty member or play director, inspection of the theater behind stage—dressing rooms, costumes, makeup, shop, and so on. This kind of tour can be capped with attendance at a play—together as a class or separately—and a discussion of the tour and the play afterward in class. Tours are especially useful on large campuses, where students are more likely not to know where offices and other places are. "Find it" geographical-type tours can also be organized as scavenger hunts to locate places or get signatures of people the student should come to know.

Having a Party. Students appreciate any opportunity to party—that is, to get together to eat and talk. Having a party can lessen the formality of the classroom and let students see their instructor as a person. You can do this any number of ways. If you live close to campus and have the space, invite the students to your home. Or go to their place—have pizza in the lounge of their residence hall. A commuter student could invite the others home, or you could meet in the student center or a local restaurant. If you feel you need to, you can always introduce a class activity—show a movie or do an informal class exercise.

PROCESSING THE ACTIVITIES

At the end of the exercise, have each small group read its report to the class while you write the summary on the board or flip chart. Encourage your students to draw conclusions about the small-group activity. These conclusions might deal with both the content and the process of the activity. Early in the term you will want to discuss the dynamics of groups. Who took the leadership? Who was the recorder and why? Did one person dominate? Did some people not talk? Did the composition of the group (for example, by gender) affect the conclusions? Did they reach consensus? If not, why not? Was it important to reach consensus? How were decisions made? Were people persuaded or just dominated? Were people comfortable with what happened? Was anyone left out?

When you talk about content, you will also want to point out inconsistencies, assumptions, or fallacies in their reasoning. This is the occasion when you can give praise for a job well done, provide additional information on the subject, or relate where and how to get more information. You should make connections to other previous or future classroom activities or readings and exercises in the text. Connections provide coherence and understanding of the objectives of the course.

Processing can be done in a similar manner with out-of-classroom activities—a speaker, play, or musical event they all attended. Have your students examine their reactions to the event; if you asked them to write about the event, read their comments aloud.

Many of the classroom activities can be fun, but their meaning or purpose is not always clear to students. **After completion of each exercise or activity, it is important to spend some time explaining the purpose of the exercise or activity in relation to the stated goals of the course.**

USING WRITING

It is almost axiomatic that writing is, as Janet Emig (1977) argues, "a central academic process." Hence, any course that introduces students to the college experience must include writing. Although the specific chapter on writing from the original edition of *YCE* has been cut from this edition, the editors of the text and this manual assume that writing must be an important part of any first-year seminar.

The Writing Across the Curriculum and the Writing to Learn movements have given increased focus to the goals and process of writing, emphasizing that "writing represents a unique mode of learning—not merely valuable, not merely special, but unique" (Emig, 1977). The objective is to use writing as a means to learn, not to "eradicate the problem of poor writers" (Herrington, 1981). These movements also suggest that a variety of types of writing beyond traditional formal papers be incorporated into the learning process. *YCE* and this course manual provide a variety of writing exercises to be incorporated into classroom and out-of-class activities.

Types of Writing

College courses frequently incorporate a variety of types of writing. These are commonly categorized as free, or informal, writing and formal writing. You will want to incorporate both categories of writing into your course. The syllabi provided in Chapter 4 of this manual indicate examples of how both types of writing might be included in the formal requirements and grading of the course as well as how they might be incorporated in the classroom.

Informal Writing. Informal writing can be used in a variety of ways. The most important and consistent informal writing activity recommended for the course is the journal, described at length in Chapter 3 of this manual. You should also consider using informal writing in class in other ways. For example, have students take 5 minutes at the beginning of the period to write about the previous class, about the chapter just read, or about a program they attended or a speaker they heard; have them do one of the exercises from *YCE* that asks them to write on something; or take some time at the end of the class meeting to write about how they felt about that day's class or to summarize what was discussed. Writing at the beginning of the class can help focus or encourage discussion of an issue. Writing at the end of the class period can help bring closure or help students summarize what was discussed.

One strategy to get students involved is for you to write while they are doing their writing, and then share your writing on the subject. The important characteristic of free writing is the activity—involvement in the process of writing and thinking. You should occasionally collect their writing and note for their individual records that they are doing it. Have them share their writing aloud occasionally. You might want to count it in some way in the course grade. Keep in mind that free writing is not judged in the same manner as formal writing. Grammar, spelling, and mechanics are not evaluated or marked. The objective is to get the ideas and the pen flowing.

Formal Writing. You will also want to include some formal writing assignments. The syllabi in Chapter 4 of this manual provide some suggestions. The writing assignments can be used directly in relationship to the various chapters in *YCE*, or they can focus on a theme or an area of your own choice, described below. If you wish to increase the formal emphasis on writing, you can excerpt materials or exercises from the original edition of *YCE* or use other readings for this objective. Or you may be able to coordinate your writing assignments with the first-year composition course.

If you plan a series of assignments, they should be sequenced so that they advance in complexity and so that each assignment prepares the student for the next one (Herrington, 1981). The assignments should both specify the topic and define the purpose and audience for the paper. "This specificity will help the writer understand what is required of them and usually will challenge them to something more than restating information for no purpose" (Herrington, 1981).

Evaluation

No matter how well designed or creative the writing assignments, if you do not treat them meaningfully, they will have little value. "If the teacher treats the resulting writing as unimportant or merely samples of writing, then the students begin to resent having to write." Conversely, "if the teacher treats the student writings as important to the course and as worthy of substantive response, then the students can be expected to feel more positively about future assignments and to invest more in them" (Herrington, 1981). The process of evaluation should be correlated with the specific assignment, and the criteria for judging the assignment should be specified clearly. An assignment from a psychology class provides an example:

Short Paper 3: Erik Erikson's Theory of Psychosocial Development

The Senses of Trust, Mistrust; Autonomy, Shame/Doubt; Initiative, Guilt; Industry, Inferiority; Identity and Role Confusion.

Question: *Using the definitions and the causes of each "sense" for the first five stages of psychosocial development, indicate which "sense," for example, trust or mistrust, is more characteristic of you and why you believe that sense is more characteristic of you than its opposite. Write your essay as if you were writing an Eriksonian autobiography to facilitate someone's understanding of your psychosocial development.*

Requirements: *In order to write this assignment, you must:*

1. *Know Erikson's definition of each sense*
2. *Know the cause of each sense, as seen by Erikson*
3. *Be able to recognize each sense in yourself*
4. *Be able to provide concrete examples of each sense in yourself*

Evaluative Criteria: *Your instructor will evaluate your essay with these criteria in mind:*

1. *Did you clearly understand Erikson's conceptualization of each sense, that is, Erikson's definition of the sense and his assertions about its cause?*
2. *Did you provide lucid examples of how each sense is evident in your psychosocial development?*

Note: *Your instructor will evaluate each short paper for content only. You will be allowed to write one revision of the content of your paper*

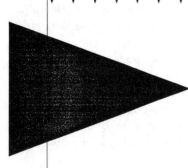

A Guide to Peer Review

The purpose of student peer review of writing assignments is to enable you to help each other improve the quality of your writing .

The process of student peer review is to pass the papers around in the group and read all the papers. As you read them make specific suggestions and comments on the papers. After all members of the group have finished reading and commenting, discuss the papers in the group as a whole.

The comments should be useful. Although it is desirable to affirm that a fellow student is doing a good job, general comments that are not specific are not very helpful. Statements like "Nice job," or "I liked what you wrote" may make the student feel good but do not give him or her much practical help on how to improve his or her writing.

Reading the paper closely for specific errors in spelling, grammar, or punctuation may be helpful, but remember, the paper will most likely be retyped. The most useful information you can give is organizational and substantive.

Organizational information includes such things as: Is the paper logically organized (does each element or paragraph follow logically from the preceding one)? Does each paragraph make sense in itself, and is it logically organized internally?

Substantive information includes such things as: Does the paper address the question (for instance, if the question asks for four examples, does the writer give four examples)? Does the paper use an appropriate form of response (for instance, if the question asks for a description, does the writer give a true *description*)?

to try to earn a higher grade. Your instructor will note your grammatical, spelling, and typographical errors, which you must correct in pencil on your paper. Correcting your errors is mandatory. However, correcting your errors will not raise your grade. If you fail to correct your errors, a grade of "F" will be assigned to your short paper (Herrington, 1981).

In this assignment the requirements are clearly outlined step by step, and the evaluation criteria are specifically stated (Herrington, 1981).

Drafting

Many first-year composition or writing classes introduce students to the concept of drafting—the process of writing, rewriting, and refining. You should incorporate this process in the way that you design your writing assignments, providing spacing and time between drafts. The syllabi in Chapter 4 in this manual indicate how drafts might be spaced for the formal papers, and they set aside one class period for peer review of papers. Peer review is a way you can incorporate the process of revising and editing into your writing design. Peer review gives students a chance for someone else to read and critique their paper before they turn in their final draft.

For peer review divide the class into groups and have the students exchange papers; then have them discuss the papers. A sample handout for the peer review process is on p. 68. You could combine both mechanical editing and content evaluation in the peer review, but you should ask your students to read and comment on only one or two specific types of errors or problems, such as subject–verb agreement and provision of supporting examples.

Computers and Writing

Computers are wonderful tools for writing and can take much of the drudgery out of the process. Encourage your students to write their papers on the computer. To help them, you should be familiar with the computing facilities that are available on your campus, including location, hours, software available, training that is provided, and laboratory assistance. Include the facilities on your campus tour. Check with your students on how much they know about using the computer. You may want to arrange individual training sessions for them in the computer center.

Using computers for writing facilitates and even encourages multiple drafts. Computers make editing faster and easier; they can encourage collaboration and can simply make writing more fun (Fulwiler, 1989). Remind students to use a spelling checker, and encourage them to try out one of the new grammar-checking programs as well. Using a computer to eliminate at least some of the irritating mechanical problems can make writing less of a chore and more rewarding for students.

USING YOUR OWN EXPERTISE

Most faculty feel more comfortable teaching "content" in their own discipline than in the unfamiliar territory of study skills and values clarification. For these instructors, and to give the course more academic credibility with the skeptics, elements can be integrated into a first-year experience course that introduce students to the instructor's content field. Some examples are provided in the syllabi in Chapter 4 of this manual.

Specifically, elements that serve to sharpen writing, research, and study skills can use the instructor's discipline as their basis. For example, a history instructor might choose to incorporate an issue or theme from American history into the course. The topic could be used for a lecture for students to practice note-taking. (See the 3 credits, 3 sessions/week, 14 week syllabus: Week 4, Day 2.) This could be followed by having the students read an article on which to do the précis (Week 5, Day 2). Designing and taking a model exam could be based on the material (Week 6, Day 1). The oral reports and the formal papers could also be tied to the discipline content.

The amount of discipline-based content material incorporated into a course depends on the particular program, the number of class sessions, and the desires of the individual instructor. The first-year experience seminar model allows the instructor the flexibility to introduce his or her expertise in a different context and with different methods if he or she chooses. It can present to students a window on a subject field they might never otherwise see, and it enables instructors to try out teaching ideas and techniques they might be reluctant to experiment with in a more traditional course.

EVALUATION AND GRADING

Students are always concerned about the evaluation of their performance. What counts and for how much? As indicated previously, your syllabus should state clearly the components of the course that are to be counted in the final grade and how much they are being weighted.

Research shows that students value a clearly and carefully organized course in which they know exactly what is expected of them. Frequent, quick, and detailed feedback is important. Students strongly indicate that the most important element for course effectiveness is rapid response on assignments (Light, 1990). You should return any exercises, quizzes, or papers you collect as quickly as possible, preferably by the next class period. The journal, as indicated previously, should also be returned on a regular schedule.

Students also have a strong preference for frequent evaluation (Light, 1990). The first-year experience seminar lends itself to incorporating a number of evaluation components and opportunities for quick feedback. You should take time periodically to assess where each of the students is cumulatively and remind them individually of the various components they have yet to complete.

CHAPTER 6 ▼▼▼▼▼▼▼▼▼▼▼▼▼▼▼▼▼▼▼▼▼▼▼▼

Getting Started

THE BASICS OF PREPARATION

Things to Have

In anticipation of your first class meeting, you will want to prepare both yourself and the classroom. You should also check that you have the supplies you will need.

The Classroom. Check out your classroom in advance to make sure that you know where it is and how it is equipped and that there are no surprises on the first day of class. Can you arrange or rearrange the furniture? Are the chairs movable? Is there a blackboard?

Supplies. Secure a sufficient quantity of supplies you will need: large flip chart tablets and markers for small-group reporting, masking tape for displaying sheets of flip chart pages, and so on. Check with the bookstore well in advance to assure that the books you intend to use have been ordered and are in stock.

Things to Know

You cannot be an expert on everything, but your students will look to you for information concerning the school. You should be prepared to answer their basic questions and know where to refer them for answers to other questions.

College Rules and Regulations. You should secure the most recent copy of the school catalog and review it carefully. If you are relatively new to the campus and have done little or no academic advising, you should take some time to meet with the appropriate person to review the advising procedures. Take advantage of any advisor training available, and arrange to meet with the director of academic advising and, perhaps, the registrar or director of registration. Obtain a copy of the faculty advisor's handbook if your school has one. Collect information on the courses that a first-year student will need for the various majors.

Campus Resources. Review all the up-to-date information you have on campus resources. Make a list of questions you think students might ask. Swap lists or brainstorm with another first-year seminar instructor. Make a list of names, locations, and phone numbers of sources of referral or information to have handy or to pass out to the students. If your institution does not have a resource manual or directory, suggest that one be created. You may want to compile with other instructors a list of "most frequently asked questions" and their answers.

Student Information. Find out as much as you can about your students before they start, or as early as possible in the term. If you know the names of your students well in advance of the first day of class, many colleges will let you review their admissions folder for general information about them—major interest, high school activities, and so on. If this information is not available, you can ask the students to fill out a brief data sheet in class the first day or answer specific questions about themselves in their journal for their first assignment. This information will help you get to know the students faster, establish a more personal relationship with them, and identify needs and problems they may have later on. For example, if you know that a student has a potential health problem, you will want to tell him or her where the health services facility is. If a student was on the high school paper, you will want to be able to tell this student how to get involved on the campus paper if he or she is interested.

Peer Mentors

If you intend to use upper-class students with your class, you should prepare them in advance as well. If possible, select and make arrangements with the students the preceding spring. Think about ways to provide "training" on what you want them to do. Clearly define their responsibilities and your expectations of them, and supply them with a syllabus that details their involvement.

THE FIRST DAY OF CLASS

If you have never taught a first-year experience seminar, or perhaps never taught at all, you may be nervous on the first day of class. You can be assured that the students will be even more nervous. Your class may, in fact, be the first class they have in college. Your objective should be to help them become at ease with you, their classmates, and the school.

You can help by beginning with some informal activity such as talking about how things are going this first day or week of class. Are they settled into their dorm room? Are they having any problems? If they are commuters, have they found a place to park? Do they know where all their classes meet?

A discussion of classes can lead you to an introduction of your seminar. Because it is not a typical content course, the students will probably not understand what the seminar is about. Begin by providing them with a general overview of the course, pass out the syllabus, and explain your expectations in more detail. Continue to put them at ease, and begin the process of group building by doing one of the exercises described in Chapter 3 of this manual.

Using *YCE* to Create an Interactive Classroom

A COMPREHENSIVE TEXT/RESOURCE FOR YOUR CLASSROOM

The authors of *YCE* recognize that, "while there is growing consensus about the aims and the means of the freshman seminar, there is also great diversity in how the 101 course is structured and in what topics are emphasized." The text, therefore, is designed to be both comprehensive and flexible. As indicated before, the units can be presented in any order, and many of the chapters are designed to be used either in their entirety or in parts. Several special features, incorporated to enliven the text and the class, can be used in class or by the students on their own.

Prompts for Discussion and Writing

Writing and classroom discussion in large or small groups are two central activities in first-year seminars. Several of the special features are designed to be used as the basis for informal classroom discussion, writing assignments, or other activities. An introductory comment representing a student point of view appears on the first page of each chapter (see p. 65 in the main text for an example). The chapters also include feature boxes, photos and cartoons, a concluding journal assignment, and suggestions for further reading. Two special icons highlight opportunities for writing or group work in the text's numbered exercises: ✍ This icon indicates a writing exercise. ♟ This icon indicates an exercise involving class or small-group discussion.

Introductory Comments: The Student's View

The opening student comment that begins each chapter can be used as a takeoff point to begin discussing the chapter or even as a concluding reflection. These comments attempt to distill into a few words the essence of student frustration—lack of knowledge about or irritation with the subject covered in the chapter. The comments can be incorporated into the class in a variety of ways. Before they have read the chapter, students can be asked to complete an in-class, 5-minute "free-writing" reaction to the quotation. Or after they have read the chapter and the discussion is concluded, they can write a response to a question like "Suppose a friend made this comment to you after you have read and discussed the chapter. How would you respond to her or him?"

For discussion, you can have small groups analyze the student comment and articulate the student's problems or concerns. If the exercise is done at the end of the chapter, the group can list some specific solutions to the student's problem. Or the students can role-play the problem. One student in a group of three plays the commenting student, one plays a friend or advisor, and one observes to discuss their responses later. Play out the "drama" with the dialogue focusing on the stated problem and possible solutions. Have the "cast" change roles and repeat the process. Consider using this approach as a midsemester review by doing the small-group discussion or having the students role-play for several chapters. Treat the cartoons and photos as you did the material in "Introductory Comments: The Student's View."

Suggestions for Further Reading

Each chapter in the main text concludes with a "Suggestions for Further Reading" section. In addition to the usual option of referring students to this section for more information if they have questions, you can put these suggested readings to practical use in the class. Incorporate them directly into the activities of Chapter 8, "An Information Age Introduction to the Library," in YCE. The text itself can be a source for identifying potential topics for the library exercise, and you can suggest that students begin their search for information with the suggested readings. This can also lead to a discussion of the use of suggested readings generally and of those in their texts for other classes.

Building Your Course and Your Program

RECRUITING STUDENTS FOR THE COURSE

Recruiting students for a first-year seminar is seldom difficult but may require some extra effort. If the seminar is required of all students, of course, there is no difficulty. Even if smaller groups such as provisionally admitted students or undecided students are required to take the course, you will find that the sections fill quickly. But if the course is not required for all students or for any special population, you will need to implement some strategies for "selling" the course.

The method by which incoming first-year students choose courses is critical to your strategy. In most situations incoming students register either by mail, by telephone, or in person. With mail or telephone registrations the students' decisions will be based on the information they receive from the college admissions or registrar's office. Be sure the registration information sent to incoming students contains information about the seminar. This information should include an attractive, separate brochure that explains the program and its contribution to the students' college success.

If possible, the specific course should be highlighted on the registration form itself with a separate listing or a specific question, such as, "Do you wish to enroll in University 101?" The office or person(s) who will answer questions about registration should understand and be able to explain the course. The director of the first-year program should discuss the registration process with those who organize it, informing them of the nature of the program and its goals and objectives. You might even send support staff to an instructor training workshop.

For walk-in or on-campus registration the task is more difficult. Again, if preregistration materials are mailed to students, first-year seminar material should be included. Otherwise, mail a brochure to students, explaining the course and its contribution to their success. If students register without contact with an advisor, the individuals doing the registrations should be made aware of the mission and objectives of the course and urged to encourage students to register for it. If the students register through special advisors or general faculty advisors, the director of the first-year program should be sure those individuals receive information about the importance of the course.

Parents, current students, and alumni can be allies in your strategy as well. In many instances parents exert a strong influence on the courses students take. The brochure to promote your first-year experience seminar should be written with an eye to the parents as well as to the entering students themselves. You might also want to send the parents a special letter about the course. Other students can also have an impact on how entering students make registration decisions, even before the first term begins. The reputation your course develops over the years will help you use those advanced students to sell the course to the new students. Students who are admissions tour guides or who are part of the first-year orientation process are important people to have as informed, enthusiastic supporters and promoters of the course. Over time, the reputation can extend beyond the campus as well. A successful course of long standing can even build an alumni following that will help prospective students become aware of the program and encourage them to sign up for it.

PROMOTING THE COURSE AMONG YOUR COLLEAGUES

If recruiting students does not present major difficulties, recruiting faculty may. The number of sections of the seminar you offer may, in fact, be more restricted by the number of faculty you are able to recruit than by the number of students available.

Faculty have many reasons for not choosing to teach a first-year seminar. They don't have enough time; their departmental responsibilities are too great; their major courses come first; the seminar is not academic enough; they do not have enough control over the course; they are not comfortable with the teaching method; and so on. Most of these reservations fall into two categories: (1) disagreement over the nature and content of the course itself and (2) the best use of the faculty member's time.

Some faculty are reluctant to teach a course that lacks a clearly specified body of knowledge and uses a method of instruction with which they are uncomfortable or unfamiliar. If you have identified faculty who have the potential to become seminar instructors and who you believe can be won over to the instructional team, several arguments may influence them positively. Some "content," you can indicate, can be built into the course. You might also point out that this course will give them an opportunity to meet first-year students whom they might not otherwise ever get to know—perhaps even interest students in taking a course in the instructor's discipline. Pointing out the individualized elements in the course may also allay the concerns of faculty who want to control their own course.

Attending the instructor training workshop may also sway them. The workshop can help them become more comfortable with alternative teaching styles. Remind them that other new instructors will be teaching the course and that they will be part of a team of instructors whom they can look to for support. Finally, you should recognize that not everyone is meant to be an instructor in this type of course. Some are convinced of this in advance or after attending the workshops. Others teach the course once and say "never again!" That's all right too.

Faculty priorities and time are a different matter. Some faculty will tell you, "I would love to teach the first-year seminar, but I have to teach these other courses for our majors." Their statement is a reflection of their and, probably, the institution's values. Leadership and support from the administration and from senior faculty are essential to create a system that values teaching first-year students. The bottom line is that faculty must be convinced that instructing first-year students is equal in importance to teaching courses in their disciplines for advanced students.

Given the historic value system of American higher education, this ideal is not likely to be created easily. Faculty recognize that tenure decisions, promotion decisions, and the support of their departmental and professional peers rest primarily on activities—teaching, research, publication—within their discipline. Pragmatically then, the director of the first-year seminar program must work with the department chair, the institution's dean(s), or whoever has authority to determine loads or establish schedules. He or she must work with the administration to find ways to free up faculty to teach in the program—by hiring replacement adjuncts; authorizing overloads; or allowing "banking" of credit taught to be collected in a later term or year—by whatever means your system allows. Moreover, the administration must be convinced that the important tenure, promotion, and salary decisions must reflect the value that teaching first-year students is important.

GETTING ADMINISTRATIVE SUPPORT

Support of senior administrators is crucial to the success of a first-year student program, for administrators have influence and control money. Provosts, vice presidents, and deans—not to mention presidents or chief executive officers—have the authority and influence to make things happen. A call from the dean may enable a department chair to find a way for a willing faculty member to be available to teach a section of the first-year seminar. A note from the provost encouraging a new faculty member to attend an instructor training workshop is likely to get an immediate positive reply. And, of course, administrators allocate the money for special programs.

The support of senior administrators is not difficult to obtain. Most senior academic administrators take an institutional view and are aware of the advantages of first-year experience programs. In many cases the dean or vice president actually initiates the first-year seminar.

If your dean is not among the converted, you should prepare a summary of some of the literature on the national freshman movement and in particular the information on student retention. This instructor's manual should provide you much of what you need. Encourage your dean to attend one of the National Conferences on The Freshman Year Experience$_{SM}$ and to participate in the instructor training workshop to get a feel for the course. Perhaps she or he might even like to teach the course.

Whether your dean is a longtime advocate or new to first-year programming, it is important to keep in touch about the program and maintain a steady flow of information on your successes. Meet with the director of institutional research and design a plan for an empirical study of the impact of your first-year program on institutional retention or whichever goals you define for your program. Also retain and compile anecdotal information from students, parents, and faculty about the course.

In addition to retention and community building, first-year programs benefit the institution in a variety of ways. If you require attendance at collateral programs, like a speakers series (discussed in Chapter 3), for example, the freshman course can generate significant audiences. No dean wants to spend $3,000 for a speaker and have an audience of only ten people. Compile data on attendance to demonstrate this additional impact on campus life.

Teaching first-year experience seminars also promotes faculty development. Faculty can be rejuvenated teaching the seminar; some carry away new teaching strategies, and almost all develop a new view of students and a renewed perspective on the first-year experience. It also can produce administrative development. Many academic and Student Affairs deans teach this course. Compiling data—on the instructors in the course and changes in their teaching style and performance and on administrators and their broadened understanding of first-year student issues—can provide compelling evidence of faculty and staff development.

A successful first-year experience program requires the support of the entire campus community—admissions, student affairs, academic administration, faculty, academic support services, and more. The more people you can make aware of your program and its goals, the more people you can convince to become involved in some way, the more support you will have. As the program gets going, it will build its own momentum and support, but it will never achieve the level of structural stability that an academic department enjoys. It will always require an extra effort of organization, coordination, direction, recruitment, and cultivation. But it is worth it!

2

Teaching the Chapters of *Your College Experience: Strategies for Success*, Concise Edition

Part 2 gives general suggestions on how to teach each chapter. The chapter-by-chapter presentation includes chapter instructional goals, the relationship of the specific chapter to the rest of the text, a list of questions students typically ask, tips on teaching the chapter, and an elaboration of teaching objectives.

CHAPTER 1 ▼▼▼▼▼▼▼▼▼▼▼▼▼▼▼▼▼▼▼▼▼▼▼▼▼

Keys to Success

CHAPTER OVERVIEW

A. Chapter goals
B. Timing and connections to other topics
C. Questions students typically ask
D. Teaching this chapter
E. Tips on teaching "Keys to Success"
F. In-class use of exercises
G. Journal exercise

A. CHAPTER GOALS

1. To introduce factors that contribute to persistence
2. To introduce a process of setting goals
3. To encourage students to set goals that will contribute to their persistence
4. To communicate that the circumstances of commuters may work against persistence
5. To encourage commuters to set goals that will overcome the obstacles they face
6. To secure the students' understanding of the outcomes of a college education
7. To stimulate the students to gain self-awareness about their reasons for attending college
8. To make all of the above especially apply to returning students.

B. TIMING AND CONNECTIONS TO OTHER TOPICS

This chapter should be assigned and discussed at the beginning of the course. The chapter is essentially an overview of both the text and the course itself.

Connections

Because this chapter provides an overview, it connects, in effect, with all the chapters in the text.

C. QUESTIONS STUDENTS TYPICALLY ASK

1. Why do I have to worry about setting goals? I like to go with the flow.
2. Persistence factors? I had no trouble getting through high school!
3. As a commuter, can I live at home and still be successful?
4. After being out of school for so many years, can I make it?
5. Why do "they" want to change me? I like the way I am!
6. Why are "they" asking me to take courses that raise issues about marriage and the family? I just want to take accounting courses so that I can make a living.

D. TEACHING THIS CHAPTER

Beginning college students often hold contradictory beliefs about their new environment. On the one hand, they believe they have been successful thus far in their lives and will continue to be successful. On the other hand, almost all begin college with some nagging doubts. They've heard from older siblings and friends who've been to college that college is significantly different from high school. Thus, they're really not quite sure that what worked in high school and in the world of work and the home will also work in college. They fear that they won't be able to discover what *does* work. As one student put it, "There's a kind of magic that some students have and others don't, and I hope I can discover the secret myself!"

The purpose of this chapter is to introduce your students to the secret, which is anything but magic. Rather, the secret to college success is in establishing a deliberate, rational plan to guide their academic and extra-curricular life. In presenting guidelines, the authors of the chapter base their recommendations on an understanding of the research about retention/persistence (in particular, the research of Alexander Astin, Vincent Tinto, and E.T. Pascarella). This research shows correlations between specific student behaviors and persistence through graduation. Although these are simply correlations (and not causal relationships), they do suggest ways to help students adopt positive behaviors that will increase the chances of completing a degree. The statistics included in the beginning of Chapter 1 (that is, that only 40 percent of American college students complete their degrees) are not gratuitous. This book and the course that you are teaching are intended to show students that they can beat these odds.

As you begin this course and this unit, please note an irony—although the book is about success, the point of departure is a list of commonly held fears of failure. This list is not intended to scare students. Rather, it is based on a very positive belief: *Students who establish a deliberate plan of action for themselves significantly increase their chances for success.* Remember the title of this book, *Your College Experience: Strategies for Success.* As you begin your course, it is important that you "accentuate the positive, eliminate the negative."

The twenty-one "persistence factors" that Jewler and Gardner enumerate constitute a touchstone that you can use throughout the course to test your students' plans of action. Take time at the beginning of the course to present these factors as simple, positive steps to success!

Many of the persistence factors are dealt with later on in the book. In this chapter, you might focus on the following:

1. Find and get to know one individual on campus who knows you are there and cares about your survival.
2. Understand why you are in college.
3. Get involved in campus activities.
4. Show up.

Because this is the beginning of the term and you are still concerned with "building the group," try this class exercise. Divide the class into four groups, one for each factor (if you decide to add factors that we have not included on our list, feel free to do so, and divide the class accordingly). Give each group the same assignment. The four factors are so important to the success of first-year students that each ought to be the subject of a separate chapter in their textbook.

1. Each group should construct an argument intended to convince the publisher's board of editors of the need for the chapter.
2. Each group should present the argument to the board of editors (that is, the class as a whole).
3. These presentations will provide the basis for a group discussion and allow you to stress the importance of the four factors.
4. At the end of the four presentations, ask the board of editors to vote on which factors they will include.

Because you are using this exercise to build the group into a coherent, working unit and to highlight the importance of these persistence factors, do not grade these presentations. The sooner your students begin to apply these factors to their behavior, the greater their chances of success. Throughout the term, you should continue to stress the importance of these factors.

Chapter 1 also does an excellent job of exploring the value of a college education. It states, up front, that college students are preparing for careers that will give them economic security throughout their lives, so there's no pretense about the primary reason motivating most students to attend college. Having stated this, the chapter goes on to explore some of the other reasons: increased knowledge and cognitive complexity; increased self-esteem, confidence, and competence; better preparation for marriage and other relationships; and so on.

Although it's important to make the students aware of the value of a college education, traditional-age students may not fully understand the significance of these abstractions this early in their college career. Of course, they'll understand the words, but will the words have the necessary impact? Try to use the nontraditional students as examples to help make the abstractions concrete.

E.   TIPS ON TEACHING "KEYS TO SUCCESS"

It is fairly important to get the attention of your students at the beginning of this chapter. One way to do this is by getting them to consider what it might be like to be on a plane flown by a pilot who doesn't have the slightest idea of the destination, flight path, and so on. When you teach the material on the value of a college education, place the responsibility for the discussion squarely on your students' shoulders by encouraging them to use the chapter as a guide to understanding the changes they expect to undergo and will continue to undergo. Doing this serves three purposes: First, it helps you avoid preachiness; second, it encourages the students to think more deeply about the issues; finally, at the end of the semester, it is a nice culminating experience.

F.   IN-CLASS USE OF EXERCISES

Exercise 1.1 "Your Reasons for Attending College"

One of the basic threads of *YCE* is the importance of goal setting. In fact, student success is linked to the process from the book's beginning to its end. Thus, it is important at the beginning of the term to take up goal setting, and Exercise 1.1 is a good starting point.

Because this is the beginning of the term and your class is not yet built into a group, the personal nature of the exercises may preclude an open discussion about personal goals. It is important, however, that the exercises be processed, and we suggest the following possibilities.

1.   If you require your students to write a journal, ask them to include the exercises in the week's journal so that you can comment on them.

2.   Require your students to submit the exercises as an out-of-class assignment, which you could then comment on.

3.   Set up individual appointments to discuss the goals and strategies. Obviously, this is the most time-consuming suggestion, but it is particularly appropriate if you are your students' advisor.

G.   JOURNAL EXERCISE

We recommend that, before ending this chapter, you make your journal expectations clear to your students. Read the boxed material (titled "A First-Year Journal") on page 21 with them. Let them know how you will treat the journal suggestions made at each chapter's end. Read the students' first journal entries, including the response to the journal exercise on p. 22. Doing so will tell you whether you need to provide your students with more instruction on writing journal entries. By all means, be sure they understand how important the journal really is to their one-way conversation with themselves and their two-way conversation with you.

CHAPTER 2

Time Management: The Foundation of Academic Success

CHAPTER OVERVIEW

A. Chapter goals
B. Timing and connections to other topics
C. Questions students typically ask
D. Teaching this chapter
E. Tips on teaching "Time Management: The Foundation of Academic Success"
F. In-class use of exercises
G. Journal exercise

A. CHAPTER GOALS

1. To show that time management is one of the keys to college—and life—success
2. To model methods of gaining control over time
3. To encourage students to adapt a method of time management that works for them
4. To analyze time management problems peculiar to commuting students
5. To encourage commuting students to adapt a method of time management that works for them

B. TIMING AND CONNECTIONS TO OTHER TOPICS

We all know that students should begin practicing effective study skills from their first days on campus, and it makes sense for instructors to introduce these skills early on. Unfortunately, beginning college students do not always see the need for improving their study skills, since the techniques they used throughout high school were relatively successful. Still, first-year students need to be introduced to effective study skills as early as possible, so don't give up. In your first-year orientation course or seminar, you should introduce study skills at the beginning of the term and continue to reinforce those skills throughout the term. We suggest that you begin the unit on study skills immediately after completing Chapter 1 and whatever other introductory exercises you plan. Then proceed in order through Chapters 2, 3, 4, 5, and 6. By the end of this five-chapter unit on study skills, you will have given your students an excellent overview.

There is, by the way, an alternate position that would have you delay teaching study skills until well into the middle of the term. This view bases the delay on the "need to know" principle, which suggests that students modify their behavior only if they have a need to do so. By the middle of the term, your students will have learned that they do "need to know" better study methods, and they will therefore have better motivation for learning the study skills you teach.

Connections

► Chapter 1, "Keys to Success," gives general advice on setting goals and relates the advice to success in college.

C. QUESTIONS STUDENTS TYPICALLY ASK

1. How do you expect me to do well if I put myself on a schedule? I work best under pressure.
2. If I do manage my time, will that guarantee success?
3. How can I manage my time when my entire household is completely disorganized?

D. TEACHING THIS CHAPTER

The students who are most in need of improving their skills are often the ones who are most resistant. Study skills in general appear to them to be rigid and confining, and these students believe that by practicing the techniques they are condemning themselves to a form of slavery. You know that just the opposite is true, so you need to make the case for study skills early and often.

When we teach study skills, we run the risk of making some students feel inferior. In offering good advice, discussions of study skills often assert generalizations about study methods that appear to suggest there is only one way of studying (for example, "good student time managers frequently have assignments finished several days before actual due dates to allow time for emergencies"). Generalizations like these can be guilt-inducing to students who manage their time differently, because they come to believe they are more like Joe than like Carmen or because they cannot, in spite of their best efforts, get everything done on time. As Chapter 3, "Learning Styles," shows, different personality types manage their lives in different ways, and we shouldn't make students feel guilty over matters of personality.

Rather, we need to show them other, more efficient, ways of doing things and allow them the opportunity to adapt methods they are comfortable with. Thus, you should avoid making negative generalizations about study methods. The last thing we want to do is lower the self-esteem of beginning students. They have enough to concern themselves with.

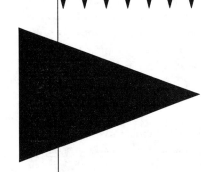

What We Know About First-Year Students

Study Hours

► **High School** Not surprisingly, few students reported significant hours of study in high school. The majority reported studying 10 hours or less per week.

► **College** Although students did recognize that increased study hours would be necessary in college, few students envisioned college as a full-time job. The majority of first-year students doubled their high school study hours and estimated that 11–20 hours of study per week would be adequate.

► **Reality** After one year of college, first-year students were surprised at how unrealistic they had been about their estimates of study hours required by college-level courses. They realized that students who expect a B average or better must study a minimum of 30–40 hours per week.

Source: Penn State Freshman Survey, summarized by James Kelly, Assistant Director, Division of Undergraduate Studies, The Pennsylvania State University.

Present a methodology so that students can gain control over their time. Recognizing, however, that using the methodology often involves breaking old habits and gaining new ones, you must constantly remind students that Carmen and Joe are caricatures—not real students—and that the students' purpose in your course is to develop study habits that they will continue to refine and develop over the next several years of college.

E. TIPS ON TEACHING "TIME MANAGEMENT: THE FOUNDATION OF ACADEMIC SUCCESS"

An effective way of sensitizing students to the issue of time management is by asking them to keep an accurate record of how they spend their time. Ask your students to read and complete Exercise 2.1. (See below for guides to in-class use of the exercise.) Figure 2.2, "Timetable and Master Plan" (p. 33), will help your students keep track of their time. They can photocopy this form.

Other than making some general observations about the chapter (discussed earlier in "Teaching This Chapter"), you will not need to explain the time management system outlined in the chapter. Instead, use class time to process some of the exercises.

F.   IN-CLASS USE OF EXERCISES

While you will want your students to do Exercises 2.1 through 2.8, you need process only Exercises 2.1 and 2.2 in class. Exercises 2.3, 2.4, and 2.5 will provide each student with invaluable information about his or her time commitments for the entire semester; there is little to be gained by processing these exercises in class. Instead, your students should make these exercises a permanent part of their notebooks or journals. Thus, this information will always be available for reference. Individual students will find Exercises 2.6 through 2.8 useful and you should assign them as homework. As always, be prepared to answer students' questions about them.

Exercise 2.1 "Identify Your Priorities"

At the end of the week, set aside about 15 minutes of class time to process the exercise. Ask students to share their observations about their priorities and how they spend their time. Divide the students into small groups in class to discuss their results. Did the results surprise them? Points for discussion might be similarities and differences among priorities; the relationship between current practices and college success; and suggestions for change. This is a good time to direct students to "How to Beat Procrastination" (p. 26).

A Word of Advice: Do not use this sharing period to preach about "the proper way to manage time." The more self-discoveries your students make, the better.

Exercise 2.2 "Basic Advice"

Divide the students into small groups to discuss Joe and Sheila. As they discuss Joe's self-defeating behaviors, the students are likely to urge each other to set unrealistic time management goals for themselves. As you move from group to group, you should caution them against trying to make extraordinary changes in their lives. Such changes are unrealistic to the point that students cannot follow through, and this leads to frustration and a weak self-image. It is better for students to set small, manageable changes for themselves and to follow through on these changes. Making those changes motivates them to set other small, manageable goals.

If you have students like Sheila in your class—i.e., nontraditional, married with children—you can almost count on a spirited discussion in which the students reveal a great deal about themselves. Be prepared for self-disclosure that is candid and personal.

G.   JOURNAL EXERCISE

When you assign this journal entry, you might remind your students once again that Joe and Carmen are caricatures, not real students, and that the last thing students should do is measure themselves against an unattainable yardstick. Remember, it's the small, manageable changes that your students should aspire to. Also, you might want to ask your students to explain the strategies they will employ to deal with distractions.

CHAPTER 3 ▼▼▼▼▼▼▼▼▼▼▼▼▼▼▼▼▼▼▼▼▼▼▼▼

Learning Styles

CHAPTER OVERVIEW

A. Chapter goals
B. Timing and connections to other topics
C. Questions students typically ask
D. Teaching this chapter
E. Tips on teaching "Learning Styles"
F. In-class use of exercises
G. Journal exercise

A. CHAPTER GOALS

1. To direct students' attention to different learning styles
2. To help students discover their own learning styles
3. To direct students' attention to different teaching styles
4. To help students analyze and adjust to the teaching styles of their instructors
5. To encourage students to form study groups

B. TIMING AND CONNECTIONS TO OTHER TOPICS

For the sake of concentration of effort and continuity, teach this chapter soon after you have taught Chapter 2.

Connections

▶ Chapter 4, "Listening and Learning in the Classroom," gives advice on approaches to listening to and taking notes on lectures.

- Chapter 5, "A Sound Approach to Textbooks," presents methods for reading textbooks.
- Chapter 6, "Making the Grade," presents an array of testing styles as well as methods for studying for tests.
- Chapter 7, "Teacher and Student: Partners in Learning," features three kinds of teachers and explains their expectations of students.
- Chapter 10, "Major, Career, and Transfer Planning," discusses personality type in terms of the MBTI.

C. QUESTIONS STUDENTS TYPICALLY ASK

1. How can you put people in these little boxes?
2. I'm 38 years old. How can I change my learning style now?
3. How do you expect me to adjust to that guy's teaching style? He doesn't make any sense!

D. TEACHING THIS CHAPTER

In our discussion of Chapter 1, we asserted that some first-year students believe a mystery surrounds the success of some students and the failure of others—that there's a kind of magic that successful students have. You know this is anything but true, and we recommend teaching study skills in general and this unit on learning styles in particular in order to:

1. Demystify the experience of being a college student
2. Provide a series of methods that will encourage being a more deliberate and organized student
3. Facilitate the students' self-development

Demystification

The opening section of Chapter 3 in *YCE* suggests that many first-year students do believe there is a mysterious process at work. A student does well in one course that he or she finds fascinating but that his or her friend hates and is failing. The friend is doing well in another course, but he or she finds the class intolerably boring and is in danger of getting a very poor grade.

By demonstrating that different students have different approaches to learning and different instructors have very different teaching styles, this chapter replaces the mystery with a logical means of analyzing classes and teachers. Thus, students should feel more in control of their success.

Deliberateness

If your students know that classes are not simply chaotic, they should be able to approach learning somewhat more deliberately than they might have without this knowledge. Teaching learning styles is another way you can reinforce one of the basic premises of *YCE*—that college success depends largely on careful planning.

Self-Development

The chapter on learning styles is not included to provide a shortcut to success by showing first-year students how to "psych out" their instructors. Instead, the chapter suggests that as first-year students develop academically, they will need to expand their learning styles to embrace a wide variety of teaching styles. This is just another way of adding to their "bag of tricks." As a writing instructor used to tell her students in response to their complaints that she was trying to destroy their writing styles, "I'm not trying to destroy your styles at all; I'm trying to help you develop a variety of styles."

E. TIPS ON TEACHING "LEARNING STYLES"

Because this chapter differentiates between two learning styles and two teaching styles, you might begin teaching the chapter by presenting two lectures, each of which demonstrates a different teaching style. You might choose to lecture on the "theme" of your first-year experience seminar, or you might choose a topic similar to what your first-year students are hearing in their more "traditional" courses. Remember, it's not the material in the lecture that's important but the styles of the lectures you deliver. At some time during your presentation, you should point out that these two styles rarely exist in their "pure" forms. Most teachers blend the two styles, although it is usually obvious that one style is dominant.

We suggest that you allocate about 20 minutes for these lectures. In presenting the two styles, remind your class that one teaching/learning style is not better than another teaching/learning style. Depending on whether you use a sensing or factual and informational teaching style or intuitive or analytical learning style, you will present very different kinds of information and stress very different issues, even when teaching the same basic subject. Perhaps you will find the following illustration helpful. Assume that you are going to lecture on the Industrial Revolution.

A Sensing or Factual and Informational Teaching Style

This teaching style:

1. Provides a precise definition of the Industrial Revolution
2. Presents a precise chronological framework
3. Outlines the lecture on the board as a conceptual framework
4. Lists primary inventions of the period and their inventors
5. Provides statistics about population shifts from rural to urban centers; about the nature of the urban working class; and about the increase in imports and exports

An Intuitive and Analytical Teaching Style

This teaching style:

1. Examines the processes that brought about the Industrial Revolution, for example, an acceptance of the belief that humankind can progress through control over nature
2. Discusses the relationship between the development of the middle class and the concept of progress

3. Analyzes the reasons that England is the first nation to experience industrialization with specific reference to England's history and geography

4. Focuses on the by-products of the revolutions (exclusive of the material products), such as the emergence of new urban problems

5. Asserts value judgments about the Revolution, for example, that quantity of life is very different from quality of life

Having presented these lectures, you can begin teaching learning styles in more detail. The exercises provided will be useful in discussing the chapter's content, and the students should complete Exercises 3.1, 3.2, and 3.4 before coming to class.

In addition, the material on page 60, "How to Develop Other Learning Styles," suggests a useful exercise for the journal. After your students have discovered their learning styles and determined which alternate styles they need to develop, direct them to this material. Ask them to choose the learning style they need to develop (for example, factual) and then during the next week complete one of the exercises intended to develop that style (for example, Exercise 3.2). As they do the exercise, ask them to write their impressions of it in their journal.

F.   IN-CLASS USE OF EXERCISES

As presented in the text itself, Exercises 3.1, 3.2, and 3.5 may be done by each student out of class.

Exercise 3.3 "Working with Other Learning Styles"

Exercise 3.3A. Follow Exercise 3.3A as explained in the text. To participate in this exercise, your students must have already done Exercise 3.2 and know the four letters of their learning style, for example, INTP, INFJ.

1. At the beginning of the exercise, have students write their four-letter type on an index card that you provide and tape it to their shirts or blouses.

2. Ask them to form into groups of three. These groups should be a mixture of similar and different learning styles, for example, INTP, ENTJ, INFJ.

3. Complete the exercise as described on page 57.

Exercise 3.3B. Form students into pairs representing opposites: S/N (sensing/intuition) types together and T/F (thought/feeling) types together. Present an out-of-class assignment to be completed for the next class period. This assignment should involve information gathering and information analysis rather than personal experience, for example, a short analysis of the current nationalistic struggles within Yugoslavia. When the students come to the next class, they should be prepared to participate in a discussion of the answers to the assigned questions in Exercise 3.3B. You need to be prepared to keep the discussion focused on learning styles.

Exercise 3.4 "Exams and Learning Styles"

To simplify this exercise, you should provide your students with a few articles that you know will "work" and allow the class to select the article they wish to use for the exercise.

Processing this exercise is critical. As students share their exams with each other, be sure to correlate the elements of their tests with the various elements of the groups' learning styles.

G. JOURNAL EXERCISE

The journal assignment is very effective because it focuses the students' attention on themselves and their fellow students with whom they are most comfortable.

▼▼▼▼▼▼▼▼▼▼▼▼▼▼▼▼▼▼▼▼▼

CHAPTER 4

Listening and Learning in the Classroom

CHAPTER OVERVIEW

A. Chapter goals

B. Timing and connections to other topics

C. Questions students typically ask

D. Teaching this chapter

E. Tips on teaching "Listening and Learning in the Classroom"

F. In-class use of exercises

G. Journal exercise

A. CHAPTER GOALS

1. To emphasize that the dominant mode of delivering information in college classes is the lecture

2. To argue that active listening, especially in a lecture class, enhances understanding of the lecture material

3. To convince students to adopt an efficient note-taking system to promote the larger goal of active listening

4. To demonstrate that an efficient note-taking system is also a powerful study aid

B. TIMING AND CONNECTIONS TO OTHER TOPICS

For the sake of concentration of effort and continuity, teach this chapter after Chapter 3.

Connections

► Chapter 2, "Time Management," urges students to adopt methods that will leave them with enough time to use effective note-taking methods.

- Chapter 3, "Learning Styles," identifies teaching styles, and knowing these styles will help students adopt effective note-taking methods.
- Chapter 6, "Making the Grade," discusses test-taking strategies that require effective listening and note-taking skills.
- Chapter 7, "Teacher and Student: Partners in Learning," classifies different types of instructors and their teaching styles.

C. QUESTIONS STUDENTS TYPICALLY ASK

1. How am I supposed to take notes from him/her? He/she doesn't make any sense.
2. Why do I need to take notes? I have a good memory.
3. Why do I have to take notes? I like to sit back and enjoy the lecture, and taking notes gets in the way.
4. Why can't I just bring in a tape recorder?
5. How can I take notes when he/she talks too fast?

D. TEACHING THIS CHAPTER

Although your students may not realize it or believe it, this chapter contains information critical to their success. Nonetheless, many students are resistant to changing their listening and note-taking strategies, and it is therefore urgent that you try to persuade them of the importance of considering appropriate changes.

We suggest that you devote some time to this task of persuasion prior to assigning the chapter. You might begin, as we do, with the statement that college classes differ significantly from high school classes in ways that make effective note taking critical. In regard to this, here are some of the points that we cover.

1. In contrast to most high school classes, which are focused on a textbook, most college classes are focused on the lectures, and the textbook is supportive rather than primary. Because of this essential difference, college students must listen attentively to lectures and write down both main ideas and supporting details in ways that are clear, comprehensive, and conducive to learning and recall later on. If they do not listen and take effective notes, there may not be a textbook to fall back on, as there was in high school.

2. Whereas testing was fairly frequent in high school, it is much less frequent in college. In fact, at some schools some instructors of first-year courses test only twice during the term and once at finals time. Consequently, long periods of time come between the delivery of information and the testing of that information. This suggests, once again, the importance of accurate and effective note taking.

After discussing these essential differences, you might also tell the students about other students who succeeded in large part because they used the method outlined in the chapter. Take our word for it: It does work, and we can cite student after student who found the method to be truly helpful.

Finally, be sure to try to convince your students that memory is the worst enemy of students. As the text points out, most forgetting occurs within 24 hours of learning. (Refer your students to page 67, Figure 4.1, "Learning

What We Know About First-Year Students

Study Skills

► **Perception** First-year students generally perceive their study skills to be in good shape as they approach their first year of college. The majority (70%–80%) rate their skills as excellent to good, while less than 10% rate their skills as fair to poor. Only on the dimension of reading speed did first-year students rate themselves lower; 53% rated their skills excellent to good, while 12% rated their skills poor.

► **Reality** After one year of college, first-year students reported that they greatly overestimated their study skills abilities, and they were surprised at how naïve they had been as entering students. Specifically, they had not expected the quantity of work (especially reading) assigned, and they reported that their comprehension, note-taking, and organizational skills should have been much better.

Source: Penn State Freshman Survey, summarized by James Kelly, Assistant Director, Division of Undergraduate Studies, The Pennsylvania State University.

and Forgetting.") What is significant about this is that it suggests a coping strategy: *Students need to take advantage of the 24-hour period after learning occurs.*

To demonstrate how easy it is to forget information, ask your students to think back to a lecture they heard the day before and to jot down as many main ideas and supporting details as they can remember. As part of the homework assignment, have them compare these lists to the notes they took in class. When we do this, our students invariably discover that their lists are seriously incomplete.

Having done this preparatory work, assign the entire chapter and ask the students to complete all exercises. If you do not want to process all of the exercises in class, you could spend class time giving them practice in using the method.

As in Chapter 3, we suggest that you deliver a lecture in class and ask the students to take notes. Because effective note taking depends on adequate preparation, give your students a reading assignment. After you have completed the lecture, give the students an additional 10 minutes to complete their notes. The most obvious subjects for this lecture, by the way, are listening and note-taking or a topic from your own discipline. (See pp. 69–70 of this manual.)

E. TIPS ON TEACHING "LISTENING AND LEARNING IN THE CLASSROOM"

One of your biggest problems in teaching this unit is getting students to believe what you and the chapter tell them. Thus, anything you can do to present evidence in support of the unit goals will help. We suggest the following:

1. Cite your own personal experiences if you can. Relate experiences you had as a student and as an instructor. If you still have your notebooks, you might want to bring them to class and show your students where your notes were helpful to you and where they could have been more helpful.

2. Invite an upper-class student to your class to talk about the importance of listening and its relationship to effective note-taking. Choose the student carefully to avoid giving the impression that good students are "nerds."

3. Deliver a lecture, but instruct your students not to take notes on it. Then deliver another lecture of equal difficulty, but this time instruct the students to take notes. During your next class meeting, quiz them on both lectures to demonstrate that their recall of the second lecture was greater.

4. Ask your students to submit one day's worth of notes they've taken in another class. Examine these notes to determine the effectiveness of the note taking, and give your students feedback.

As we've already indicated, study skills—like any other skills—need to be constantly reinforced. *It is not enough simply to teach the skills.* A good way to reinforce the skills of active listening and effective note-taking is to give mini-lectures throughout the course, requiring your students to take notes on those lectures. After you've delivered the lecture, give the students some time to write in recall cues. Then pass out a set of model notes to show what information the students should have recorded and to emphasize the importance of discerning between main ideas and supporting details.

Subjects for these mini-lectures can be drawn from the topic you happen to be teaching at the moment. For example, if you are teaching career planning, you might give a short lecture on the importance of discovering where one's personality, interests, abilities, and values overlap. Thus, you kill two birds with one stone: giving important information and requiring the use of an active listening, note-taking method.

F. IN-CLASS USE OF EXERCISES

The instructions for completing the exercises are clear and require no further explanation. Should you decide to process the exercises in class, simply follow the directions. An alternative to processing the exercises in class is to have the students share results with you. You can do this by having the students submit the completed exercises either separately or as part of their journal/notebook.

Exercise 4.1 "Determine Main Ideas and Major Details"

For the purpose of sharing their notes, the students should work in small groups. Your most important function in the sharing is to be able to explain why you consider some ideas to be main ideas and some details to be major details. Because this distinction is so critical to student success, we often replicate the exercise using additional paragraphs.

Exercise 4.2 "Use a Recall Column"

If you choose to process this exercise in class, the most efficient method is to place the students in pairs.

Exercise 4.3 "Compare Notes"

The assumption behind this exercise is not that all your students are taking a class in study skills but rather that they are studying those skills in your class. The exercise, then, refers to the work they are currently doing with you.

Exercise 4.4 "Apply an Active Listening and Learning System"

Rather than process this in pairs or small groups, ask your students to complete the exercise at home. In class, begin a full class discussion by asking whether any of your students expect to have difficulty following the chapter's advice.

G. JOURNAL EXERCISE

As a way of monitoring your students' note-taking progress, you might ask them to submit samples of class notes where they have been unsuccessful with the method. This will give you further opportunity to help develop their skills. You might recommend that a student having difficulty see his or her instructor.

A Sound Approach to Textbooks

CHAPTER OVERVIEW

A. Chapter goals
B. Timing and connections to other topics
C. Questions students typically ask
D. Teaching this chapter
E. Tips on teaching "A Sound Approach to Textbooks"
F. In-class use of exercises
G. Journal exercise

A.   CHAPTER GOALS

1. To distinguish between reading a textbook and reading for pleasure
2. To urge the continuation or adoption of systematic approaches to reading textbooks effectively

B.   TIMING AND CONNECTIONS TO OTHER TOPICS

For the sake of concentration of effort and continuity, teach this chapter immediately after Chapter 4.

Connections

► Chapter 2, "Time Management," urges students to adopt methods that will leave them with enough time to use effective reading techniques.

► Chapter 6, "Making the Grade," discusses test-taking strategies that require effective reading skills.

► Chapter 7, "Teacher and Student: Partners in Learning," classifies different types of professors and their expectations.

C. QUESTIONS STUDENTS TYPICALLY ASK

1. How can this reading method save me time? It looks like it takes more time.
2. Wouldn't it be easier just to take a speed-reading course?
3. Why aren't there Cliff Notes for textbooks?

D. TEACHING THIS CHAPTER

As we pointed out earlier, high school students are accustomed to getting most course information from textbooks. This is not to say, however, that they are also accustomed to ferreting out the information on their own. Rather, many high school teachers use their class time to explain the chapters, thereby eliminating the need for students to read on their own. Some high school instructors actually spend class time reading the chapters aloud. Thus, many students have less than adequate experience in reading textbooks.

Moreover, it is probably safe to say that the current generation of first-year students is not a generation of readers. Although some still read voraciously, others limit their reading severely—to *Sports Illustrated*, *USA Today*, and Harlequin romances. The bottom line is that many students are unprepared for the "boredom" and hard work involved in reading textbooks, and, in the face of boredom and difficulty in understanding, they are quick to give up.

For these reasons, it is imperative that they eliminate reading deficiencies by learning a method for reading effectively, *the sooner the better!* Thus, your first task in teaching this chapter is convincing them that the skills taught in the chapter are essential for quality college survival.

Your second task is to deal with an issue of self-esteem and self-destructive behavior that's particularly important on residential campuses. Quite simply, first-year students eagerly compare themselves to other students, and often the comparison is invidious. That is, they look at their roommates, slouched on a bed, jambox blaring, reading a difficult chapter on economics or biology. At the same time, there they are, struggling to finish their own reading assignment, with some degree of comprehension. Many of our advisees over the years have come to us asking, "What's wrong with me? My roommate reads her textbooks in minutes and gets A's. I spend an hour reading the same material."

One of the chief virtues of this chapter is that it allows students to individualize a reading technique—to test their own attention spans and to build their reading method on their self-perceived skills and abilities. Thus, the chapter provides positive reinforcement, and its content is critical to their success. In teaching this chapter, you need to stress the importance of avoiding such negative and useless comparisons and dwell on their good fortune in having at their disposal a method they can tailor to their own needs and abilities. As the chapter points out, reading effectively is like jogging; the more you do it, the better you get at it.

A third task is to emphasize a responsibility that the students themselves must accept. They must make sure they understand just what's expected of them in regard to reading their textbooks. Some instructors make daily assignments; some make reading suggestions; some expect students to know textbook material in detail; others want students to use the textbooks only for background information. Unfortunately, instructors do not always make clear how or when they want their students to read, and you will do your students a favor by urging them to learn their instructors' expectations. *A proactive student is a successful student.*

Finally, in response to the inevitable cry that a systematic reading method requires excessive amounts of time, it's important to emphasize that the methods only appear to be time-consuming. The initial reading of a chapter may take more time than the students' untutored methods, but there are several advantages. One is that they will understand more of the chapter using our method. Thus, they will not have to spend additional time rereading the chapter. Another advantage is that the reading method is also a study method. That is, writing recall cues followed by recitation is a way of learning the material. Thus, when students review for tests, they will remember more of the material. In short, the methods increase both comprehension and recall and will ultimately save time.

E. TIPS ON TEACHING "A SOUND APPROACH TO TEXTBOOKS"

Reading a textbook, like other study skills, needs to be constantly reinforced. *It is not enough simply to teach the skill.* A good way to reinforce the skill is to distribute short excerpts from textbooks throughout the course and to require your students either to read them using the method described in the chapter or to write a précis of the excerpt. In either case, be sure to check that the students are distinguishing properly between main ideas and supporting detail. Obviously, the sentences or phrases they choose to underline, highlight, or write recall cues for will provide evidence of effective reading, as will the actual content of the précis.

Excerpts can be drawn from any area as long as the writing is expository in nature (that is, writing whose purpose is to report the findings of analysis or research). Wherever possible, try to correlate the information with the material you are currently teaching. Where this is not possible, choose from typical introductory textbooks or writing on subjects of interest to students, such as athletics, entertainment, or the environment.

In addition to these short reinforcing exercises, the obvious reinforcement is to require that students use one of the two methods to read the remaining chapters of *YCE*.

F. IN-CLASS USE OF EXERCISES

Exercise 5.1 "What's Your Current Reading Attention Span?"

While the instructions suggest that students share their results with each other and with you, remember that some may be embarrassed because they fall short of others' accomplishments. Therefore, an alternative you might consider is having the students share their results only with you.

Exercise 5.2 "Prepared Reading"

The same advice applies to this exercise.

Exercises 5.3, 5.4, and 5.5 "The Well-Marked Page," "Handling Different Types of Reading," and "Write a Précis"

After the students share in class, you might want to check these exercises yourselves so that you can correct mistakes. Do not assume that the methods are so easy that the students will catch on right away. Some will have trouble finding main ideas, and many will want to summarize the content of paragraphs rather than write recall cues to be used later as a test of recall and understanding.

G. JOURNAL EXERCISE

The excellent questions posed in this journal exercise pave the way for a nice discussion on your students' expectations of their instructors. It anticipates the content of Chapter 7, "Teacher and Student: Partners in Learning."

CHAPTER 6 ▼▼▼▼▼▼▼▼▼▼▼▼▼▼▼▼▼▼▼▼▼▼▼▼

Making the Grade

CHAPTER OVERVIEW

A. Goals for section on test-taking strategies
B. Timing and connections to other topics
C. Questions students typically ask
D. Teaching the section on test-taking strategies
E. Tips on teaching this section
F. In-class use of exercises
G. Goals for the section on academic integrity
H. Timing and connections to other topics
I. Questions students typically ask
J. Teaching the section on academic integrity
K. Tips on teaching this section
L. In-class use of exercises
M. Journal exercise

A. GOALS FOR SECTION ON TEST-TAKING STRATEGIES

1. To demonstrate that all of the study skills taught in Chapters 2–5 come together in preparation for tests
2. To teach strategies for preparing for and taking different types of exams

B. TIMING AND CONNECTIONS TO OTHER TOPICS

For the sake of concentration of effort and continuity, teach this section after Chapter 5. In general, try to teach test-taking strategies sometime before the students take their first spate of exams.

Connections

- ► Chapter 2, "Time Management," urges students to adopt methods that will leave them with enough time to study effectively for tests.
- ► Chapter 3, "Learning Styles," identifies teaching styles, and knowing these styles will help students adopt effective test-preparation techniques.
- ► Chapter 4, "Listening and Learning in the Classroom," emphasizes the use of the recall column for test preparation. It also stresses the need for discovering main ideas and major details.
- ► Chapter 5, "A Sound Approach to Textbooks," emphasizes use of the recall column for test preparation. It also stresses the need for discovering main ideas and major details.
- ► Chapter 7, "Teacher and Student: Partners in Learning," classifies different types of instructors and their teaching/testing styles.

C. QUESTIONS STUDENTS TYPICALLY ASK

1. Why can't I wait until the last minute to study? I always do better under pressure.
2. How will I ever learn 6 weeks' worth of information in time to pass this test? I have over 100 pages of notes!
3. Why do I have to study at all? I never did in high school.
4. Why should I bother studying for tests? The important thing is whether or not I know the material.

D. TEACHING THE SECTION ON TEST-TAKING STRATEGIES

As we've pointed out in other chapters on study skills, students who use the suggested methods are generally successful, and students who do not use them are generally unsuccessful. Your basic task, therefore, is to convince your class of what we know to be true: that—all other things being equal—students who follow the advice of this unit as they prepare to take their tests will be more successful than those who don't. To convince them of this, you can do the same things you've already done: cite personal anecdotes, invite upper-class students, and so on.

At the same time that you are doing this, you will want to caution your students against having unrealistic expectations. The study techniques promise only to improve students' performance, not to perfect it. Perfection, as a humorist said, takes a little longer! The longer your students use the techniques, the better at them they will become.

Perhaps the most persuasive technique is to examine the chapter in detail, giving every section equal attention. In a manner of speaking, test preparation is the culmination of the other study skills, all of which lead up to preparing for and taking the exam. Spending time teaching the chapter in detail is thus a validation of the previous chapters and the skills they teach. It is also a way of emphasizing their importance.

When we teach this chapter, we assign the chapter to be read in advance of the class. We ask that the students think about the exercises but not actually do them. Completing the exercises is reserved for the actual class, during which we explain each study technique. After completing our

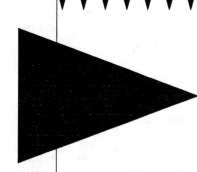

What We Know About First-Year Students

Grades

► **Expectation** The majority (96%–99%) of first-year students expect to earn a B average or better in their first year of college. Both bachelor's (4-year) and associate (2-year) degree students expect this kind of average, and students who have weaker academic credentials (lower high school grades, SAT scores, and placement test scores) have the same high expectations as students who are academically well prepared.

► **Reality** At the end of one year less than 40% of first-year students earn a B average and less than 5% earn an A average.

Source: Penn State Freshman Survey, summarized by James Kelly, Assistant Director, Division of Undergraduate Studies, The Pennsylvania State University.

discussion of each study technique, we ask the students to complete the appropriate exercise in class, and then we process each exercise.

In light of the importance of this chapter, you will probably devote at least two class periods to a full discussion. If you time this properly, you will be discussing test preparation at about the time your students are preparing to take their first major exams. This is also a good time to talk about test anxiety and those students who fall prey to their fears about testing. Perhaps some of your students will share their anxiety with the rest of the class, and you can lead a discussion on techniques for overcoming anxiety. Your college counselor (or other appropriate person) might be willing to visit your class to help teach strategies. Finally, you might consider having your students report the results of their first tests after they take them. (More about this later.)

E. TIPS ON TEACHING THIS SECTION

Essay Tests

1. To explain the process of studying properly from notes (explained in *YCE*, pp. 94–96), have your students bring in the notes from one of their classes. If you discover that some of them have not been using the method recommended in Chapter 4, this is a good time to explain why they should use the method. Make it clear that studying for tests is the culmination of the study skills you have been teaching.

2. The section on the mind map (pp. 96–97, Figure 6.1) affords the opportunity to remind your class that different people have different

learning styles. The mind map is particularly useful for people with visual learning styles.

3. Be sure to bring in concrete essay questions illustrating the different key task words (pp. 102–103). Do not assume that students will understand them without the examples. Your colleagues teaching introductory courses are good sources for such questions.

4. Perhaps you could give your students a timed essay on a topic related to one of your class themes.

Multiple-Choice, True-False, and Matching Exams

5. Even though the chapter cites examples of objective exams, your students will pay more attention if you provide samples from your colleagues' tests. We have found that most instructors of introductory courses are willing to provide samples.

General

6. Exercise 6.4, "Design an Exam Plan," can also be reversed as a "postexam" exercise. We recommend that students analyze their exam study plan after they take their tests (as well as before) as a way of evaluating the adequacy of their study. This usually brings to light problems that, when solved, will bring about improvements on later exams.

7. As you circulate around the room while monitoring the exercises, take note of students who are having difficulty. Depending on the degree of difficulty, you might want to schedule an appointment to see these students. If you make an appointment, ask your students to bring along the exercises themselves, notebooks, textbooks, and so on.

8. Another effective study technique to share with your students is the study group. A well-chosen study group provides each student with the opportunity to assess his or her understanding of the material. Group discussions confirm or deny understanding. The study group also provides an opportunity to fill in any blanks that may exist—through either misunderstanding, oversight, or absence. Also, different students will bring different approaches to studying, and these differences will create a desirable richness. Finally, the will of the group to study can overcome individual procrastination.

   The key to effective study groups is their composition. Students should invite others based on their serious commitment to doing well. Otherwise, study groups turn into social sessions. If you suggest study groups, caution your students to avoid including rank opportunists who join the group only for what they can get out of it. Every member of a study group should make a contribution, and those who do not should be asked to leave.

F. IN-CLASS USE OF EXERCISES

Exercise 6.1 "Essay Strategies"

To save time, you might want to have students answer only one question in class. For sharing, divide the class into small groups. You will probably want to circulate among the groups in order to monitor the questions and answers.

Exercise 6.3 "Key on Task Words"

In addition to the three brief essays provided, you might want to add others. Following are some examples.

1. Contrast this class with other classes you are taking.
2. Discuss the potential benefits of this class.

G. GOALS FOR THE SECTION ON ACADEMIC INTEGRITY

1. To argue for academic integrity
2. To define forms of academic misconduct in general and at your institution in particular
3. To discuss reasons for academic misconduct
4. To explain how to avoid the temptation to cheat

H. TIMING AND CONNECTIONS TO OTHER TOPICS

Timing for this unit is really a toss-up. There's good reason to talk about academic integrity at the beginning of the semester since students begin writing papers and taking tests then. But there are a host of competing subjects that should also be talked about then, and you will need to use your judgment. One tip we can offer is that if you assign papers in your college experience seminar, assign this unit immediately prior to assigning the first paper. This will make the subject timely.

Connections

▶ Chapter 1 enumerates goals that will be undermined by lack of academic integrity.

▶ Chapters 2, 3, 4, and 5, the "study skills" chapters, help prepare students for success and thus eliminate one of the reasons for dishonesty, that is, lack of adequate preparation.

I. QUESTIONS STUDENTS TYPICALLY ASK

1. Is it cheating if I didn't intend to cheat?
2. Our school's policy on cheating is really tough! One mistake and you're out. Is that fair?
3. All this stuff on when to footnote. Isn't it just a matter of individual judgment?
4. Why can't I change a verb tense just because it's in quotation marks?
5. How many words do I have to change so that I don't have to use quotation marks?

J. TEACHING THE SECTION ON ACADEMIC INTEGRITY

As the statistics in the chapter indicate, today's student is no stranger to cheating. This does not mean that all your students have cheated, but it does mean that some have and that some may continue to cheat. Consequently, this subject often produces in first-year students a very defensive response. Some react as if the subject is actually an accusation or an assault on their integrity. For these reasons, teaching this unit is difficult.

In our course we have resolved the problem by assigning a unit on academic integrity, including a series of exercises. But we have not spent much class time on the rights and wrongs of academic dishonesty—not because we consider the subject unimportant but because we assume the students have already developed their values. We believe our best efforts are made in reinforcing the positive. In this regard we suggest that you relate the unit to the previous chapters on study skills. The unit asserts that cheating often results from a feeling of desperation, which in turn results from poor study habits. This provides another occasion to argue for the need for effective study habits. In addition, you can help students overcome academic deficiencies that may promote cheating by referring them to the proper campus resources, such as the math clinic or the writing center. In short, you may be able to help head off some potential problems.

K. TIPS ON TEACHING THIS SECTION

Be careful not to "play the heavy" when you present this material. The students will listen up to the point that you become heavily moralistic. Instead, why not take a Socratic approach? Through carefully structured questions, you can perhaps lead the students to articulate a view of academic integrity consistent with their goals as well as the goals of colleges and universities.

L. IN-CLASS USE OF EXERCISES

Exercise 6.6 "Know Your School's Academic Code"

If you choose not to process this exercise in class, have your students record their answers in their journals or notebooks. This will allow you to check to be sure they understand the rules.

M. JOURNAL EXERCISE

When you assign this journal exercise, you might ask students to keep track of the changes they make in the way they study for tests. We usually ask our students to indicate the grades they receive on their tests. This provides an opportunity to monitor progress as well as to give praise for positive results.

In addition, the journal entries on academic integrity lead directly to a discussion of values. Thus, you might use this journal exercise as preparation for a class discussion of personal values. If you do, be sure not to reveal any confidences related in the journals.

Teacher and Student: Partners in Learning

CHAPTER OVERVIEW

A. Chapter goals

B. Timing and connections to other topics

C. Questions students typically ask

D. Teaching this chapter

E. Tips on teaching "Teacher and Student: Partners in Learning"

F. In-class use of exercises

G. Journal exercise

A.   CHAPTER GOALS

1. To shift the focus of the student from himself or herself to the academic environment, that is, the teacher

2. To demonstrate that an understanding of the teacher is a significant key to college success

3. To get each student to meet with a teacher

B.   TIMING AND CONNECTIONS TO OTHER TOPICS

Perhaps the best time to teach this chapter is sometime prior to your students' preselection of next semester's courses. (This assumes, of course, that your students preselect the second semester's courses during the first semester. If they do not, then the timing of this chapter is not critical, and you can teach it whenever it fits into your overall plan.)

One way to prepare your students for preselection is to engage them in a discussion of what constitutes good teaching. This can help to head off some misconceptions—for example, that a content-oriented teacher who lectures without engaging students in discussion is necessarily a bad or boring teacher or that an easy grader is a good teacher—as well as to help students make intelligent choices about the next semester's courses. If your school has a drop period, the discussion can also help students understand that they should "cut their losses" while they still have time to drop a course or "stick it out" in another course.

Connections

► Chapter 3, "Learning Styles," provides a system for understanding teachers in terms of their teaching styles.

► Chapter 11, "Yourself and Others," helps students understand themselves, their interactions, and the need to be assertive in dealing with their teachers.

C. QUESTIONS STUDENTS TYPICALLY ASK

1. (On visiting a teacher's office) Did you really read all these books?
2. Why do I have to put up with boring teachers?
3. Why don't my teachers outline the unit on the board the way they did in high school?

D. TEACHING THIS CHAPTER

Because the students' academic experience has mostly been with elementary and high school teachers who did not necessarily share the profile of the college teacher, you need to give your students the chance to understand their teachers and to learn how best to relate to them. Thus, you should discuss the material in this chapter enough to help students understand their teachers.

This chapter, like others, focuses on student success by suggesting ways to modify behavior. In this case, through an understanding of their teachers, students can gain insight into the behaviors their teachers will admire most. Most college instructors, for example, were model students: They loved learning in general; they sought out research opportunities (through either reading or laboratory work); they attended classes regularly; and they submitted their work on time. Naturally, they will relate best to those students who demonstrate the same kind of behavior.

This should not suggest a foolish dissimulation of model student behavior in which students pretend to love to read. Most teachers see through such pretenses. It should suggest instead the foolishness of submitting sloppily prepared work; being constantly absent; and being generally inattentive and uninterested in class. In other words, this chapter lets you discuss some very practical tips on success.

One such tip involves the need for students to be fairly assertive. As the chapter points out, teachers expect students to take care of themselves (although it is fair to say that many of today's college teachers are more obviously concerned with their students' success and thus practice more interventions). That is, when students do not understand class material, it is up to them to seek out the teacher for clarification. A student who has not done well on a test or paper should not expect the instructor to inquire about the reasons. Instead the student will have to make an appointment. Even though this chapter focuses on the teacher rather than on the student, you cannot stress enough the responsibility of the students for their own success. We believe in helping the students to develop the skills of assertiveness and then in constantly reinforcing those skills.

E. TIPS ON TEACHING "TEACHER AND STUDENT: PARTNERS IN LEARNING"

1. As you teach this chapter, especially the section on "finding a good teacher," you may find yourself juggling a political hot potato. Not everyone on a campus agrees on what makes a good teacher or who the good ones are, but you will find no such uncertainty among your students on who the poor ones are. They make no bones about announcing publicly and loudly that such and such stinks! It goes without saying that this chapter invites indiscretion from the students and that you will have to be very discreet in your responses. We cannot really advise on the proper responses, but we can warn you what to expect.

2. Earlier we indicated that students must learn to be assertive in pursuing their interests, especially when they are having problems with the way a course is taught. Students find it very difficult to approach a teacher in these situations. One way you can assist is by setting up role plays in which you play the role of a teacher with whom the students are having difficulties. For example, you can establish a scenario in which students believe the teacher "doesn't give good notes." In a fishbowl in which you and a student are surrounded by the class, try to act out the conversation between the teacher and the student. After the conversation is over, ask the class to critique the role play and make suggestions. A final suggestion is to ask your students to provide situations for future role plays based on actual experiences they have throughout the semester. As students submit such scenarios, you might actually act them out from time to time.

3. As tip 2 indicates, assertiveness is an important skill, and anything you can do to help your students learn positive assertiveness will help them. Therefore, you may want to consider teaching Chapter 11, "Yourself and Others," immediately after teaching this chapter.

F. IN-CLASS USE OF EXERCISES

Exercise 7.3 "Interviewing a Teacher"

Different instructors view this exercise differently. Some find the exercise, as described in the text, to be a wonderful experience for their students. Others believe that freshmen find interviewing a teacher singly to be an intimidating experience. In a small group, however, they get over their fear relatively quickly. Moreover, in their groups students perform a more successful interview because they can divide tasks. Thus, instructors often will assign students to complete this exercise in small groups.

A variation of the exercise is to have the students give group reports to the entire class in place of writing the essay. These group reports (approximately 5 minutes each) provide a foundation for discussion of the chapter.

G. JOURNAL EXERCISE

This journal entry is excellent for encouraging your students to use the journal as a means of communicating with you. When they raise questions, try to answer them as honestly and completely as you can.

CHAPTER 8 ▼▼▼▼▼▼▼▼▼▼▼▼▼▼▼▼▼▼▼▼▼▼▼▼▼▼

An Information Age Introduction to the Library

CHAPTER OVERVIEW

A. Chapter goals
B. Timing and connections to other topics
C. Questions students typically ask
D. Teaching this chapter
E. Tips on teaching "An Information Age Introduction to the Library"
F. In-class use of exercises
G. Journal exercise

A. CHAPTER GOALS

1. To convince students of the importance of information and the ability to retrieve it
2. To provide an extended and a detailed exercise in the use of the library for information gathering

B. TIMING AND CONNECTIONS TO OTHER TOPICS

This chapter may be taught anytime during the term. If, however, you expect your students to complete a research project in your course or if you know they will be doing research projects in other courses, the sooner you teach this chapter, the better prepared they will be.

C. QUESTIONS STUDENTS TYPICALLY ASK

1. Why do I have to do this? I already know how to use the library.
2. What's the matter with this place? They never have the books I need.

3. Why doesn't the library keep newspapers and magazines? The microfilm reader is a real pain!

4. Why do I have to go to the library at all? The people who work there intimidate me.

D. TEACHING THIS CHAPTER

Until recently, colleges have relied on a short lecture-tour as a way of introducing students to the library. In our experience, this is inadequate. Because at the time of the tour the students have no obvious need to know about the library, the lecture is "nectar in a sieve" for most students. In addition, the quick tour is a lecture; it requires nothing of the student and is often regarded as just another boring lecture.

For these reasons we believe that Chapter 8 will be of most use to your students if you connect it to a research project that is a significant part of your course. Under these circumstances the information they will retrieve as they go through the library will be directly relevant to the project. Moreover, you are replacing the lecture-tour with an active learning experience, and actual learning should be greater. Finally, if you make the research project a group assignment, students will be motivated, we hope, by a sense of responsibility to the group.

You can increase the students' perception of the importance of this chapter if, from the moment you assign it, you behave as if it is important. You can do this by indicating from the beginning that you intend to give their project a grade that carries a specific weight in relation to other grades in the course. We recommend fairly rigorous grading as a means of preventing students from taking too many shortcuts. As well-intentioned as first-year students may be and as much as they value information and information retrieval, they often require strong motivators. (See pp. 28–29 of this manual.)

E. TIPS ON TEACHING "AN INFORMATION AGE INTRODUCTION TO THE LIBRARY"

In assigning projects to your class, you might want to increase the list of possible topics to include specific topics relevant to themes you are developing in your class, such as gender relations. Similarly, you might want to eliminate items on the list so that the remaining topics are relevant to your course themes. Because involving students in the course is always a good idea, you might want to expand the list by asking your students to suggest topics of particular concern to them.

F. IN-CLASS USE OF EXERCISES

This chapter is an extended exercise and needs to be treated as such. As you know, the directions for the exercise are quite explicit and require little explanation.

Exercise 8.1 "Retrieval, Organization, and Presentation"

Paragraph 1 of the exercise makes a significant statement about the library staff and affords you an opportunity to discuss the library staff and their function. As question 4 of "Questions Students Typically Ask" suggests, first-year students often have the wrong idea about librarians and their usefulness, and you can use the exercise to disabuse them of some of these notions (such as that all librarians are women).

One of the main stumbling blocks for students completing this exercise is the fact that they must work in groups. We know that working in groups pays off in terms of student achievement, involvement in courses, and enthusiasm (see p. 64 of this manual). We also know that in the world of work, tasks are often accomplished by groups of employees working in quality circles, continuous improvement teams, and so on. Although most first-year students are not thinking specifically about their work lives after college, collaborative exercises in college will help prepare them for the workplace. In spite of this, we also know that students are not accustomed to working in groups. In fact, the payoff throughout grade school and high school was to the individual for individual effort. Even in your course, each student will receive an individual final grade, in spite of the fact that the grade was derived in part from group work. In short, students are unaccustomed to working in groups, and the academic reward structure militates against group work.

Group work also presents first-year students (and others) with another challenge—organizing the group and motivating all members to pull equal weight. As adults we know the difficulty of organizing effective group projects. How difficult must it be for freshmen!

In light of these problems, we recommend that you conduct a full-class discussion about group work—its rewards and its problems—in which you try to be both upbeat and honest. The former is not difficult. Group work allows students to share the workload. It also takes advantage of the talents of the group, which often exceed the talents of individuals in the group. Introduce the notion of synergy (an interaction or combined effort such that the total effect is greater than the sum of its individual parts), and try to suggest ways for groups to achieve synergy. A discussion of group dynamics, the stages of group formation, and the different roles people play in groups (for example, the task-oriented role or the caretaker role) can be very helpful. (For a complete discussion of group dynamics, see Applbaum et al., 1979.)

You should also forewarn students about the problem areas of group work. People have different ability levels, and some people therefore make greater contributions than others. Students are also on different time schedules, and getting a group to meet—even a small group—is not always easy. Students inexperienced in arranging meetings need to be reminded to exchange phone numbers and schedules.

Finally, groups may contain members who simply will not cooperate. You should make provisions for students to give feedback on the effectiveness of the other members of the group and require regular submission of these feedback reports (a sample is provided on p. 114). If, as a result of reading these reports, you discover a student who is uncooperative, you will have to decide on an intervention strategy, such as speaking to the individual or speaking to the entire group. This may seem like a lot of effort, but, in terms of the rewards students reap, it is well worth it.

As we said earlier, you should grade this project and include the grade when you determine final grades. In assigning a grade to the library project, you might consider the following: the actual worksheets that each student submits; effectiveness of the presentation; and effectiveness of each student as a member of his or her team. You will already have collected the

Feedback Report

Name _____ Date _____

Group Member 1 _____

	yes	no	explanation
Attended Called Meeting	_____	_____	
Completed Assigned Task	_____	_____	

Group Member 2 _____

Attended Called Meeting	_____	_____	
Completed Assigned Task	_____	_____	

students' worksheets. After each presentation, you should have your entire class submit their evaluations of the presentation (see *YCE*, p. 147, "Evaluation Checklist"). Finally, the Feedback Reports will provide you with insight into each student's performance on the team. Naturally, we recommend that you provide feedback on all three areas.

G. JOURNAL EXERCISE

In light of the importance of collaborative work, you might instruct your students to include in their journals a brief analysis of the experience of collaborating on the library project. How was collaboration helpful? What were the problems they encountered? If they were doing the project again, how would they change their behavior in relation to the other members of the group?

Finding Answers: Your College Catalog and Academic Advisor or Counselor

CHAPTER OVERVIEW

A. Chapter goals
B. Timing and connections to other topics
C. Questions students typically ask
D. Teaching this chapter
E. Tips on teaching "Finding Answers"
F. In-class use of exercises
G. Journal exercise

A. CHAPTER GOALS

1. To introduce the students to the key components of the college catalog
2. To make the students aware of the specific degree requirements that will be applied to them
3. To enable students to find information that they need in the college catalog
4. To define the role of a college academic advisor
5. To encourage an effective relationship between advisor and advisee
6. To prepare each student to meet with his or her advisor

B. TIMING AND CONNECTIONS TO OTHER TOPICS

Whether you choose to spend class time on the catalog will depend on your specific class objectives, the time you have available, and whether someone else, like the students' advisors, will be spending time with them. Ask yourself, "How important is it for the students to learn this information?" and "Are they likely to learn it somewhere else?"

The college catalog may be introduced at almost any time in the term or at any point in the course. Or you may prefer just to make reference to it and suggest that the students read it on their own. The material on academic advising/counseling can be taught anytime during the term. In determining the right time, you need to consider the importance of the unit in relation to two factors: (1) your institution's philosophy of advising; (2) the other topics you intend to teach.

If your institution supports a holistic approach to advising (one in which the advisor assumes partial responsibility for the students' overall development rather than their cognitive development within the context of an academic major), you will want to teach this unit relatively early in the term. Remember that the beginning of the first year can be a time of anxiety for new students, and an early explanation of the role of the advisor can encourage students to seek their advisors' help. Also, many studies on student persistence show a strong correlation between persistence to graduation and relationships established early in the first term between a first-year student and a significant adult in the community. The academic advisor can serve as this significant adult.

Many topics will compete for your attention early in the term, and you must choose carefully among them. Probably the best guide is the students' "need to know." For example, most first-year students need help with study skills early in the term, and thus study skills should be taught before the unit on the academic advisor. As is almost always the case, making these choices is a juggling act.

Connections

▶ Chapter 3, "Learning Styles," and Chapter 7, "Teacher and Student: Partners in Learning," classify instructors by teaching style. In some cases teaching style and advising style are related; that is, some teachers/advisors are concerned primarily with students' cognitive development in an academic area, and others are concerned also with their advisees' overall development.

▶ Chapter 11, "Yourself and Others," stresses the need to be assertive. Taking full advantage of one's academic advisor often requires a high degree of assertiveness, especially on the part of a first-year student.

C. QUESTIONS STUDENTS TYPICALLY ASK

1. If I'm not signed up for accounting my first term, can I still major in business?
2. Another student told me I had to take biology this term or I couldn't be pre-med; is this true?
3. When can I change my schedule and how do I do it?
4. What are midterm grades used for? Will my parents see them?
5. What does an advisor do?
6. What if I don't get along with my advisor?
7. How do I change advisors?

D. TEACHING THIS CHAPTER

It is important to emphasize that the catalog is *the* institution's most important document. It is the contract with the school that both the student and the college must adhere to in pursuing and awarding a degree. Consequently, students should be made aware of their catalog year and should note any time limit on the catalog, for example, 5 years to complete the degree. This later information is particularly important for nontraditional and part-time students. In general, all students should be encouraged to keep their entering catalog.

It is obvious, therefore, that the instructor should see to it that the students have a copy of their entering catalog. If the student does not have a catalog, he or she should be provided one or told exactly how to get one.

Reviewing the main headings in your catalog that correspond to the sections in Chapter 9 is an easy way to begin familiarizing students with the catalog. Although you cannot review every detail, you should emphasize a few key sections, including the academic calendar, the general education requirements, and the academic programs.

The calendar can be discussed with reference to principles of sound time management. Important dates that students should be aware of, for example, are the last dates to add or drop classes. This can also lead to a discussion of the procedures for adding or dropping a course, the meaning of certain grades—for example, W or WF—and strategies for determining if students should stay in a course or drop it.

The general education requirements can be discussed in terms of the purpose of general education and its relationship to the liberal arts and the school's mission. It is important to reemphasize that the students alone and not their advisors are ultimately responsible for understanding and meeting those requirements. It is useful for students to establish a special file for their registration/degree progress materials. This file should contain all grade reports, a general education check sheet, a major program check sheet, and the catalog. Ideally the advisor should retain an identical file folder for each student and cross-check the folders at each preregistration.

As discussed in Chapter 10, "Major, Career, and Transfer Planning," although many students come to college with a clear idea of their personal career and major goals, an equal number have only a vague idea of their plans. It is not easy to remain undecided very long. The registration process forces the student to begin to make decisions, and the catalog gives them the options. Review the section of the catalog on academic programs to explain to students how they can determine exactly which courses their program requires. Many catalogs provide model courses of study for the first year or even for 4 years. If the catalog does not provide these models, frequently the department or the registrar's office has them. The registrar's office almost always has a form for the "senior check" or "degree audit" for each major.

First-year students probably have little or no idea of what an academic advisor is. They often think of the academic advisor in terms of their high school guidance counselors, which means you may have to overcome some negative attitudes.

E. TIPS ON TEACHING "FINDING ANSWERS"

Discussing the catalog can be a good opening activity in the early days of the term. It introduces the students to some important practical information and serves as a reminder to save their catalog for later reference and to begin building a file of important papers from the beginning of the term. Such a discussion of the catalog and the students' major plans is a nonthreatening way to begin the process of group building.

This chapter also can be discussed, or rediscussed, later in the term. Another good time to introduce this material is either just before preregistration for the next term or (if there is no preregistration) at the end of the term in preparation for the next term's registration. At preregistration/registration time students are anxious to know what the rules and expectations are. Going over the degree requirements and the preregistration process will ease that anxiety.

The catalog is a document that you should become familiar with, especially if you are also an academic advisor. It provides answers to a great number of questions about programs, requirements, course offerings, and so on. Nevertheless, you cannot be an expert on everything. Don't hesitate to call the people who know the answers or to refer students to them. The department or division chairpersons should be able to answer any questions about programs, major requirements, and schedules of courses offered. The registrar's office is also an important place for information. At many institutions the registrar is the person who does senior degree audits and certifies the candidates for graduation.

The catalog is not an inherently interesting book. It should be treated as a reference and kept on the shelf for answers to important questions. Knowing what kinds of questions it can answer and where to find the information is important.

The material on the academic advisor/counselor teaches itself. That is, after your students read the unit, there's really not much for you to explain. Therefore, you can use class time to process whichever exercises you choose to assign.

F. IN-CLASS USE OF EXERCISES

Exercise 9.4 "Academic Advising at Your School"

You can do this exercise in one of two ways. One is to have the students actually ferret out the information themselves. This will involve much of their time, but the effort and what is discovered may be worthwhile. The second way is simple and efficient: Answer the questions yourself in class. In either case, you can use the class discussion of the answers as a transition to a discussion of the philosophy of advising on your campus and the role of the advisor.

Exercise 9.7 "Questions to Ask Advisors"

Part 1 lends itself to an active, in-class group exercise that reinforces the discussion in Exercise 9.4. While some of Frank's questions involve course selection, others will get at some basic issues of holistic advising. For example, questions about lifestyle can lead to discussions about life choices (anticipating the unit on career advising). Questions about campus involvement can lead to discussions of time management. These issues will reveal the academic advisor as a mentor rather than as merely someone who helps students register for classes.

Exercise 9.8 "Prepare to Meet with Your Advisor"

To assure that students get the most from this exercise, assign it shortly before they are to choose courses for the following term. (This assumes that your students meet with advisors each term to preselect or preregister for courses for the following term. If your campus uses another system of course preselection, you will have to rethink the timing of this exercise.)

G. JOURNAL EXERCISE

In assigning this, keep in mind that you may be the advisor being discussed in the journal. If this is the case, you might want to modify the exercise.

CHAPTER 10 ▼▼▼▼▼▼▼▼▼▼▼▼▼▼▼▼▼▼▼▼▼▼▼▼▼

Major, Career, and Transfer Planning

CHAPTER OVERVIEW

A. Chapter goals

B. Timing and connections to other topics

C. Questions students typically ask

D. Teaching this chapter

E. Tips on teaching "Major, Career, and Transfer Planning"

F. In-class use of exercises

G. Journal exercise

A. CHAPTER GOALS

1. To introduce a timely process of career planning and the selection of a major

2. To identify career-related interests, skills, aptitudes, personality characteristics, and values

3. To see how career planning, choice of academic courses, and lifelong career decisions and activities are interrelated and involve a specific process

4. To relieve stress resulting from unclear career goals

5. To help students plan for transferring from one institution to another

B. TIMING AND CONNECTIONS TO OTHER TOPICS

A good time to introduce this material is either just before preselection/preregistration (as mentioned previously) for the next term or near the end of the term as a summary.

Connections

► Chapter 3, "Learning Styles," discusses personality as it is described by the Myers-Briggs Type Indicator. The MBTI is also useful in career advising.

C. QUESTIONS STUDENTS TYPICALLY ASK

1. I'm only a first-year student. Why should I be concerned with careers now?
2. If it's true that my generation will change careers five times, why is career planning so important?
3. I already know what I want to do. Why do I have to go through all this boring stuff?

D. TEACHING THIS CHAPTER

Goal setting in general and career planning in particular are real problem areas for students, especially first-year students. In teaching this chapter, then, don't expect miracles. Probably only a minority of your students are self-disciplined enough to engage in rigorous career planning. Others are simply not developmentally ready to undertake career planning. Still others, especially the older student, are so sure of the choices they've already made that they will regard any time you spend on career planning as a waste of their time.

Therefore, at best, you can expect your students to understand the process of career planning by the end of this chapter. They should know the major steps of the process, how to perform them, and what resources exist on your campus to help them as they move along the path of goal setting and career planning. The same cautionary advice applies to the materials on transfer planning. Only the most precise students will undertake to use the methods outlined in the chapter. Perhaps the most to expect is an understanding on the students' part that transfer planning should be a careful process and that they should be fairly methodical in that planning.

This is not meant to discourage you from teaching the chapter. This apparently "modest" achievement is really very important in that it gets the students to begin thinking about the process, lets them know that there is a process they can follow, and informs them of who can help them when they are ready. It is also another way of demonstrating your concern for them.

Before beginning this chapter, you should decide how much time you want to devote to it. If your intention is consciousness raising, one 50-minute period will probably be more than enough. More extensive goals will require more time, but remember, given student attitudes toward career planning, you might decide to spend the time on other activities.

Think back to your own first year. Did you begin college knowing what career you wanted, and did you stick to that decision? Were you uncomfortable with that inevitable question, "What's your major?" Did you feel that you were alone in feeling clueless about your future?

Many students come to college with very clear ideas of their personal career goals. But an equal number have only the vaguest idea of their plans. It is important to help these students feel comfortable in their "undecidedness."

What We Know About First-Year Students

Choice of Major

► **Certainty** More than 80% of first-year students are uncertain about a choice of major. Contrary to popular belief, engineers and science students are as uncertain about a major as liberal arts, education, or undecided students.

► **Chances of changing majors** More than 82% of first-year students expect to change majors at least once during their college careers. Some students may change majors as many as five or six times and are still making changes well into their junior and senior years.

► **Knowledge and participation** Only 12% of students report having a great deal of knowledge about their intended majors, and only 13% report a great deal of participation in activities related to intended majors.

► **Top 20 majors of interest** The majority (54%) of students attend college to prepare for a vocation or career. It is no surprise then, that when given an opportunity to choose among 200 majors, first-year students concentrate themselves in just a handful of majors. Between 50% and 60% of students see themselves in one of 20 majors related to professions such as engineering, business, medicine, law, education, journalism, or architecture.

Conclusion

The narrow range of first-year student choices illustrated by the top 20 majors combined with other educational planning factors such as grade expectations, study hours, study skills, certainty, knowledge, and participation indicate how little students know about college and how unprepared they are to deal with the academic realities of the first year. It is clear that the first year is a sorting out, learning year, but the rate of change of major that often persists well into the junior and senior years makes it equally clear that adjusting to college academic life is a continuous developmental process that extends from the first year through the last year.

Source: Penn State Freshman Survey, summarized by James Kelly, Assistant Director, Division of Undergraduate Studies, The Pennsylvania State University.

You will probably want your students to share their career goals (or the lack of goals) with each other. This will help them realize that many of their fellow students are as undecided as they are. You want to let them know that being undecided is okay. Teaching the chapter is also a way of letting the first-year students know that there are methods to help them make decisions and that you will be teaching those methods.

First-year students who are undecided may actually reach conclusions about career choices. But more likely they will just begin the process of reaching conclusions. Beginning the process is a very significant step for them, and you should praise their efforts and encourage them to continue.

Career planning can help convince the decided students that they made the right choice or show them that they made the wrong choice. In a typical class you're bound to find a little of each.

One theme of *YCE* is that student success and the ability of students to set meaningful goals for themselves are related to each other. Students who know what they want to do with their lives have a far easier time motivating themselves to be successful students. Career development is another means of helping students succeed.

In this world of Star Wars and Patriot missiles, students are often forced into highly structured, complex majors. Thus, the sooner the students know what they want to major in, the sooner they can start on the proper sequence of courses.

E.   TIPS ON TEACHING "MAJOR, CAREER, AND TRANSFER PLANNING"

You don't have to be a career counselor to teach this chapter effectively. What you need to understand is some of the methodology that career counselors use in helping students. In a nutshell, career counseling is based on the following: the students' discovery of who they are in terms of personality, interests, skills, aptitudes, and values and the intersection of those five factors.

In the best of all possible worlds, students will discover the major or career that satisfies all five factors. Your expectation should be more modest. Basically your objective in teaching this chapter is to teach your students enough to get them started on the road to self-discovery.

Here are some ways to stimulate interest before you assign the chapter. Begin class by reading excerpts from *Working* by Studs Terkel. These excerpts will illustrate that some workers are very happy with the work they do, whereas others (perhaps the majority) are terribly unhappy with their work. This can open up a discussion in which your students explore their notions about work and the kinds of satisfaction they expect to get from their future jobs. Is a job just a way to make a living? Is happiness in a job important? Must a job provide satisfactions beyond the paycheck or job security? In conducting this discussion (and others), don't be afraid to cite your own experiences, but avoid being preachy. Be sure to capitalize on the nontraditional students in your class. They can be a treasure trove of experience.

The discussion can also emphasize choice. Your students are among the first generations to have the privilege of career choice. They not only can choose their careers now but also will be able to change their careers later in life if they so desire. Encourage students to think about members of their families and the attitudes they have toward their work. Try to end the discussion by having them discover how lucky they are to have this choice.

After this discussion, ask your students to submit at least two questions each about career choices. Specifically, what do they want to learn from the chapter? You might then compile these questions in a list and distribute them to the whole class to be used as a guide to the chapter. These questions will also be a guide to you as you teach the unit.

Invite a graduate of your institution into the classroom to discuss his or her experiences in searching for a major and finding a career. A graduate who had trouble choosing a major or who has had more than one career would be of special interest. Or arrange for a small panel of several graduates from your local area to discuss such experiences. (See p. 52, 14 week syllabus, week 14, day 2.)

A good ending for this chapter is either a class visit from your career counselor or a class visit to the counseling center. In either case, the career counselor can provide an authoritative summary of what you have already taught. Also, this is a good way of demonstrating the commitment of your campus to the students' ultimate success.

Whether or not you choose to invite the career counselor to class, at the close of this unit your students will have identified, articulated, and started to integrate their interests, current skills, aptitudes, personality characteristics, and values.

F.   IN-CLASS USE OF EXERCISES

As presented in the text itself, these exercises may be done by each student out of class. The suggestions that follow are intended to help you use the exercises collaboratively in class. When used collaboratively, the exercises are quite lengthy. Therefore, you will probably choose only one or two for in-class use.

Exercise 10.2 "What Are Your Interests?"

When you assign this exercise, be sure the student has or knows where to get a copy of your college catalog. In class, one way to process the exercise is to divide the class into small groups. After sharing their lists with each other, students in each group draw some conclusions about the courses on their lists (for example, that laboratory courses offering hands-on opportunities are inherently more interesting to them than courses that are entirely bookish). They should record these conclusions on sheets of newsprint and post them around the room. You could then help the class draw additional conclusions, for example, that students who prefer laboratory courses may be revealing an interest in the practical rather than the theoretical, in the concrete rather than the abstract. Knowledge of this sort can be critical to students who are searching for career paths.

Part 2 of the exercise also allows you to divide the class into small groups. In these groups, the students draw conclusions about activities (such as clubs, part-time jobs, volunteer experiences) that interest them and the reasons for their interest. For example, some students enjoy the opportunity to take leadership roles, whereas others enjoy the opportunity to work alone on projects (for example, working in a darkroom as photography editor of the yearbook). Again, you can use this information to help students understand their interests and to show how these relate to future majors, jobs, or careers.

Note: The chapter states that "you can take standardized inventories or tests through the counseling services at your school." You should have information about the kinds of tests that are available at your counseling center and perhaps use this as a lead in to get them to go there for an investigative project. The tests used most often include the Strong-Campbell Interest Inventory.

Exercise 10.3 "What Are Your Current Skills?"

After your students have identified their five skills, ask them to speak or write about concrete examples demonstrating those skills. As gently as possible, push the students to move beyond hasty generalizations they may make about their skills.

After they have identified the skills they would like to develop, ask them to speak or write about how they would go about developing those skills. Perhaps they can identify the courses in the catalog that would help them develop those skills. This could be connected to Exercise 10.2 about courses they found interesting. In addition, ask the students to think about other nonclassroom resources—both on and off campus—available to help them gain skills.

Exercise 10.4 "What Are Your Aptitudes?"

This exercise can also be dealt with similarly to Exercise 10.3. After the students have identified the areas in which they believe they are strong, ask them to speak or write about concrete examples demonstrating those aptitudes. They should then address, orally or in writing, the question asked in the exercise: "Are they in the same family as the skills you previously checked?" Obviously, the intersection of skills and aptitudes suggests a degree of ability that should be considered in the major/career planning process.

Exercise 10.5 "What Are Your Personality Characteristics?"

This can be done individually out of class.

An alternative or supplement to this activity is to incorporate the Myers-Briggs Type Indicator into your activities for this chapter. The MBTI is a personality inventory based on the work of the psychiatrist Carl Jung. Used in many first-year programs, the MBTI divides personality into sixteen profiles, each a combination of four dimensions: introversion-extroversion; sensing-intuitive; feeling-thinking; and judging-perception.

Exercise 10.6 "What Are Your Life Goals?"

This can be done individually out of class.

Exercise 10.7 "What Are Your Work Values?"

This can be done individually out of class.

Alternatives or supplements to this and other career-related activities are SIGI+ and Discover, two popular career planning software programs. These programs include a section asking the students to rank their "work values." If your school has one of these computer software programs, you could require that your students work through the program. Students could then be asked to discuss the results in groups in class or to meet with their instructor/advisor individually for discussion at the time of preregistration.

Information about SIGI+ and Discover may be obtained from the following sources:

SIGI+
Educational Testing Service
P.O. Box 6403
Princeton, NJ 08541-6403

Discover
American College Testing
Discover Center
230 Schilling Circle
Schilling Plaza South
Hunt Valley, MD 21031

Exercises 10.9 and 10.10 "The Holland Categories" and "The Holland Hexagon"

To help students understand the Holland categories, ask them to imagine that the classroom is a party and that there are six groups of people at the party. Each group corresponds to one of the six Holland categories. Direct students to the group with whose interest they have most in common. Thus, students who view themselves as realistic will go to the Realistic group, and so on. Have each group collectively prepare a list of jobs that match their interests. Students should then go to their second choice and do the same.

As you bring this unit to a close, help students synthesize the self-knowledge they have gained. Ask them to select one or two jobs from their Holland lists and identify the skills, aptitudes, life goals, values, and personality characteristics they have or need to develop for those jobs. You can also make integration of interests, skills, life goals, aptitudes, and personality characteristics the subject of a journal entry or other writing. Students might also do a specific research assignment in the library or elsewhere on the job they have selected.

Exercise 10.11 "For Returning Students: Exploring New Fields"
Exercise 10.12 "Follow Up on Careers"

Because the life/work experiences of your returning students are so individualistic, these exercises are best done by each student and shared not with the class but with the academic advisor and/or college counselor.

Exercise 10.13 "A Personal Transfer Assessment"
Exercise 10.14 "Ask Questions About Transfer Schools"

The highly individualized students' responses to these exercises make class discussion inappropriate. Because choosing a transfer school is such an important decision, encourage your students to work with their advisors and/or college counselors. You might also give students the opportunity to include their responses in their journals.

Exercise 10.15 "Compare Sample Course Descriptions"

To prepare your students to complete this exercise at home, you might distribute sample course descriptions from a variety of schools. After dividing them into small groups, ask them to find the similarities and differences in course terminology and content and to list these.

G. JOURNAL EXERCISE

The point of this journal entry is personalized synthesis of the chapter's content. As your students prepare to answer the six questions, remind them that there is nothing wrong with being undecided and that they are now in a position to begin the process of choosing.

Yourself and Others

CHAPTER OVERVIEW

A. Chapter goals
B. Timing and connections to other topics
C. Questions students typically ask
D. Teaching this chapter
E. Tips on teaching "Yourself and Others"
F. In-class use of exercises
G. Journal exercise

A. CHAPTER GOALS

1. To provide an additional opportunity for self-evaluation, focusing on habits of interpersonal communication
2. To promote more effective interpersonal communication skills, leading to appropriate social relationships
3. To define assertiveness as a behavior that involves mutual respect and personal responsibility
4. To provide a methodology for self-examination with reference to assertiveness
5. To promote the development of assertiveness through chapter exercises and the use of external resources
6. To encourage students to become involved in the co-curricular life of the college
7. To help students understand the benefits of involvement
8. To help students identify organizations that satisfy their personal needs and interests

B. TIMING AND CONNECTIONS TO OTHER TOPICS

This chapter can be taught anytime. The advantage of teaching it early is that establishing good relationships and developing assertiveness skills can be significant for the success of some first-year students. The decision of when to teach the material on co-curricular involvement may be influenced by whether or not involvement in co-curricular activities is an integral part of your course. If you require students to join a campus organization, it may be beneficial to teach the chapter early.

Connections

► Chapter 2, "Time Management," advises students to take control, another way of urging them to be assertive. It also cautions against over-involvement.

► Chapter 7, "Teacher and Student: Partners in Learning," encourages assertiveness in order for students to establish meaningful relationships with their professors.

► Chapter 9, "Finding Answers: Your College Catalog and Academic Advisor or Counselor," encourages assertiveness in order for students to establish meaningful relationships with their academic advisors.

► Chapter 10, "Major, Career, and Transfer Planning," urges students to look for connections between campus and off-campus activities and possible careers.

► Chapter 12, "Healthy Decisions: Sexuality, Drugs, and Stress," suggests the importance of good personal relationships and the need for assertiveness in sexual relations.

C. QUESTIONS STUDENTS TYPICALLY ASK

1. Why are we even doing this stuff? Aren't my relationships my business?

2. Are you telling me I should make friends with everybody?

3. What about this advice about honesty? I would have lost most of my friends already if I'd always been honest.

4. How can people always be so careful about the way they express themselves? When I'm angry, I can't control whether I say "I'm angry when you . . ." or "You make me angry when . . ."

5. How can I be more assertive? I've always avoided conflict.

6. Isn't assertiveness just another word for pushiness?

7. Why are you trying to make me more assertive? I'm happy the way I am!

8. I have no trouble being assertive when I do exercises. But how do you do this in real life?

9. Isn't there anything to do on this campus? I wish I could find some people who share my interests.

10. Why should I go to these dumb events? They're boring!

11. Why should I get involved? I came to college to get a job.

D. TEACHING THIS CHAPTER

This is another chapter that you may choose "not to teach" in the sense of lecturing on the subject. Rather, we suggest approaching the unit tangentially, perhaps in relation to assertiveness, for the purpose of involving students in discussions of some very important topics.

Why is this important? For one thing, personal relationships among students have a direct bearing on their connectedness to their colleges or universities, and connectedness, in many cases, has a direct bearing on persistence to graduation. Research shows that students who develop significant relationships tend to have higher graduation rates than those who do not. In this sense, then, relationships do affect college success.

For another thing, the chapter involves matters of great importance to your students. Many years ago, when we first began assigning journals to first-year students, we were shocked to learn that the telephone call they received—or did not receive—was more important to them than Plato's *Republic* or Aristotle's *Ethics*. In short, this chapter is very much "where your students are at," to put it in their words.

In leading discussions on relationships, you can almost always rely on gaining your students' attention from the onset. You can also rely on having the discussions become very personal, sometimes embarrassingly so for those of us who are trained in the traditional academic disciplines and are accustomed to dealing with classroom matters in fairly scholarly and impersonal terms. For example, several years ago in a discussion of Chaim Potok's novel *My Name Is Asher Lev*, a student used the novel as a departure point for some very personal revelations about his relationship with his parents. It would be fair to say that most people in the class were at first shocked and embarrassed. Nonetheless they were sympathetic and, in the long run, became a source of support to someone who had become a real person to his fellow students through self-disclosure.

Like some of the other late chapters in *Your College Experience*, this chapter on assertiveness involves some very personal issues and therefore must be taught with some delicacy. As you plan this unit, you must think about your own level of comfort in approaching the subject. In addition, you will almost certainly have, in your class, some very shy and passive students. In our experience, exercises on assertiveness invariably make such students uncomfortable. They do not want to be put on the spot.

For this reason, you should focus your efforts on helping your students understand the important concepts. You should also take pains to respect their privacy and yet find ways to give them feedback on the exercises they complete in private. The journal is a fine place for such feedback. Remember, your students always have the option of bringing up in class ideas they would like discussed further.

Perhaps the most efficient way to teach the key concepts about assertiveness is through a brief lecture, which can serve double duty—that is, as a way of communicating a body of information and as the basis for another note-taking exercise. You might also ask that your students write a précis of the paragraphs that define assertiveness, passive and aggressive behavior, and specificity. Still another technique is to require students to write test questions (essay and objective) covering the major concepts in the chapter. Finally, you might choose to give a brief quiz. Whatever you choose, you need to be sure that students understand the key concepts.

This material on involvement poses two kinds of difficulties related to two kinds of students and their social habits. Some students are natural joiners and need little encouragement to become actively involved in college life. The danger these students face is becoming over-involved. Others need to be encouraged every step of the way. For whatever reason, they are reluctant to join organizations, and this puts their instructors in the position both of encouraging their involvement and respecting their right to remain uninvolved.

As you design your course, you will consider ways of encouraging involvement. In general, we are aware of three basic approaches. One is to allow each student to choose his or her own path. These students will join whichever organizations they like at the time that best suits them. The second is to require each student to join at least one organization during the first term. (Keep in mind that while joining an organization has benefits for the majority of students, it may be counter-productive for the extremely shy, the highly individualistic, the student who prefers to remain aloof, or a student who is already adequately involved. For these kinds of students, you need to have appropriate alternatives.) The third is to require that students attend a specific number of co-curricular events as a means of introducing the students to campus life. This method is proactive, yet respects the right of individual students to make choices.

At the same time that you plan involvement in organizations, we suggest that you think about the importance of co-curricular events outside of organizations. Most campuses abound with film and lecture series, musical and dramatic performances, art exhibitions, and athletic events. Although we grant diplomas to students for the completion of academic courses, we also know that co-curricular events constitute an important part of learning, and we need to encourage students to learn outside the classroom as well as inside. In our first-year seminar, we require that students attend and report on a specific number of co-curricular events, and we factor this into their final grade.

E.   TIPS ON TEACHING "YOURSELF AND OTHERS"

It is virtually impossible to discuss relationships meaningfully with your students unless you have already established an environment of trust. Only after you have achieved a high degree of rapport with your students will they be comfortable disclosing themselves to you and their classmates. Remember too that relationships are a two-way street. If you want students to be honest with you, you should not be fearful about disclosing yourself to them.

Some of our colleagues feel that this kind of mutual self-disclosure borders on "counseling" and constitutes an invasion of the students' privacy. As for the first, talking honestly with each other is only "counseling" if it occurs within the confines of a counselor's office; in ordinary discourse, it is merely openness. Regarding the second, faculty members invade students' privacy all the time. Consider the instructor who asks students to write the famous "What I did on my summer vacation" theme. Our experience has taught us that, just as we limit our disclosures to students, so they limit theirs to us.

Of equal importance is the "group feeling" that you have worked to establish throughout the class. Without it, and the civility that it implies, students usually will not be honest with each other.

Perhaps the most significant suggestion we can make about teaching assertiveness is that you teach this chapter as objectively as you possibly can. Present the material as if the students' major requirement is to understand the concepts, but, as you do so, urge the students to practice these concepts for the purpose of developing assertiveness skills. Let your students know that you are interested in monitoring the development of these skills, and that you will look forward to reading the journal entries in which they record their progress. Finally, use class time to invite your students to raise the issues that are of most concern to them. Although the exercises will guide them, the decision of what to bring up is theirs.

From the beginning of the term to the end, you should encourage your students to become involved—in organizations and in co-curricular events. In addition, for this unit, assigning the readings and exercises is sufficient.

F. IN-CLASS USE OF EXERCISES

As you will see when you examine the exercises, most are really intended to be completed in private. Only exercise 11.3 is appropriate for in-class use.

Exercise 11.3 "Improving Relationships"

This may well be the key exercise in the chapter. Because your students will have established a good relationship with each other by this point in the term, the sharing should be exceedingly productive. As a rule of thumb, we recommend removing yourself as instructor as much as possible from this exercise.

Exercise 11.5 "Affirm Your Personal and Interpersonal Rights"

While this exercise should be done in private, some of the rights listed can be used as vehicles for class discussion. For example, "the right to control my own time, body, money and property" is something of an oversimplification and ignores some basic obligations that children—even college students—have to their parents and spouses, and that significant others have to each other. You might choose to extend the discussion beyond the boundaries of assertiveness and cross into the area of values.

Exercise 11.7 "Take the Plunge"

Having your students report on their experiences in a student organization is a good way to spread information about such organizations. To make this more interesting, you could ask your students to deliver their reports as commercials for the organization. Should a student deliver a negative report, you might brainstorm with the class on how to make the organization more effective.

G. JOURNAL EXERCISE

The more specific your students are, the more helpful you can be in your response. Therefore, you should urge them to consider this entry as an opportunity to take advantage of your assistance. If you think particular students have real assertiveness problems, you can use the response to refer them for appropriate help.

Healthy Decisions: Sexuality, Drugs, and Stress

CHAPTER OVERVIEW

A. Chapter goals
B. Timing and connections to other topics
C. Questions students typically ask
D. Teaching this chapter
E. Tips on teaching "Healthy Decisions: Sexuality, Drugs, and Stress"
F. In-class use of exercises
G. Journal exercise

A. CHAPTER GOALS

1. To explain proper nutrition, fitness, and sexuality as components of wellness
2. To encourage positive habits of nutrition, fitness, and sexuality
3. To demonstrate the dangers in using alcohol and other drugs
4. To define stress as a part of the human condition
5. To teach stress reduction methods

B. TIMING AND CONNECTIONS TO OTHER TOPICS

Although this chapter may be taught anytime, its information is so important to your students' well-being that it should be presented as early as possible. If you choose to defer discussion of the information until after you cover other material, at least assign the chapter to be read early on.

Connections

► Chapter 2, "Time Management," suggests a key strategy for avoiding stress.

- Chapter 10, "Major, Career, and Transfer Planning," focuses on a primary cause of stress—concern about one's own future.
- Chapter 11, "Yourself and Others," concerns itself with assertiveness, relationships, and getting involved, all of which are related to the concerns of Chapter 12.

C. QUESTIONS STUDENTS TYPICALLY ASK

1. Who are you to interfere with my personal life? What I put into my body is my business.
2. Why do we have to hear this crap about nutrition? Soon they'll discover that we can't eat anything.
3. Why do I have to wear a condom? I can't become pregnant.
4. Why do they expect us not to drink and smoke when they all drink and smoke?

D. TEACHING THIS CHAPTER

As indicated previously, we believe the information presented in this chapter is critical to student well-being and success. Without belaboring the notion of *mens sana in corpore sano*—the "sound mind in the sound body"—we assume an institutional responsibility to provide students with information about lifestyle that will encourage them to make positive choices. This is not to suggest a return to the 1960's policy of *in loco parentis*. As faculty and staff, we are not surrogate parents. We are concerned adults in possession of information that can help first-year students cope with the freedom that is often cited as their number one problem.

The reference to *in loco parentis* suggests one of the difficulties in teaching this chapter. It is all too easy to become preachy, heavy-handed, and parental in discussing these issues, and nothing will shut down your students' hearing so much as preachiness. As our students have told us many times, "We've heard it all before." This should not, however, militate against your teaching wellness. The fact is that students eat badly, sleep too little, indulge in alcohol and other drugs, become "stressed out," and sometimes suffer the negative consequences of sexual activity (such as sexually transmitted diseases or unwanted pregnancies).

Another difficulty implicit in the nature of the chapter's material is that the information here is more personal than that of other chapters. Consider the subjects being presented: nutrition, fitness, sexuality, alcohol and other drugs, and stress. What could be more personal than the lifestyle choices one makes about his or her body? Furthermore, these subjects have not been the traditional concern of academic classrooms. Many faculty are unaccustomed to and uncomfortable with treating these issues in an academic setting.

Finally, there is a danger in not knowing your particular campus. There may be those who would charge you with intellectual flabbiness for even taking up the topic of wellness. There may also be those who would charge you with moral flabbiness for discussing (and in their minds therefore promoting) sexuality.

If you assume, as we do, that the material must be taught, you will need to consider the resources of your own campus in deciding on a teaching approach. If your campus has a limited staff of Student Affairs professionals, you will have to commit a significant amount of class time to teaching and processing the chapter's information. If your campus has the resources, you might simply assign the chapter to be read and hope that your students will get explanations and the opportunity for discussion in their residence halls.

Should you not want to rely on chance for this important chapter, you should arrange with your Student Affairs staff to present residence hall programs on issues of wellness. In this case you might require that students attend wellness sessions and write about them in their journals. We also suggest that you spend class time discussing the important issues presented. This approach obviously requires careful coordination with your Student Affairs staff.

If you accept responsibility for teaching this material in your course, here are our suggestions.

Sexuality

Regardless of the fact that information on sexuality has been made available to your students throughout high school, Student Affairs and medical professionals tell us that first-year students practice sexuality in what appears to be a conspiracy of misinformation. It is essential that we take the opportunity to clarify the subject.

Unfortunately, many of us—especially those of us from traditional academic backgrounds—are not entirely comfortable with the prospect of teaching sexuality. The truth is that our students are also not entirely comfortable. One way to begin the unit is by admitting your discomfort and explaining its basis, that is, that you feel inadequate to present the information with complete accuracy or that you feel a little uncomfortable talking openly about the subject. We have been reared not to be open about sexuality. You could then indicate that the subject is important enough to warrant going ahead, even in the face of personal discomfort.

Once you begin the discussion, you will probably find, as we have, that the students are eager to explore issues of sexuality. This is a topic that is very much on their minds. At this point in the semester, you should be able to capitalize on the trust and rapport you have established with the group.

One way around personal discomfort is to bring in an "expert" to talk about sexuality: the campus physician or other medical personnel or medical professionals from the community or a nearby university or medical center. The University of South Carolina has made excellent use of the university physician and two Master's level health educators in a program called "Sex and the College Student."

As for teaching the unit, the minimum is to go over the essential facts, even if you choose to lecture on forms of contraception; the use of condoms as both contraceptive and prophylactic; varieties of sexually transmitted diseases, especially AIDS; and rape. We recommend going beyond the lecture by giving your students a chance to discuss the information with each other, examine how this information can have an impact on their lives, and finally discuss decisions regarding their sexuality. Your students need the chance to ask you questions about the information, and, if you don't have the answers, simply let them know that you will get the answers by the next class. They also need the opportunity to explore some of the myths about sexuality, such as you can't get pregnant the first time you have sex, or you can't get AIDS if you're a straight male having sex with a "good girl." These myths are best explored in small groups and are most easily discussed by the entire class if each group lists myths on newsprint. (If you want to supply a number of these myths for your students, you could consult your Student Affairs and counseling professionals for the prevalent myths.) You might also ask your students to provide some of the conventional wisdom for these discussions. Finally, role playing is a very effective way of allowing students to think about how to communicate with sex partners on the subject of sexuality. For such role-playing exercises, we recommend a fishbowl in which a couple acts out dialogues on the sexual issues that have surfaced throughout the previous discussions. Naturally, you should arrange in advance for particular students to do the role playing. Some students will be eager to help. After the fishbowl, divide the class into small groups to discuss the effectiveness of the dialogues and to develop alternatives.

As for the issue of rape and date rape, a good technique for initiating discussion is to show videotapes. Several professional tapes are available, and your librarian should be able to make recommendations. Feel free to contact the Assistant Dean for Campus Life Activities, Marietta College, Marietta, Ohio 45750, (614) 374-4784 to secure a videotape of a mock trial concerning date rape. In addition, use the boxed material in the chapter itself to initiate discussion.

Alcohol and Other Drugs

Teaching this unit presents challenges similar to teaching the unit on sexuality. The students have heard it and heard it and heard it, and they don't want to hear it again. The unit differs from the unit on sexuality, however, in an essential way. Here, for the most part, the students know the information contained in the chapter, and they reject it. Many of them like to drink, some of them enjoy other drugs, and they don't want anyone telling them they shouldn't.

Nonetheless, the message is important enough to deliver one more time, and we are committed to teaching a unit on drugs and alcohol. If, by the time you teach this unit, you have developed a good relationship with your students, they will at least be certain of the good will you bear them, and they should be somewhat tolerant of what they will probably consider your intrusion into their lives. If, however, you are unsure of yourself or fear that you might fall into the trap of preaching, try to find a professional who can present the information without becoming pious and moralistic.

In doing exercises about alcohol and drug use, we have found that students invariably ask instructors whether or not they drink or use other drugs (they usually ask the latter out of class). Should this happen, we recommend an honest answer, even if that means you admit to drinking or using or having used drugs. This will almost surely lead to questions about why you had them read the chapter, and this will let you explain your own views. Note, however, that you will be doing so in the context of explaining your personal policies, not preaching to them about what they should do.

Stress Management

We have found that first-year students are very skeptical about the possibility of managing stress. They are convinced not just that stress is a part of life but also that the conditions of college life make stress management impossible. In the face of this skepticism, you should nevertheless assign the chapter to be read and the exercises to be completed. You might even ask students to keep track of their stressful periods as well as the strategies they employ for dealing with those periods. If you feel you must do more, you can invite a counselor to lead the students through some stress management exercises.

One proactive thing you can do regarding stress management is to remain alert to your students' moods, especially at critical times during the term. For instance, students generally take their first major exams between the fourth and sixth weeks of the term, and first-year students often experience stress at that time. If you notice that some students are showing signs of stress, you might direct them to the exercises on stress reduction and also inform them of the campus resources available for help.

E. TIPS ON TEACHING "HEALTHY DECISIONS: SEXUALITY, DRUGS, AND STRESS"

This is the most sensitive chapter in the book, and you must therefore be especially careful to approach the subjects with tact, delicacy, and confidence. Above all else, don't preach! If at all possible, lead your students through discussions in which they will raise all the important points and sides of the various issues. This will lessen their perception that you are preaching. Remember that you are approaching this material not as an expert but as an adult mentor to your students.

F. IN-CLASS USE OF EXERCISES

Exercise 12.4 "The College Readjustment Rating Scale"

To process this exercise, ask students to submit the results of their surveys anonymously. If you find many of your students scoring 150 or higher, you might invite your college counselor to discuss stress management and to demonstrate stress reduction techniques.

Exercise 12.5 "Divide and Conquer"

Role-playing exercises can be very useful when students are adequately prepared and comfortable with such play-acting. Give students who are not comfortable the option of watching and commenting rather than role-playing. Be sure to assign the exercise in advance of the class, and encourage your students to practice the roles with each other, if possible.

G. JOURNAL EXERCISE

The focus of this entry is extremely personal. As you respond, be sure to avoid a confrontational tone.

How to Manage Your Money and Obtain Financial Aid

APPENDIX OVERVIEW

A. Appendix goal: "How to Manage Your Money"

B. Timing

C. Questions students typically ask

D. Teaching this section of the appendix

E. Tips on teaching "How to Manage Your Money"

F. Appendix goals: "How to Obtain Financial Aid"

G. Timing

H. Questions students typically ask

I. Teaching this section of the appendix

J. Tips on teaching "How to Obtain Financial Aid"

Note: We have divided the material into two sections: (1) "How to Manage Your Money" (pp. A1–A5 in *YCE*) and (2) "How to Obtain Financial Aid" (pp. A5–A9).

A. APPENDIX GOAL: "HOW TO MANAGE YOUR MONEY"

To provide students with a method for controlling their finances

B. TIMING

Whether you choose to spend class time on managing personal finances will depend on your specific class objectives and the time you have available. This material is placed in the Appendix section of the text because the subject of managing personal finances might be introduced at almost any time in the term.

It is not necessary to spend a great deal of time on personal finances. You can cover most of the information in 20 to 30 minutes.

C. QUESTIONS STUDENTS TYPICALLY ASK

1. How can I manage my personal finances when no one even tells us about all the extra charges?

2. How am I supposed to call my girlfriend/boyfriend once a week when long distance calls are so expensive?

3. Do I have to pay all my college bills at once?

4. How can I manage my money when I don't have enough to go around?

D. TEACHING THIS SECTION OF THE APPENDIX

Like financial aid, personal finances are very much an individual case. You may find that some students are embarrassed by discussions of personal finance, since they are convinced that other students have significantly more money than they do. Consequently, when you discuss personal finances, you might want to keep the discussion fairly general.

A good focus is the number of pitfalls that await college students unaccustomed to managing their money. For example, one pizza may not cost very much, but pizza every night begins to add up—in more ways than one. Credit cards are sometimes too convenient, and they do have to be paid off.

As *YCE* points out repeatedly, the key to handling personal finances successfully is deliberate planning. The appendix provides a method.

E. TIPS ON TEACHING "HOW TO MANAGE YOUR MONEY"

Take your cue of when to teach this unit from the students themselves. At a certain point in the term, we have found that students begin to write in their journals about the problems they are having managing their money. When you notice a significant number of such references, you might decide to teach this part of the appendix.

If you want to be more proactive, you might simply ask your students whether they are having financial problems. If they answer affirmatively, you might assign this part of the appendix and suggest that they set up an expense journal similar to the samples.

F. APPENDIX GOALS: "HOW TO OBTAIN FINANCIAL AID"

1. To provide students with a definition of financial aid and introduce them to the four basic types of financial assistance: grants, scholarships, loans, and work

2. To enable students to examine the cost/benefit of a college education

3. To introduce students to the process of applying for financial aid

4. To provide students with an introduction to issues in higher education financial aid

G. TIMING

Whether you choose to spend class time on financial aid will depend on your specific class objectives, the time you have available, and whether you believe that the students' questions about financial aid are being adequately answered elsewhere. This material is placed in the Appendix of the text because the subject of financial aid might be introduced at almost any time in the term.

It is not necessary to spend a great deal of time on financial aid. You can cover most of the information in 20 to 30 minutes. If you use the subject as a springboard for a more general discussion of the value of higher education, you will want to devote a whole period to it.

H. QUESTIONS STUDENTS TYPICALLY ASK

1. Why is financial aid such a hassle? I never get a straight answer from those people.
2. Why can't I get more financial aid? My family's not rich!
3. Why can't I declare myself independent and get more aid?
4. How am I supposed to get all my school work done, play varsity sports, have fun, and do 10 hours a week of work/study?

I. TEACHING THIS SECTION OF THE APPENDIX

Although financial aid can be a very arcane and complex subject and terms and conditions of awards vary from person to person, the rudiments and the basic categories of aid are fairly straightforward and are clearly explained in the text. The important point to make to the students is that each individual's financial aid situation is different and that they must investigate their own situations without making any assumptions based on what other students tell them.

Although financial aid arrangements are ultimately a very personal and private matter, this can be a good place to discuss the cost/value of higher education—both the financial and nonfinancial costs and rewards. You may want to connect this section with the discussion in Chapter 1, "Keys to Success," on the value of college.

Most students who are enrolled have already applied for financial aid for the current term, but some may be confused about the process, and the status of others may have changed. Changes in parental income, the number of family members in college, or changes in other family/personal circumstances may alter their eligibility.

Applying for aid is frequently a bureaucratic and time-consuming process; the students should be advised to begin well in advance of any deadlines. At some colleges registration will be denied if all financial aid paper work is not completed. You should know the regulations at your institution.

J. TIPS ON TEACHING "HOW TO OBTAIN FINANCIAL AID"

A good time to introduce this material may be near the end of the term in preparation for the next term, as some students' financial aid eligibility may be changing for the next term or year.

Financial aid is a complex subject that most faculty do not feel comfortable dealing with in any detail. The instructor may feel more at ease with this material by consulting with the financial aid office and being briefed on current college/government regulations or by inviting someone from that office to make a presentation to the class. Alternatively, the class could visit the Financial Aid Office as part of a campus tour to help the students literally find "financial aid."

▼▼▼▼▼▼▼▼▼▼▼▼▼▼▼▼▼▼▼▼▼▼▼▼▼▼

Ten Good Questions About Computers

APPENDIX OVERVIEW

A. Appendix goals
B. Timing and connections to other topics
C. Questions students typically ask
D. Teaching this appendix

A. APPENDIX GOALS

1. To provide first-year students with a brief overview of how computers work and the terminology used to describe their operation
2. To explain the ways in which computers can be useful to students
3. To provide tips on buying a computer

B. TIMING AND CONNECTIONS TO OTHER TOPICS

This unit may be taught anytime. In light of the usefulness of computers, however, the earlier it is taught, the better.

C. QUESTIONS STUDENTS TYPICALLY ASK

1. How can I even think about using a computer? I don't know anything about them, and I'm not very technical.
2. How can I afford a computer? I can barely afford a typewriter.
3. What's the point of buying a comptuer now? Everyone knows the current models will be obsolete soon.

D. TEACHING THIS APPENDIX

Rather than "teaching the appendix," assign it to be read early in the term, and be prepared to answer questions. You might also check your campus resources to see if anyone is available to provide students with advice on understanding, using, and buying computers. Perhaps you could arrange for students to visit the campus computer center, if you have one.

You might also inquire if your campus has special "higher education" discounts on computer purchases. Apple Macintosh® offers campus discounts under HEPP II (Higher Education Purchase Plan). IBM sales division should be contacted to determine whether your school qualifies for discounts.

PART

3

▼▼▼▼▼▼▼▼▼▼▼▼▼▼▼▼

Other Resources

► Resources for Educators of First-Year Students
► Complimentary Copy of The Freshman Year
  Experience_{SM} Newsletter
► Teacher Training Seminars and Workshops
► Bibliography
► Videography
► Transparency Masters

▼ ▼

Resources for Educators of First-Year Students

NATIONAL RESOURCE CENTER FOR THE FRESHMAN YEAR EXPERIENCE_{SM}

Established in 1987, The National Resource Center for The Freshman Year Experience at the University of South Carolina collects and disseminates information about the first year of college. To that end, the center engages in research and publishes a scholarly journal, newsletter, and monograph series. These publications are dedicated to expanding available knowledge about first-year programming and to studying factors that enhance the success of first-year students. The center also conducts national surveys on first-year experience seminars, hosts faculty on sabbaticals, and serves as a clearinghouse for information on first-year programming. Under John Gardner's direction, the center works closely with and in support of the University 101 first-year experience seminar and The Freshman Year Experience Conference series. For more information or to order the publications listed below, contact the National Resource Center for The Freshman Year Experience, 1728 College Street, University of South Carolina, Columbia, SC 29208; phone: (803) 777-6029.

PUBLICATIONS

Journal of The Freshman Year Experience
A semiannual refereed journal providing current research and scholarship on the first year of college.

The Freshman Year Experience Newsletter
A quarterly newsletter offering innovative and practical ideas for improving programs for first-year students.

Guidelines for Evaluating The Freshman Year Experience
Comprehensive guidelines developed by John Gardner for assessing the quality of first-year student life on the college campus.

Monograph Series

#1 *Character Development in the Freshman Year and Over Four Years of Undergraduate Study*
Longitudinal research study of a living–learning curriculum intervention to enhance character development in college students.

#2 *Perspectives on the Freshman Year: Selected Major Addresses from the Freshman Year Experience Conferences*
Views on the critical first year from renowned educators Alexander Astin, Lee Knefelkamp, Arthur Levine, Reginald Wilson, Lee Upcraft, and Peter Scott.

#3 *Annotated Bibliography on The Freshman Year Experience*
Comprehensive annotated listing of books and articles pertinent to the first year of college.

#4 *The Freshman Orientation Seminar: A Research-Based Rationale for Its Value, Delivery, and Content*
An extensive review of available research on the first-year experience orientation seminar, providing a framework for decision making, administration, and course content.

#5 *Residence Life Programs and The First-Year Experience*
A joint publication with the Association of College and University Housing Officers, International. Research and programming ideas for improving the residential first-year experience.

#6 *The First National Survey on Freshman Seminar Programs: Findings, Conclusions, and Recommendations*
Presents results of a 1988 national survey of first-year experience seminar programming. Data include information about the institutions, the course itself, and related faculty development programs.

Additional monographs are being developed on the following topics: university colleges, supplemental instruction, a follow-up national survey comparing different types of first-year seminars, college–high school partnerships, first-year orientation, writing in the first-year seminar, and character development.

THE FRESHMAN YEAR EXPERIENCE CONFERENCE SERIES

Initiated in 1982, the Freshman Year Experience Conference Series brings together faculty, student affairs administrators, and academic affairs administrators with a common interest in improving the status of the first college year. Through the concurrent session format, educators share information on campus-based programs and engage in discussion sessions on a variety of topics of interest to first-year student educators. Keynote and plenary session speakers include prominent national figures in American higher education. Full-day and half-day workshops are offered as pre- and post-conference sessions.

An annual meeting is held each February in Columbia, SC. In addition to this annual meeting, a variety of special focus meetings are held at various locations around the United States on such topics as the first-year experience in small colleges, diversity, teaching first-year students, and science and technological education of first-year students. International meetings are also held annually during the summer. Past international conferences have been held in England, Scotland, Canada, and Denmark. Upcoming international conferences are scheduled for Victoria, British Columbia, in May 1992, for Boston in July 1993, and again for England during the summer of 1994.

ONE-DAY RESOURCE SEMINARS AND INSTRUCTOR TRAINING WORKSHOPS

In 1991–1992, the National Resource Center for The Freshman Year Experience and The Freshman Year Experience Conference Series collaborated to develop a new series of six 1-day drive-in/fly-in seminars and workshops that were held on campuses of co-sponsoring institutions around the country. The Resource Seminars are designed to provide educators with an intensive, practical, interactive experience that focuses on the theory and practice of effective first-year programming. The Instructor Training Workshops highlight cognitive and affective faculty training techniques designed to prepare participants to teach an extended first-year orientation seminar. These seminars and workshops will continue to be offered at campus locations nationwide in successive academic years.

FOR MORE INFORMATION ABOUT PUBLICATIONS, SEMINARS, CONFERENCES, AND WORKSHOPS

For information about publications from the National Resource Center for The Freshman Year Experience or about resource seminars, instructor training workshops, or conferences, contact The Freshman Year Experience at 1728 College Street, University of South Carolina, Columbia, SC 29208; phone: (803) 777-6029.

Contact persons for The Freshman Year Experience are:

► Barefoot, Betsy
  Co-Director for the National Resource Center for The Freshman Year Experience, (803) 777-2247

► Berman, Dan
  Co-Director for Instruction and Faculty Development, (803) 777-9506

► Fidler, Dorothy
  Senior Managing Editor, (803) 777-5193

► Hunter, Mary Stuart
  Co-Director for Conferences and Administration, (803) 777-4761

► Gardner, John
  Director for University 101 and Associate Vice Provost for Regional Campuses and Continuing Education, (803) 777-3480

The Freshman Year EXPERIENCE *Newsletter*

The University of South Carolina, Columbia, SC 29208

A Complimentary Copy*

Another new beginning for The Freshman Year Experience

You are receiving a complimentary copy of this newsletter published quarterly by the National Resource Center for The Freshman Year Experience, University 101 Program, University of South Carolina.

This newsletter is designed to distribute information about programs and research from institutions across the country which are making strides in creating a more productive first year for college students and in retaining freshmen.

The National Resource Center for The Freshman Year Experience evolved from of the freshman seminar course at the University of South Carolina, University 101, and The Freshman Year Experience Conferences. Since 1983, regional, national, and international conferences on the Freshman Year Experience provided a forum to discuss freshman programs. From this ground swell of interest, the National Center for the Study of The Freshman Year Experience grew with the following goals:

✧ to publish this newsletter of trends in freshman programs;

✧ to establish a national database for disseminating information about successful freshman programs;

✧ to provide an on-site research facility for visiting scholars on sabbatical;

✧ to publish a scholarly journal emphasizing freshman retention research as well as design, implementation, and assessment of freshman programs.

The staff of the National Resource Center for The Freshman Year Experience consists of John Gardner, Director; Dorothy Fidler, Co-Director; Betsy Barefoot, Associate Director; Mary Hendricks, Editorial Assistant; and Rachel Stokes, Graduate Assistant. We encourage you to submit ideas and articles for publication in the Newsletter. Please call us at (803) 777-6029 or send an article to:

Dorothy Fidler
National Resource
Center for The Freshman
Year Experience
University 101
1728 College Street
The University
of South Carolina
Columbia, S.C. 29208.

We hope to receive your news and your subscription to help us keep you up to date on innovative programs for freshmen from colleges and universities around the world by sharing trends and ideas from campus to campus.

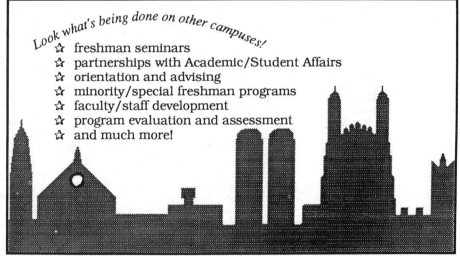

Look what's being done on other campuses!
☆ freshman seminars
☆ partnerships with Academic/Student Affairs
☆ orientation and advising
☆ minority/special freshman programs
☆ faculty/staff development
☆ program evaluation and assessment
☆ and much more!

* This complimentary copy is composed of a selective sampling from several issues.

Note: The Freshman Year Experience Newsletter is reprinted with permission of the National Resource Center for The Freshman Year Experience.

From the Director

John N. Gardner
Director, University 101
Vice Chancellor for University
Campuses and Continuing Education
Professor of Library and Information Science

When Dorothy Fidler, the editor of this newsletter, gave me the task of writing a column along with the request that it be limited to 200 words, this was truly more than I could do. How could I possibly describe in 200 words for readers of this first edition how my hopes and dreams for such a publication had come to fruition after 16 years of work with University 101 and The Freshman Year Experience concept at the University of South Carolina and in American higher education? Nevertheless, the purpose of this column is to share a few of my reasons to start this newsletter in the first place and what I hope it will do for all of us who have a keen interest in enhancing The Freshman Year Experience.

First of all, the newsletter will be a critical organ of the developing National Resource Center for The Freshman Year Experience. Why did we start this Center in 1987? Because the University of South Carolina had long been a de facto clearing house for information regarding freshman programs and it seemed high time we legitimized this function. There is also a crying need for more research on the effectiveness of the hundreds of new freshman programs which have been spawned in the 1980s and for the dissemination of the findings from such research. Even though many institutions have made enormous changes in the way they are treating first-year students, there are hundreds more who still do business the way they did even prior to 1965 in terms of how they assimilate, or in many cases, don't as-similate, first-year stu-dents. There's literally not a day that goes by when I don't receive a letter or phone call from some desperate soul wanting information that can be used to persuade conservative faculty groups who don't see why we need to bring about changes in the freshman year.

A purpose of this newsletter is both to introduce ideas and share perspectives on The Freshman Year Experience. The newsletter will describe current practices, model programs, and research findings. It will feature stimulating and provocative ideas from those who are doing important work on behalf of enhancing the freshman experience. Over my sixteen years of work on behalf of this concept, I have collected a large number of gems in terms of great people/educators who are doing important things to improve the education and the lives of students but most of whom have lacked forum in which to share their ideas. Consequently, th have also lacked a platform to help legitimize such ide. We want this newsletter to serve that kind of a purpo.

There are all kinds of experts on The Freshman Ye Experience. Since 1982, approximately 7,000 edu. tors from more than a dozen countries have attend our conferences. They are undertaking extraordina approaches to enhance the freshman year. It's the kinds of people that we want to feature in this Newslet which means, in all probability, you, the readers of t first edition. We want your ideas, so please send th to the newsletter editor, Dr. Dorothy Fidler.

This first issue is complimentary to those of y whom we know are interested in enhancing the fres man year and to any of your colleagues who reques copy of this issue. Unfortunately, there's no way we c produce a fine newsletter "free." This is an expens process to collect the information, and to devote t staff time and resources to write such a newslet including all the costs of ultimate production, maili etc. Therefore, we have to sell subscriptions becau this activity like all continuing education activit sponsored by the University 101 program, must entirely self-sufficient in terms of recovering all of th costs. In the event that there are any residuals from t publication of this newsletter, such monies will be us to support further research and dissemination activit of the National Resource Center for The Freshman Y Experience. One way or another, this publication a all related proceeds will be plowed back into the hancement of The Freshman Year Experience in Ame can higher education and beyond.

I want to take this opportunity to thank my c leagues here at University 101: Cherie Bishop, D Berman, Dorothy Fidler, Vicky Howell, Stuart Hunt Betsy Barefoot, Carol May, Penny Smoak, and Beve Windham for their ideas, their efforts, their loya support, and inspiration. Without them, John Ga ner's dream of a freshman year experience newslet would be just that, a continuing and very incompl dream. We thank you for sharing in our vision and hope that we will hear from you with your ideas. Tha you, too, for whatever you're doing to enhance T Freshman Year Experience.

2

About the Staff

Dorothy Fidler is the Co-Director for the National Resource Center for The Freshman Year Experience. She edits *The Freshman Year Experience Newsletter* and the *Journal of The Freshman Year Experience*. She is also Assistant Director of Adult Student Services and teaches in the Psychology Department.

Dan Berman, Co-Director for Instruction and Faculty Development, supervises the three-credit freshman seminar course, faculty development workshops, and the University 101 Forum, a series of programs to promote collaboration among faculty, professional staff, administrators, and students. He also is a faculty member in the Department of Media Arts in the College of Applied Professional Sciences.

As University 101 Co-Director for Conferences and Administration, **Mary Stuart Hunter** assists educators in learning methods for enhancing the freshman year. Through more than 7000 educators from some 20 countries who are alumni of the Freshman/First-Year Experience Conferences, she stays in touch with current trends in higher education. She also teaches University 101 and is Director of Academic Advising for the University of South Carolina's Division of Continuing Education.

Newsletter Staff

The Freshman Year Experience Newsletter is published quarterly by the National Resource Center for the Freshman Year Experience at the University of South Carolina, University 101, Columbia, S. C. 29208. Telephone (803) 777-6029. One year subscription is $50 for individuals or $60 for institutions. The Center, a nonprofit organization, will use proceeds from the newsletter to defray publication costs, support research, and disseminate information.

Director:
John N. Gardner
Co-Director:
Dorothy S. Fidler
Associate Director:
Betsy Barefoot
Editorial Assistant:
Mary Hendrix
Graduate Assistant:
Rachel Stokes
Publications Designer:
Kelley C. McDonald

ISSN 1053-2048

Betsy Barefoot is Associate Director of the National Resource Center for The Freshman Year Experience. In addition to her various duties in the National Center, she currently serves as coordinator for the University Instructional Development Project to train graduate teaching assistants at the University of South Carolina in methods of college teaching. She also is a doctoral candidate in higher education from the College of William and Mary.

Carol May, Associate Director for Domestic Conferences, is responsible for planning and implementing regional conferences on The Freshman Year Experience. She also teaches University 101, the freshman orientation seminar at the University of South Carolina.

Vicky Howell has been the Administrative Assistant for University 101 since 1980. She and Administrative Specialist **Penny Smoak** perform administrative duties for the program including the conference series on The Freshman/First-Year Experience and the National Resource Center for The Freshman Year Experience. **Beverly Windham** is Conference Coordinator and **Cherie Bishop** is Assistant Conference Coordinator. They coordinate and organize the myriad of details involved in conference planning and implementation.

Left to Right: **Cherie Bishop, Vicky Howell, Beverly Windham, Penny Smoak.**

3

Legislature Mandates Help for Freshmen

Universities within Pennsylvania's system of higher education are required to provide an opportunity for all students to develop their fullest educational potential. The Educational Opportunities Program/ Act 101 at Clarion University strives to accomplish this goal through two programs: Pre-College and the Freshman Year.

Pre-College: Freshmen admitted into EOP/ Act101 must attend a Pre-College Experience for six and a half weeks. During this time they enroll in an intensive skills development curriculum consisting of basic composition, basic mathematics, seminars in reading and study skills, personal development, and career orientation. This curriculum emphasizes reading and writing skills, logical reasoning, and critical thinking. They also receive comprehensive academic advising for a full schedule of classes for the fall semester.

Freshman Year: EOP/Act 101 freshmen enroll in a two-credit *Reading and Study Skills Course* with lab. For four additional hours per week they must also attend a *Learning Skills Lab* where they work on class assignments. Lab time is recorded each week to monitor their time spent in academic preparation for classes.

Also during their first academic year, these freshmen participate in a required non-credit *college skills seminar* which meets twice a week. Here they discuss topics relating to adjustment to college life such as self-image, values clarification, self-defeating behaviors, anxiety management, understanding college expectations, scheduling of courses, and planning academic programs.

Faculty *monitor their academic progress* on written forms. Advisors discuss the comments with each student and then encourage freshmen to meet with faculty to discuss their performance. This monitoring process continues through the sophomore year.

The EOP/Act 101 staff works with freshmen to provide a sound academic program including skill development, career and personal counseling, and the identification of resources on campus to address their needs.

Contact:
Isaiah Sessoms, Director, Educational
Opportunities Program/Act 101, Clarion University
Clarion, PA, 16214. Phone: (814) 226-2321

Data Show Effectivenes of Freshman Semina

For over a decade Paul Fidler has collected retention data for the University 101 Program at the University of South Carolina. Recently he reviewed research from over a dozen other institutions on freshman seminars conducted for credit and published his findings in *The Freshman Year Experience* edited by Lee Upcraft and John Gardner, and published by Jossey-Bass. The research includes several variables: retention, academic performance, use of student services, and personality development.

Fidler found ample evidence across institutions that freshman seminars are associated with improved retention rates among college freshmen. Since 1972, in ten of the thirteen years that the University of South Carolina collected retention data, students participating in University 101 returned for their sophomore year at a significantly higher rate than non-participants. The remaining three years showed trends in the same direction. He also cited a recent longitudinal study conducted by Mark Shanley at the University of South Carolina that found students enrolled in University 101 as freshmen had a significantly higher *graduation* rate than did non-participants.

Fidler's chapter reviewed data from eight other institutions across

the country that replica retention findings. For ample, a study conduc at Sacramento City Col used matched con groups to compare eff of three different type orientation programs academic performa and retention. Stud attending a freshn seminar earned a **hig GPA** and a **lower attri** rate.

Reviewing data f several institutions le the conclusion that ticipation in freshn seminars also correl with improved freshr academic performa and more frequent us student services. A few leges studied the effect freshman seminars on sonality variables.

Fidler suggested the freshman seminar vides an example of colleges and universi can "front-load" their sources to meet the ne of freshmen. So that re ers may contact reseai ers cited in his chapter included names, mai addresses, and teleph numbers of professioi from over a dozen inst tions that have conduc research on freshn seminars.

Contact:
Paul P. Fidler
Assistant Vice Presider
for Student Affairs
Russel House
University of South
Carolina
Columbia, S C 29208
(803) 777-4172

4

Recruitment, Remediation, Retention, and Research: Creating success for "at-risk" freshmen

The Penn State-McKeesport Campus combines academic and non-academic services to offer an all-campus approach to meet the needs of academically underprepared freshmen through the Four Rs: Recruitment, Remediation, Retention, and Research.

Recruitment

Penn State's Admissions Office identifies students with low SAT scores and low GPAs from high school. These "at risk" students are then offered admission provided they enroll in the remediation curriculum listed below.

Remediation

Since the "at risk" freshmen are weak in basic skills, the following thirteen-credit curriculum is required of these students

COURSE	CREDITS
Basic Math	3
Basic Reading	3
Basic English	3
Sociology or Psychology	3
Freshman Seminar	1

In the introductory sociology or psychology course, these "at risk" students are integrated with the regular college freshmen, and all students in that class participate in a Mastery Learning Program, the components of which are:

✦ three chances to master each test, with mastery defined at 80% or more of the total score;

✦ the opportunity to review non-mastered tests in preparation for the retakes.

The course also features extra small group recitation sessions to review and prepare for tests. The instructor meets with students at these recitation sessions.

In addition, all "at risk" students are encouraged to use the services of the Learning Center where a reading specialist diagnoses and remediates reading difficulties and offers help in English. Professional and peer tutoring is available in most subjects; study skills workshops are offered on a regular basis.

Retention

With the help of the Advising Center, designated faculty advisors monitor the progress of the "at risk" students and oversee their activities by meeting with them at the beginning of the semester, the fifth week, and the tenth week. These advisors also meet with faculty to update and coordinate their students' progress.

A career counselor offers the following workshops: career planning, career choices, math anxiety, and test anxiety.

Research

After two years, preliminary results indicate that the program was successful in improving the achievement of "at risk" students. A longitudinal study is also underway to track these students after their first year.

Research indicates that colleges and universities need a better understanding of the changing student population to include those who do not fit traditional guidelines for admission. In sum, many students who do not meet admission requirements have shown that, with the proper services and curriculum, they can succeed.

Contact:
Judy Merisko
Department of English
and Reading
Penn State-McKeesport
University Drive
McKeesport, PA, 15132
(412) 462-7048

President's Discretionary Fund Enhances Freshman Year at Duke

In Fall, 1988, the President's Discretionary Fund for Undergraduate Education at Duke University funded a five-fold increase in the number of freshman seminars taught by regular and distinguished faculty. "Freshman seminars, with a maximum of fifteen students in each class, provide significant opportunity for enhanced student-faculty interaction during the freshman year," reports Richard White, Dean of Arts and Sciences and Trinity College, in the publication, *Duke Campaign Thresholds*. "That the president of the university taught a course this spring reflects the important intellectual contribution these seminars will make." President Keith Brodie's seminar focused on the biological bases of human behavior; other seminars dealt with topics ranging from economics to zoology.

5

Assessing and Advising Freshmen
during Orientation at Santa Barbara City College

*B*ecause assessment, orientation, and advising are mandatory for freshmen at Santa Barbara City College, the college offers the following orientation activities to enrich this process.

For high school seniors
Pre-enrollment activities for high school seniors include a Senior Assembly at the local high school and an on-site assessment of their English and math skills. Then in May, these high school seniors come to Santa Barbara City College for a Senior Orientation Day to learn more about college life and academic expectations. They tour the campus and sit in on selected classes. They also attend a general orientation session and meet in small groups with a counselor to plan their coursework for the fall semester. The college provides lunch and the opportunity to register early for fall classes. These pre-enrollment activities serve local, in-town high school seniors. These activities become both a recruitment tool and a way to spread out orientation/advisement over time so that more individual attention is given each prospective student.

Summer orientatio
Out-of-town high sch graduates attend summ orientation for assessme advisement, and regist tion for the fall semest Summer orientation cludes social activities give new students an portunity to get acquain with each other and to more relaxed about th college experience. T participate in non-cc petitive games and i breaker activities. A sc enger hunt acquaints th with the campus and location of special supp services. Lunch is provi along with a fashion sl featuring items from campus bookstore. Th items are then raffled c

**During their first
semester**
During their first sem ter, new students atten series of orientation wc shops to help develop c lege survival skills. S dents select workshops t appeal to them and rec half-a-unit of credit as inducement to atte Workshops are videota and housed in the Car Center so that those una to participate can view workshops later on v otape.

Contact:
Margo Handelsmar
Counselor
Debbie Mackie-Bur
Counselor
Santa Barbara City
College
721 Cliff Drive
Santa Barbara, CA
93109-2394
(805) 965-0581

Seminars for First-Year Students Explore
Women's Issues

*F*reshman seminars provide an ideal place to explore women's issues with entering college students. Seminar instructors can find resource people in women's studies department or among faculty and students affairs staff. Topics may include: a women's studies curriculum, the importance of recognizing sexism, and how to report incidents of sexual harassment. The following exercises can introduce freshmen to a variety of women's issues.

Values From Three Generations of Women.
Have students interview women of their generation, their mother's generation, and their grandmother's generation. Ask questions about women's roles (wife, professional, decision-maker, care-giver, etc.). In a paper, students should report differences in value systems and reflect on what this means.

Assertiveness For Women.
Contact an assertiveness training specialist from the counseling center for a presentation in class. If this is not an option, perhaps a specialist within your community is available to speak to classes. Men who tend to be aggressive in their communications rather than assertive need this training as well.

Be Sensitive to Sexist Language in Your Class.
Make it a point to refer to professors as both "he" and "she". Avoid equating the terms "men and girls." For example, use the terms "men and women" or "boys and girls". Gently but firmly point out any use of sexist language from students and faculty alike.

The above exercises can be used in many classes. However, such exercises seem tailor-made for freshman seminars with reserved sections for entering women students. In seminars composed of both sexes, these exercises often become the vehicle for introducing new students to women's issues.

Contact:
Sue Rosser, Director, Women's Studies Program, 1710 College Street
University of South Carolina, Columbia, SC 29208. Phone: (803) 777-4007

6

Freshman Orientation Seminars for Adult Students

Adult students contend with many barriers to entering and remaining in college. Home and work responsibilities of necessity take precedent over educational responsiblities; and yet adult students are typically the most motivated folks on campus.

A reserved section of a freshman seminar for adult students is often the most effective way of incorporating them into academe. They come on campus with rusty study skills, but within a semester they are up to speed and often outdistance traditional-aged freshmen. In fact, on many campuses the GPR of older students is significantly higher than that of younger students. But, during their first semester, they do need extra help and different kinds of assistance with learning the ropes. They are a pleasure to work with because they are among the most motivated, highly committed, intensely interested students you will ever teach. One of the most effective ways to capitalize on their strengths and minimize their weaknesses is through a reserved section in a freshman orientation seminar. In a section reserved for only adult students you can build a peer support group and adapt the curriculum to meet their special needs. For example, they show little interest in fraternities, homecoming dances, meal tickets, and adjusting to homesickness or roommates. They are critically interested in child care; study skills; library skills; content courses reviewing high school math and grammar; combining demands of job, home, and school; feeling accepted as a student despite their age; and discovering that they are not too old to learn. In short, their unique needs call for a unique curriculum in a freshman orientation seminar.

The National Resource Center for The Freshman Year Experience at the University of South Carolina recently designed a curriculum for freshman orientation seminars for adult students which can be adapted to other campuses. To receive a free copy, contact the Center.

Contact:
National Resource Center for The Freshman Year Experience, University 101, 1728 College Street, The University of South Carolina, Columbia, SC, 29208. Phone: (803) 777-6029

The Terminal Introductory Course

excerpted from *Notes: On Teaching and Learning* **by Dr. W. Lee Humphreys, University of Tennessee**

It has the ring of an oxymoron: The Terminal Introductory Course.

Many introductory courses are taught as if they were the first stage on a trajectory that filters the chosen few on to the Ph.D. Yet the majority— a vast majority in many cases— of those enrolled in introductory courses have no intention of pursuing formal study in that particular discipline.

Thus the idea of the terminal introductory course. This is the course designed, in part at least, with this question clearly in mind: What fundamental things do I want students who will never have another course in my discipline to know and be able to do at the end of this term? Addressing this question means taking on hard choices.

It means paring and winnowing, and it entails distillation of complex material into essences. It means constant flirtation with gross simplification. It quite likely also involves less attention to facts and more to the processes by which these facts were and other facts will be discovered. It may mean more explicit formulation of those modes of inquiry, frames of questioning, and distinct perspectives that so fundamentally define our disciplines, and of which we who have lived in and with them so long are no longer fully conscious.

The terminal introductory course provides a refreshing new challenge for experienced faculty by offering a distinct perspective on their discipline as it fits into the larger world of human inquiry and as it connects with the lives of men and women.

Contact:
W. Lee Humphreys, Director of Learning Research Center, 1819 Andy Holt Avenue, University of Tennessee, Knoxville, TN 37996. Phone: (615) 974-2459

7

Freshman Interest Groups
Building Academic Community

Creating a sense of community for freshmen is a special challenge at a large research university. Freshman programmers at the University of Washington have met this challenge by developing academic learning communities called Freshman Interest Groups or FIGs.

FIGs generally consist of 20-25 incoming freshmen who take a cluster of courses that provide some curricular coherence. For example, students might enroll in a cluster entitled "The Individual and Society" that includes a sociology class, a speech class, and an English class. Or they might choose a pre-science/pre-engineering cluster with courses in math, chemistry, and English composition. Typically, at least one course in the cluster is a small class in which only the students in the FIG group are enrolled. The other courses may be larger lecture courses where FIG participants comprise only a fraction of the students taking the course but where the members of the FIG are all in the same discussion section.

In addition to enrolling in the same cluster of courses, students in each FIG meet periodically for discussion facilitated by an upper class peer adviser. These meetings provide opportunities for the freshmen to share their knowledge, vent their fears, learn about university resources, establish friendships, and develop a supportive learning environment.

In the first year of the program, 83 students enrolled, by choice, in four different FIG clusters during autumn quarter. During the second year, nearly 200 students enrolled in eight clusters. Fall 1989, the third year of the program saw enrollments climb to nearly 400 students enrolled in 20 freshman interest groups.

Peer advisors for this program are upper class students chosen on the basis of their leadership, their academic interests, and their knowledge of the university community and its resources. They assume important roles in the program, functioning as facilitators of discussion sessions, as resources to provide support and information, and as liaisons between the students and faculty to teach FIG courses. Peer advisors undergo a training program that consists of a three-hour session before the start of classes and weekly sessions throughout the quarter.

The FIG program is regularly evaluated by faculty, peer advisors, and students. Students comment that through FIGs, they have obtained help with their classes, developed supportive friendships, gained information, increased interest in their classes, and adjusted more readily to the university. Peer advisors suggest that they have gained hands-on experience as leaders of small groups as well as skills in interacting with others. Faculty report that students who participate in FIGs seem better prepared, more enthusiastic, and mutually supportive.

Contact:

Ken Tokuno
Special Assistant to the Dean for Undergradu[ate] Affairs
University of Washingt[on]
Seattle, WA 98195
(206) 543-2551

Reference:

Sullivan, C. and Wulff (1990, Winter). Freshm[an] interest groups at the U[ni]versity of Washingt[on] Building community [among] freshmen at a large univ[er]sity. *News.* 4 (2) 19[90]. Washington Center for [Im]proving the Quality of U[n]dergraduate Educa[ti]on, The Evergreen St[ate] College, Olympia, Wa[sh]ington.

Outcomes Assessment
What Freshmen Need to Know

Kean College of New Jersey initiated an outcome[s] assessment program upon receiving a Governor['s] Challenge Grant on "Excellence and Equity". Sin[ce] 1985, two faculty members with release time fro[m] half their teaching load coordinate the program f[or] Assessment of Student Learning and Developmen[t].

Freshmen at Kean participate in assessment [in] various ways. They complete entering student que[s]tionnaries, receive data on outcomes, respond [to] assessment measures within their major, and a[t]tend program assessment committees. To ensu[re] the willing and enthusiastic participation of freshme[n] in the assessment effort, freshman seminars inclu[de] presentations on the process and diagnostic value [of] assessment outcomes which, in turn, have led [to] modification of programs and improvement of cu[r]riculum. Freshmen expressed an interest in t[he] processes, outcomes, and changes based on asses[s]ment results.

Contact: Michael E. Knight, Donald Lumsde[n,] Coordinators, Assessment of Student Learning a[nd] Development, Kean College of New Jersey, Union, N[J] 07083. Phone: (201) 527-2000

Residential Programs Enhance Student Development at the University of Delaware

In six freshmen-only buildings at the University of Delaware, residential programs encourage students to deal with the following developmental tasks:

1 **Resolving Child-Parent Relationships;**

2 **Developing a Sexual Identity;**

3 **Formulating a Personal Value System and Making Lifestyle Choices;**

4 **Developing Intimacy in Relationships;**

5 **Developing Intellectual Academic, and Career Skills;**

6 **Dealing with Difference**

7 **Alcohol and Substance Abuse.**

In the first developmental task, "Resolving Child-Parent Relationships," freshmen must deal with issues related to parental independence/dependence. "Can You Go Home Again?" is a program presented by parents to discuss some of the major conflicts that occur after their children go to school. Another issue with which freshmen must grapple is the maintenance of long-distance relationships with parents and high school friends. A large number of freshmen come to campus leaving significant others behind and must learn how to continue or dissolve those relationships across the miles and over time.

Other programs help freshmen establish good eating habits. Dieting, anorexia/bulimia, and the "Freshman 15" (i.e., the extra 15 pounds that most students add their first year in college)...these are important issues for eighteen-year-olds who for the first time without parental guidance must learn to manage their eating behaviors.

Managing Freedom

Most freshmen are very interested in receiving information on alcohol, drugs, and sex. Since for many of them this is their first taste of "freedom," they often show concern about the effects of alcohol and drugs on their bodies. Also for many freshmen, this is their first involvement with sex and intimacy. Programs on "Date Rape" and contraception/birth control help freshmen confront issues of sex and intimacy. One popular program is the "Sex Question Fishbowl" in which males and females write down questions on slips of paper — questions that they want to ask about the opposite sex. These questions are read aloud and then followed by lively discussions which are moderated by faculty or professional staff. "Sex trivia" - done in the format of Jeopardy Game Show - also encourages frank and open discussion of issues dealing with developing intimate relationships.

During fall orientation an all-day "freshmen olympics" pits teams of freshmen, captained by members of residence life staff, against each other (and the clock) in moderately competitive games. And also during the first week of school in the fall, the student alumni association sponsors a picnic entitled "The Student Connection," in which freshmen are paired up with an upper-class student for the purpose of providing support for the first year student.

Reading Program

Faculty at the University of Delaware work closely with the residence life staff to promote an undergraduate reading program in which students, faculty, and staff read several books over the summer and discuss them during the year. Separate reading lists have been prepared for freshmen, sophomores, juniors, and seniors. Faculty members and residence life staff serve as discussion leaders.

Faculty and professional staff at the University of Delaware are designing and implementing programs for freshmen to help them master the developmental tasks of late adolescence. In addition to helping students grow into adulthood, these programs often impact directly on retention of academically able students who need assistance in resolving developmental issues in order to survive in college.

Contact:
Rob Longwell-Grice, Assistant Director for Residence Life, 5 Courtney Street, University of Delaware, Newark, DE 19716. Phone: (302) 451-2260

9

A common concern across the spectrum of American higher education is the effective management of cultural diversity on campus. While open admissions institutions often struggle to meet the needs of ethnically diverse student populations, many elite private colleges and universities are seeking ways to attract larger numbers of minority students.

"Building Foundations for Cultural Diversity" was the theme for the 1990 West Coast Freshman Year Experience Conference. This event provided a forum for institutions to share their programs and policies for the management of cultural diversity, especially during the fresh man year. Several articles in this section of the Newsletter are based on presentations at this special focus meeting.

Parents/Community/University
An Essential Collaboration for Hispanic Students

San Diego State University sits high above the freeway in east San Diego County, a predominately white institution of 36,000 students in a region where Hispanics are the largest and fastest growing ethnic minority. In order to increase its Hispanic enrollment and to meet more effectively the educational needs of these students at all educational levels, San Diego State has become part of an ongoing community effort to involve Hispanic parents directly in the educational achievements of their children.

George Hutchinson, Director of San Diego State's Student Outreach Program, reports that "San Diego State has conducted outreach programs to parents in local schools for

several years, but attendance by Hispanic parents has generally been low." By chance, Hutchinson learned about a group of Hispanic parents, residents of a 400-unit subsidized housing project in south San Diego County called Villa Nueva, who have formed a "Pro-Education Coalition" to encourage educational goals of Hispanic students. These parents had already raised the necessary funds to furnish a special study lounge in the apartment complex and had established a program to award small scholarships to Villa Nueva's college-bound students.

Hutchinson determined that San Diego State could effectively work through this parents' coalition to provide information to the

Hispanic community about available scholarships and other educational opportunities. The sixty parents in Villa Nueva's Pro-Education Coalition were invited to the San Diego State campus for a day of presentations in Spanish by the university president, by Hispanic students and their parents, as well as faculty and administrators. Since that time, San Diego State has continued to work with the parents' coalition by donating computer equipment for the study lounge and by providing counseling and tutoring services.

Coalition spokepersons report that parents, university administrators, and the students themselves have all played a vital role in promoting the value of higher education. Father

John Blethen, Director of Social Services at Villa Nueva states that, in recent years, the number of Hispanic students going to college has increased dramatically. George Hutchinson adds that San Diego State is now considering requests from other housing projects in South San Diego for assistance similar to that given Villa Nueva. At present, students from other nearby apartment complexes can come to Villa Nueva's study center for tutoring and academic guidance provided by the university.

Contact:
George Hutchinson
Director, Student
Outreach Services
San Diego State University
5300 Campanile Avenue
San Diego, CA 92182-077
(619) 594-6966

10

Kean College's Freshmen Gain a World View

Treatment of multiculturalism has always been a staple component of Kean College's freshman seminar. But recently, Kean has found a way to integrate other basic course goals into a dynamic multicultural experience, The World Game.*

The World Game is a multi-media, participatory event that takes place on a map of the world about the size of a basketball court. Each player on the map represents one percent of the world's population. The countries and larger geographic areas represented are South America, Central America, North America, Japan, China, India, Middle East, Southeast Asia, Soviet Union, Europe, Africa, and Oceania.

Throughout the game, players must contend with a variety of factors that will affect the living conditions of a given region and the world at large. These factors include population, food production, food consumption, energy production, illiteracy, military spending, and nuclear weapons. Depending on the size of the group (which should number at least 100), other players might represent the media, multinational corporations, the World Health Organization, and even the earth's atmosphere. At the game's end, student players discuss ideas about ways that they can act as advocates to make the world a better place to live.

Dr. Michael Searson, Director of the Freshman Seminar at Kean, reports that The World Game is an effective vehicle for developing basic skills such as reading and note taking. In addition, follow-up research indicates that participation in the World Game enhances student knowledge of global issues and sensitivity about cultural diversity.

Contact: Michael Searson, Director, Freshman Seminar, Kean College of New Jersey Morris Avenue, Union, NJ 07083. Phone: (201) 527-3114.
*For more information, contact The World Game, University City Science Center, 3508 Market Street, Philadelphia, PA 19104.

The University of Maine Introduces
The Freshman Seminar via Television

To expand access to a university education for increasing numbers of ethnically diverse, part-time, older students, the University of Maine system has developed a state-of-the-art interactive telecommunications system over which is broadcast a wide variety of college courses leading to an associate's degree in general studies. In September of 1989, over 2,500 students were enrolled in university courses via television, and these numbers are expected to increase dramatically over the next few years.

Since most of the students enrolled in telecourses have not attended college previously, one of the required courses which must be taken during the first twelve semester hours of course work is the three-credit hour freshman seminar.

The content of the course is similar to that found in other freshman seminars. It includes sessions on academic policies, student services, understanding professors, time management, stress management, study skills, library skills, critical thinking, wellness, and understanding the university. The requirements for successful course completion include written assignments, a journal, and class participation.

Course facilitators and resource people teach simultaneously to a classroom on campus and to students at distant locations. In the classroom, a camera focuses on the instructor, while an overhead camera focuses on charts or visual materials. Students at distance sites see and hear the instructor on television monitors. A talk-back system allows students at these locations to interact with the instructor and other students. Individual classes are videotaped so that students can review a class, or watch a class that has been missed. Class materials are mailed to students, while assignments are mailed to the instructor.

Course evaluations indicate that the freshman seminar course offered over the interactive television system has met, and in some ways, exceeded the expectations of both facilitators and students.
Contact: Jon Schlenker, Professor of Sociology & Anthropology, University of Maine at Augusta, Augusta, ME, 04330. Phone: (207) 622-7131

11

ORDER FORM

	Cost	No. of sub-scriptions/ copies	Amount
Journal of The Freshman Year Experience (Annual subscription = 2 issues. Back issues are available at $20 each.)	$40.00		
The Freshman Year Experience Newsletter (Annual subscription = 4 issues. Back issues are available at $15 each.)	$60.00		
Monograph #1 *Character Development in the Freshman Year and Over Four Years of Undergraduate Study*	$15.00		
Monograph #2 *Perspectives on the Freshman Year: Selected Major Addresses from the Freshman Year Experience Conferences*	$20.00		
Monograph #3 *Annotated Bibliography on The Freshman Year Experience*	$10.00		
Monograph #4 *The Freshman Orientation Seminar: A Research-Based Rationale for Its Value, Delivery, and Content*	$20.00		
Monograph #5 *Residence Life Programs and The Freshman Year Experience* (Published with ACUHO-I)	$25.00		
Monograph #6 *First National Survey on Freshman Seminar Programs: Findings, Conclusions, and Recommendations* (available 9/91)	$30.00		
Guidelines for Evaluating The Freshman Year Experience	$ 5.00		
Proceedings from The Freshman Year Experience Conferences Annual (for a complete listing, call (803) 777-6029) Others	$25.00 $15.00		

Select your option payable to the University of South Carolina: **TOTAL**

❑ Institutional Purchase Order Enclosed   ❑ Invoice Institution   ❑ Check Enclosed

Department/Name _____

Institution _____

Mailing address _____

City _____ State _____ Zip _____

Mail to: The National Resource Center for The Freshman Year Experience, University 101, 1728 College Street, University of South Carolina, Columbia, SC 29208
For more information call (803) 777-6029

The Freshman Year Experience
University 101
University of South Carolina
1728 College Street
Columbia, SC 29208

Non-Profit
Organization
U. S. POSTAC
PAID
Permit #766

Note: Contact Dorothy Fidler, Senior Managing Editor, (803) 777-5193, for up-to-date information on availability of and prices for these publications.

▼ ▼

Teacher Training Seminars and Workshops

For information about on-campus two-day first-year experience seminar faculty training by **Jerry Jewler**, contact him directly at his home address: 3508 Boundbrook Lane, Columbia, SC 29206; phone: (803) 787-7174.

John Gardner is available for one-day campus visits to evaluate existing first-year programs or to address the campus community on the importance of the first-year program and to bolster the institution's commitment to such programs. Occasionally, he is also available for one- or two-day first-year seminar instructor training workshops. He can be reached at his home address: 212 Rose Lake Drive, Lexington, SC 29072; phone (803) 951-6355 (home voice mail) or (803) 957-3735 (evenings/home).

Art Acton, Bill Hartel, and **Steve Schwartz** provide in-house faculty training workshops tailored expressly to the needs of your institution. They also will work with a consortium of institutions should you want to assemble one in order to reduce costs. For information contact Steve Schwartz. Daytime: (614) 374-4760. Evening: (614) 374-8760.

Bibliography

Applbaum, R. L., et al. 1979. *The Process of Group Communication*. Chicago: S.R.A.

Association of American Colleges. 1985. *Integrity in the College Curriculum: A Report to the Academic Community*. Washington, DC: Association of American Colleges.

Astin, A. W. 1977. *Four Critical Years: Effects of College on Beliefs, Attitudes, and Knowledge*. San Francisco: Jossey-Bass.

Astin, A. W., 1984. "Student Involvement: A Developmental Theory for Higher Education." *Journal of College Student Personnel* 25(4): 297–307.

Astin, A. W., Green, K. C., and Korn, W. S. 1987. *The American Freshman: Twenty Year Trends, 1966–1985*. Los Angeles: University of California at Los Angeles, Higher Education Research Institute.

Beal, P. E., and Noel, L. 1979. *What Works in Student Retention*. Iowa City: American College Testing Service.

Boe, J., and Jolicoeur, P. 1989. "The Evolution of a Freshman Seminar." *NACADA Journal* 9(1): 51–59.

Boyer, E. L. 1987. *College: The Undergraduate Experience in America*. New York: Harper and Row (The Carnegie Foundation for the Advancement of Teaching).

Clarke, J. H., Miser, K. M., and Roberts, A. O. 1988. "Freshman Programs: Effects of Living-Learning Structures, Faculty Involvement, and Thematic Focus." *Journal of College and University Student Housing* 18(2): 7–13.

Coburn, K. L., and Treeger, M. L. 1988. *Letting Go: A Parents' Guide to the College Experience*. Bethesda, MD: Adler and Adler.

Cohen, R. D., and Jody, R. 1978. *Freshman Seminar: A New Orientation*. Boulder, CO: Westview Press.

Commission on Minority Participation in Education and American Life. 1988. *One Third of a Nation*. Washington, DC: American Council on Education.

Cuseo, J. 1991. *The Freshman Orientation Seminar: A Research-Based Rationale for Its Value, Delivery and Content* (Monograph No. 4). Columbia, SC: University of South Carolina, National Resource Center for The Freshman Year Experience_{SM}.

Emig, Janet. 1977. "Writing as a Mode of Learning." *College Composition and Communication* 28: 122–128.

Fulwiler, Toby. 1989. "Programs for Change: Computers and Writing Across the Curriculum." *Composition Chronicle* (December): 8.

Gardner, J. N. 1986. "The Freshman Year Experience." *College and University* 61: 261–274.

Gilligan, Carol. 1982. *In a Different Voice: Psychological Theory and Women's Development*, pp. 128–150. Cambridge, MA: Harvard University Press.

Goodwin, Doris Kearns. 1987. *The Fitzgeralds and the Kennedys*. New York: Simon and Schuster.

Gordon, V. N. 1989. "Orientation Courses and Freshman Seminars: Yesterday and Today." In M. L. Upcraft, J. N. Gardner, and Associates, *The Freshman Year Experience*. San Francisco: Jossey-Bass.

Gordon, V. N., and Grites, T. J. 1984. "The Freshman Seminar Course: Helping Students Succeed." *Journal of College Student Personnel* 24(4): 315–320.

Greene, Bob. 1981. "American Beat." *Esquire* (November), pp. 17–18.

Herrington, Anne. 1981. "Writing to Learn: Writing Across Disciplines." *College English* 43: 4.

Lenning, O. T., Beal, P. E., and Sauer, K. 1980. *Retention and Attrition: Evidence for Action and Research*. Boulder, CO: National Center for Higher Education Management Systems.

Light, Richard J. 1990. *The Harvard Assessment Seminars, Explorations with Students and Faculty about Teach-*

ing, Learning and Student Life: First Report. Cambridge, MA: Harvard University.

National Commission on Excellence in Education. 1983. *A Nation at Risk: The Imperative for Educational Reform.* Washington, DC: U.S. Government Printing Office.

Noel, L., Levitz, R., Saluri, D., et al. 1985. *Increasing Student Retention.* San Francisco: Jossey-Bass.

Pascarella, E. T., and Terenzini, P. T. 1977. "Patterns of Student-Faculty Informal Interaction Beyond the Classroom and Voluntary Freshman Attrition." *Journal of Higher Education* 48: 540–552.

Pascarella, E. T., and Terenzini, P. T. 1980. "Predicting Freshman Persistence and Voluntary Dropout Decisions from a Theoretical Model. *Journal of Higher Education* 51: 60–75.

Schuster, M. R., and Van Dyne, S. 1985. *Women's Place in the Academy: Transforming the Liberal Arts Curriculum.* Totowa, NJ: Rowman and Allanheld.

Simon, S., Howe, L., and Kirschenbaum, H. 1972. *Values Clarification.* New York: Hart.

Smith, Page. 1990. *Killing the Spirit: Higher Education in America.* New York: Penguin.

Study Group on the Conditions of Excellence in American Higher Education. 1984. *Involvement in Learning: Realiz-*

ing the Potential of American Higher Education. Washington, DC: U.S. Department of Education.

Terenzini, P. T., and Wright, T. M. 1987. "Students' Personal Growth During the First Two Years of College." *The Review of Higher Education* 10(3): 259–271.

Tinto, V. 1975. "Dropout from Higher Education: A Theoretical Synthesis of Recent Research." *Review of Educational Research* 45: 89–125.

Tinto, V. 1987. *Leaving College: Rethinking the Causes and Cures of Student Attrition.* Chicago: University of Chicago Press.

Transitions: University 101 Resource Book: The Freshman Year Experience. 1991. University of South Carolina.

Upcraft, M. L. (Ed.). 1984. "Orienting Students to College." *New Directions for Student Services* 25.

Von Frank, J. 1985. "Setting Up a Special Program for Freshmen: Mastering the Politics." *College Teaching* 33(1): 21–26.

Young, R. B., Backer, R., and Rogers, G. 1989. "The Impact of Early Advising and Scheduling on Freshman Success." *Journal of College Student Development* 30(4): 309–312.

▼ ▼

Videography

Videos and films can be valuable tools to supplement class lectures, communicate information, and stimulate class discussion. Below is a list of videos and films you may want to consider for your course. For more information about specific titles (except those distributed by New Day Films), contact Will Covington, Audio-Visual Services, The Pennsylvania State University, Special Services Building, 1127 Fox Hill Road, University Park, PA 16803-1824, 1-800-826-0132. For New Day Films only, contact them at 121 West 27th St., Suite 902, New York, NY 10001, Tel: 1-212-645-8210, Fax: 1-212-645-8652.

AGAINST HER WILL: RAPE ON CAMPUS
1989, 46 minutes, color, video
Docudrama about the epidemic proportions of acquaintance or date rape on college campuses. Kelly McGillis, herself a rape victim, presents facts about acquaintance rape and dispels many of its myths, and three other victims tell their stories. Explains why college women are particularly vulnerable, examines men's attitudes toward sexual relationships, and shows what colleges can do to prevent sexual violence.

AIDS: CHAPTER ONE
1985, 57 minutes, color, video
Traces the intensive efforts to solve the mystery of the deadly ailment AIDS (acquired immune deficiency syndrome) since its discovery in 1981. Covers the work of the Centers for Disease Control in Atlanta in fitting together the pieces of the puzzle and the way in which two laboratories, one in the United States and one in France, simultaneously close in on the solution. Produced by WGBH for the *Nova* series.

AIDS: THE SURGEON GENERAL'S UPDATE
1987, 32 minutes, color, video
Presents statistics on AIDS for high- and low-risk groups, facts about the HIV virus and how it spreads, and infor-

mation about AIDS and pregnancy, blood transfusions, and contact with AIDS patients. Also assesses the impact of AIDS on individual behavior and on schools, health-care systems, government, and business. Presentation is by former U.S. Surgeon General C. Everett Koop.

AIDS: WHAT EVERYONE NEEDS TO KNOW (Revised Edition)
1987, 19 minutes, color, video/film
Illustrates the effects of AIDS on the immune system, explains how the disease is transmitted, and describes preventive measures the average person can take to avoid it. A family in which the husband has AIDS tells its story. Made in cooperation with the UCLA AIDS Center.

AIDS-WISE, NO LIES
1988, 22 minutes, color, video
By David Current and Anne Rutledge
Distributor: New Day Films
"Ten young people whose lives are affected by AIDS reveal thoughts, feelings, and experiences in their own words from their own environments. Deeply moving, not sentimental, their stories break through the youthful sense of being invulnerable, ultimately leaving viewers feeling empowered, knowing they have choice and control over

Note: This material adapted from information supplied by *Audio-Visual Services Collection of The Pennsylvania State University* and *New Day Films.*

contracting AIDS" (*New Day Films Catalog*). (Award: Gold Apple, National Educational Film & Video Festival)

ALCOHOL, PILLS, AND RECOVERY
1978, 28 minutes, color, film
Dr. Joseph A. Pursch describes the effect on the body and mind of sedative-hypnotics like alcohol, barbiturates, tranquilizers, and sleeping pills, explaining how they simultaneously sedate and stimulate, how cross-tolerance and cross-addiction develop, and how the half-life of drugs complicates withdrawal symptoms.

ALCOHOLISM: A MODEL OF DRUG DEPENDENCY
1972, 20 minutes, color, video/film
Examines the physiological and psychological effects of alcohol. Can be used as a guide for understanding all the different kinds of addictive conditions, dependency states, and drug abuses in general. From the Life and Health series. Produced by Tom Lazarus.

ALCOHOLISM: I WAS GOING TO SCHOOL DRUNK
1975, 26 minutes, color, video/film
Emphasizes the increasing problem of alcohol addiction among young people, physical and emotional effects, and consideration of use vs. abuse of alcohol in a society that applies a double standard to the consumption of alcoholic beverages.

ALCOHOLISM: LIFE UNDER THE INFLUENCE
1984, 57 minutes, color, video/film
Alcoholism has been called one of the nation's most widespread and least admitted diseases, and it is related to 90 percent of all physical assaults, half of all homicides, and a quarter of all suicides. Offers an interdisciplinary report on the disease of alcoholism and interviews therapists, researchers, and alcoholics. Produced by WGBH for the *Nova* series.

ALL OF US AND AIDS
1988, 30 minutes, color, video
Produced by Peer Education Health Resources and Catherine Jordan
Distributor: New Day Films
"Nine teenagers make a videotape on postponing sexual intercourse, condom buying and condom use, personal fears of AIDS exposure, gay sexual decisions, and conflicting attitudes. By empowering themselves to discuss responsible sexual decision-making, the teens challenge viewers to become informed and conscious about AIDS prevention" (*New Day Films Catalog*).

AM I BEING UNREALISTIC?
1978, 25 minutes, color, film
This study of a young man suffering from cerebral palsy shows how the disease diminishes his physical functions but in no way impairs his intellectual abilities. Depicts his progress through special schools, mainstreamed schools, and a university. Produced by the BBC for the British Open University.

THE AMERICAN EXPERIENCE 3: LOS MINEROS
1991, 60 minutes, color, video
Documents the nearly half-century battle by Mexican-American workers in Arizona copper mines to be treated equally with their white coworkers. Depicts life within the Mexican community as seen through the eyes of the miners and their families, focusing on 73-year-old David Valasquez, who led the 1946 strike that abolished the exploitive two-tier wage system. Interviews former miners and company employees. Produced by Hector Galan.

AMERICAN TONGUES
1987, 56 minutes, color, video
By Louis Alvarez and Andrew Kolker
Distributor: New Day Films
"*American Tongues* examines the diversity of American culture in a fascinating way: by listening to the different ways Americans talk, and investigating how we feel about each others' speech. From Boston Brahmins to Black Louisiana teenagers, from Texas cowboys to New York professionals, *American Tongues* elicits funny, perceptive, sometimes shocking, and always telling comments about our society" (*New Day Films Catalog*). (Awards: Peabody Journalism Award; Silver Apple, National Educational Film & Video Festival)

ANOREXIA
1987, 28 minutes, color, video
Recovered anorexics join Dr. Ronald Liebman, director of the Philadelphia Child Guidance Clinic, in exploring how the eating disorder anorexia nervosa starts and how it can be detected and cured. The program notes that women are ten times more likely than men to become anorexic in their unrelenting pursuit of thinness, leading to a loss of control over their bodies, destruction of body balances and systems, and ultimately, death by starvation. Host: Phil Donahue.

AT THE EDGE OF A DESERT: RENEGOTIATING A CONTRACT
1987, 29 minutes, color, video
Shows the challenge of helping an older adolescent girl come to grips with her alcohol problem and establish some commitment to a therapeutic plan. From the Wediko series. Dr. Edward A. Mason.

BECOMING AMERICAN
1983, 30 minutes, color, video
By Ken and Ivory Waterworth Levine
Distributor: New Day Films
"Hang Sou and his family, preliterate tribal farmers, await resettlement in a refugee camp in Thailand after fleeing their war-consumed native Laos. *Becoming American* records their odyssey as they travel to and resettle in the United States. As they face nine months of intense culture shock, prejudice and gradual adaptation to their new home in Seattle, the family provides a rare insight into refugee resettlement issues which are also addressed by teachers, sociologists, anthropologists, and refugee workers" (*New Day Films Catalog*). (Awards: Best of Fest, National Educational Film Festival; Special Merit, Academy of Motion Picture Arts & Sciences)

BERKELEY IN THE '60S
1990, 118 minutes, color, video
Chronicles student participation in protest movements at the University of California, Berkeley, from the 1960 demonstration against the House Un-American Activities Committee in San Francisco to the 1969 People's Park

confrontation. Covers anti-Vietnam protests, civil rights sit-ins, the free-speech and women's movements, and the rise of the Black Panthers. Directed and produced by Mark Kitchell.

BIRTH CONTROL: MYTHS AND REALITIES
(Revised Edition)
1988, 28 minutes, color, video
Describes birth-control methods available with and without a doctor's prescription, including the cervical cap, and tells how they are used, their advantages, disadvantages, and possible side effects. Also covers natural family planning. Directed by Judy Reidel. Preview by the instructor is suggested.

BLACK AND WHITE AMERICA
1987, 26 minutes, color, video
Tells the story of five students at Rutgers University—two black, two white, and one a child of a mixed-race marriage—and shows how they negotiate the routine of their lives based on what they feel about their own race and that of others, and how they perceive others feel about theirs. Host: Marty Goldensen. Directed by Tony Marshall and produced by Kate Manning.

BLACK AND WHITE UPTIGHT
1969, 35 minutes, color, film
An examination of the myths which perpetuate prejudice and of the subtle ways hate is learned. Explores the social and economic differences between blacks and whites caused by historical inequalities in education and opportunity. Looks at ways in which government, business, and individuals have attempted to wipe out racial prejudice. Narrated by Robert Culp. Produced by Max Miller.

BLACK HISTORY: LOST, STOLEN, OR STRAYED
1968, 54 minutes, color, film
Bill Cosby compares the real history of the black American with prejudiced and subverted history, citing black historical figures never mentioned in usual history texts. Looks at the white stereotype of the black perpetrated by radio, television, and films. From the *Of Black America* series. Written by Andy Rooney and produced by CBS.

BLACK URBAN PROFESSIONALS:
PROBLEMS OF BUPPIES
1988, 28 minutes, color, video
A discussion of the problems black urban professionals face in climbing the corporate ladder. Phil Donahue is joined by guests Edward D. Irons, author of *Black Managers: The Case of the Banking Industry*; Darrell Gay, attorney and chairman of the Coalition of Black Professional Organizations; Gregg Watson, co-author of *Black Life in Corporate America*; and Beverly Hawkins, president of the National Black MBAs Association. Donahue provides statistics demonstrating the plight of the "buppies" and gets reaction from the mostly black audience of professionals.

BLACK VIEWS ON RACE:
ADAM CLAYTON POWELL
1970, 4 minutes, color, film
Adam Clayton Powell contributes to a series presenting a broad spectrum of black opinion in the United States through public remarks that summarize an individual's philosophy at a given time and place. Powell states: "We

want to be called black. It means that we're not antiwhite but we're problack . . . black is the way you think . . . there are a lot of you who can think black and still be white."

BLACK VIEWS ON RACE: BOBBY SEALE
1970, 4 minutes, color, film
Bobby Seale contributes to a series presenting a broad spectrum of black opinion in the United States through public remarks that summarize an individual's philosophy at a given time and place. Seale states: "If you're going to talk about liberation . . . you must have the proper liberation tools and the proper liberation tools are guns. We want to begin to implement free medicine, free health clinics in the black communities."

BLACK WOMAN
1972, 52 minutes, b&w, film
Poet Nikki Giovanni, singer Lena Horne, Bibi Amina Baraka (wife of poet/playwright Amiri Baraka [né LeRoi Jones]), and other black women discuss the roles black women play in society today and their problems. Topics include the relationship of black women to black men, to white society, and to the black liberation struggle. Singing by Roberta Flack, dance by Loretta Abbott, poetry by Nikki Giovanni. Produced by NET.

BULIMIA
1987, 28 minutes, color, video
The pressure to be thin may lead to a self-destructive eating disorder known as bulimia: bingeing and purging. Low self-esteem, depression, and anger are both cause and effect of the illness—a vicious cycle usually reversible through psychotherapy. Dr. Craig Johnson of the Psychosomatic-Psychiatric Center in Chicago, Dr. Susan Wooley of the Clinic for Eating Disorders in Cincinnati, and bulimic patients discuss the illness. Host: Phil Donahue.

BULIMIA: THE BINGE-PURGE OBSESSION
1986, 25 minutes, color, video/film
Interviews with bulimia victims are interwoven with presentations by psychologist Anita Siegman, who explains the classic chain of events that leads many young women into the binge-purge behavior of bulimia. The program explores the physical and psychological risks of bulimia as well as strategies for coping with the eating disorder. Produced by Eugene Ferraro.

BUSING: A ROUGH RIDE IN SOUTHIE
1976, 29 minutes, color, film
Looks at the 1974 busing crisis in Boston through interviews with three Boston families. Two white families, residents of South Boston, hold opposite views: One wants to obey the law and reduce problems through black-white cooperation; the other is adamantly opposed to forced busing of their children. A black family living in the Roxbury section explains why they are willing to accept the inconvenience, and even the danger, of busing. Produced by Sam Kauffmann and Ellen Boyce.

CAN AIDS BE STOPPED?
1986, 58 minutes, color, video
Explores the ongoing campaign to combat AIDS by focusing on new insights into the unusual retrovirus family to which the AIDS virus belongs. Cites experts who claim that this lethal disease will remain for years to come, an

epidemic for which no vaccine and no effective treatment will be available. Produced by WGBH for the *Nova* series.

CARBO CHOICES: A QUIZ ON CARBOHYDRATES
1989, 16 minutes, color, video
The program's quiz format provides answers to typical consumer questions about carbohydrates—fiber, starch, and sugar—and helps viewers to make the healthy dietary choices of increasing fiber and starch while decreasing sugar. Developed by the Penn State Nutrition Center and produced by Penn State Television/WPSX-TV.

CASUAL ENCOUNTERS OF THE INFECTIOUS KIND
1979, 23 minutes, color, film
Focuses on the diagnosis, treatment, and cure of sexually transmitted diseases, and talks about coping with the sexual revolution on the "morning after." Using animated diagrams and nonmoralistic dialogue, the program illustrates the damage that these diseases can do if they are not medically treated.

THE CHEWS BLUES
1987, 23 minutes, color, video
Current information about smokeless tobacco is presented through a story describing the negative physical and social consequences of its use. The program examines the tobacco industry's motives and marketing strategies in promoting smokeless tobacco, and describes the need for oral self-examination among its users.

CHICANO
1971, 23 minutes, color, film
Presents the goals of the Chicano movement and its organizations. Reveals manifestations of bias, oppression, and discrimination.

CHOLESTEROL, DIET, AND HEART DISEASE
1980, 60 minutes, color, video
Identifies three primary factors that can increase the likelihood of heart attacks: smoking, high blood pressure, and elevated cholesterol levels. Dr. Byran Brewer describes the ways that cholesterol affects the blood flow, reviews recommended dietary levels of fat and cholesterol, and suggests other ways to reduce the risk of heart disease.

CHOLESTEROL: LOWERING THE RISK
1989, 18 minutes, color, video
A nontechnical and entertaining presentation about cholesterol's role in increasing the risk of coronary heart disease. Explains the difference between high- and low-density lipoproteins and shows how to lower serum cholesterol levels through diet and exercise.

A CLASS DIVIDED
1985, 54 minutes, color, video/film
Looks at the long-term effects of an experiment conducted in 1968 by a teacher in Iowa to deprogram racial stereotypes among youngsters by treating children with blue eyes as superior to children with brown eyes. Updates the acclaimed 1970 documentary *Eye of the Storm*. Produced for PBS's *Frontline* series.

COCAINE: ATHLETES SPEAK OUT
1986, 34 minutes, color, video
Through interviews with coaches, counselors, physicians, professional athletes, and former drug abusers, the program makes the point that cocaine use by athletes doesn't overcome off-the-field boredom, that even occasional use of the drug isn't safe, and that users don't control coke—coke controls them. Shows the medical and legal hazards of cocaine use and the strategies for "saying no."

COCAINE BLUES: THE MYTH AND REALITY OF COCAINE
1983, 30 minutes, color, film
Cites statistics which estimate that in the early 1980s 22 million Americans had tried, or were then users of, cocaine. Examines the history, dangers, and cultural impact of cocaine in the United States. Includes interviews with medical and legal experts, narcotics officers, underworld figures, convicted dealers, and "average" Americans who use the drug. Narrated by Hoyt Axton.

COCAINE COUNTRY
1986, 34 minutes, color, video
Observes that cocaine, once the glamour drug of the rich and famous, now can be purchased in stronger, deadlier forms on the street corners of virtually every city in America. Correspondent Tom Brokaw investigates the dangers of cocaine and its powerful derivatives and asks what can be done to prevent the widespread use of these destructive drugs. Produced by NBC.

THE COLOR OF YOUR SKIN
1991, 56 minutes, color, video
A powerful, intimate journey into America's great racial divide. For sixteen weeks, behind a two-way mirror in a small room during the U.S. military's intensive race-relations course, a dozen individuals of different races confront each other with their feelings. Useful for diversity courses and programs because participants can see/become aware of their own feelings in a nonthreatening manner. Produced for PBS's *Frontline* series.

COPING WITH THAT THING CALLED . . . STRESS!
1981, 16 minutes, color, video
The first series of dramatic vignettes depicts individuals floundering in stressful situations. The second series shows these same people identifying stress and learning to cope with it.

DAUGHTERS OF THE BLACK REVOLUTION
1988, 28 minutes, color, video
Daughters of slain civil rights leaders Martin Luther King, Jr., Medgar Evers, and Malcolm X talk with Phil Donahue. Yolanda King, Reena Evers-Everette, and Attallah Shabazz discuss how their fathers' lives and work affected them and what, a generation later, their fathers' dreams and struggles appear to have achieved.

DEAR LISA: A LETTER TO MY SISTER
1990, 45 minutes, color, video
By J Clements
Distributor: New Day Films
"The filmmaker questions her sister, herself, and others about the dreams and hopes they had growing up as girls in contrast to the reality they face in the 1990s as women. Topics include: play, sports, careers, motherhood, body image, sexual assault, and self-esteem" (*New Day Films Catalog*).

DEEP SOUTH TOWN: GREENVILLE, MISSISSIPPI
1983, 22 minutes, color, film
Shows how Greenville, Mississippi, is shedding the heavy burdens of its racist reputation, traditional agricultural industry, and undereducated population. Produced by the BBC.

DEPRESSION: BEATING THE BLUES
1983, 28 minutes, color, video/film
Investigates the nature of clinical depression, the most common form of mental illness. Examines its biochemical basis and the theory of genetic causation, and discusses treatments: chemical therapy, psychotherapy, and electroconvulsive therapy. Considers the role of the family and other support systems in helping victims of depression. Produced by the Canadian Broadcasting Corporation.

DEPRESSION: DARK SIDE OF THE BLUES
1986, 25 minutes, color, video/film
Examines the causes of a major mental health problem in the United States, clinical depression. Illustrates, through docudramas about five depressives, that this affliction is much more than a simple case of the "blues"; it is a level of despair causing serious emotional and physical damage. Points out warning signs and shows methods of treatment. Commentary is by Dr. Michael Gitlin of the UCLA Neuropsychiatric Institute.

DEVELOPING YOUR STUDY SKILLS: EXAM PREPARATION
1985, 13 minutes, color, video
Discusses how a student should approach an examination. Explores studying effectively, dealing with exam anxiety, developing an exam writing strategy, and scheduling exam study along with other daily activities. Emphasizes the necessity for developing a specific strategy long before the actual day of the exam.

DEVELOPING YOUR STUDY SKILLS: READING A LECTURE
1983, 16 minutes, color, video
Outlines the different forms a lecture may take and explains the necessity for a student to assess the content of the lecture and to determine how much participation is expected. Presents a concise three-stage approach to effective note-taking.

DEVELOPING YOUR STUDY SKILLS: STEP TO TOMORROW
1985, 13 minutes, color, video
Serves as an introduction to the issues and adjustments a new student faces soon after arriving on a college campus. Examines common fears and misconceptions, and suggests way of adapting to new academic surroundings. Advocates an honest evaluation of attitudes and abilities in order to set realistic goals and maintain a lifestyle conducive to academic achievement.

DEVELOPING YOUR STUDY SKILLS: TACKLING TEXTBOOKS
1983, 18 minutes, color, video
Addresses a student's typical difficulty in keeping up with a large volume of required reading. Recommends first an analysis of existing reading habits, then application of the SQ4R technique (survey, question, read, record, recite, and review) as a means of increasing speed, comprehension, and retention of course material.

DEVELOPING YOUR STUDY SKILLS: TIME ON YOUR HANDS
1983, 12 minutes, color, video
Demonstrates the obvious academic consequences of a student's inability to schedule time. Illustrates the principles and importance of time management, providing effective methods for developing a system to monitor and evaluate progress in meeting specific goals.

A DREAM IS WHAT YOU WAKE UP FROM
1979, 62 minutes, color, film
A look at the values and contrasting lifestyles of two contemporary American black families whose situations may be representative of many: the low-income family beset by financial problems, marital discord, lack of self-esteem, and general helplessness and hopelessness, and a middle-class suburban family living the American Dream, which ironically has the potential to be equally as inescapable a trap. Coarse language is used throughout the film. Directed by Larry Bullard and Carolyn Johnson.

DRUNK DRIVING: AN ACT OF VIOLENCE
1984, 25 minutes, color, video
Makes the point that young people comprise the vast majority of those who are killed and injured as a result of alcohol-related vehicular accidents. Discusses the effects of raising the legal drinking age and increasing the severity of punishment meted out to those found guilty of driving while intoxicated. Narrated by Brooke Shields. Produced by WNBC.

AN EARLY FROST
1986, 120 minutes, color, video
Depicts the traumas experienced by a young homosexual and his family and friends when it is discovered that he is stricken with AIDS. Stars Aidan Quinn, Ben Gazzara, Gens Rowlands, and Sylvia Sidney. An NBC made-for-television feature film directed by John Erman and produced by Perry Lafferty.

EAT, DRINK, AND BE WARY
(Revised Edition)
1984, 22 minutes, color, video/film
Shoppers, cooks, children, and critic Dr. Jean Mayer express their views about eating habits that ignore use of controversial food additives, nutritional loss in processed and refined foods, and dangerously high levels of sugar, salt, and fat in diets. The program discusses the physical consequences of changes in the American diet and makes suggestions for nutritious meals containing a high proportion of unprocessed, natural foods.

EPIDEMIC! DEADLIEST WEAPON IN AMERICA
1985, 30 minutes, color, film
Citing statistical projections that show the vast numbers of Americans who will be killed or injured by drunk drivers in coming years, this program points out the magnitude of the drunk driving problem in the United States. Calls automobiles "potential weapons," captures the human toll in scenes of victims and their families, and urges stiffer penalties for drunk drivers. Narrated by Collin Siedor.

ETHNIC NOTIONS
1986, 58 minutes, color, video
Traces the historical origins of specific antiblack stereotypes established to justify black oppression from the early 19th century through the 1970s. Identifies the carica-

tures—loyal toms, carefree sambos, faithful mammies, grinning coons, savage brutes, and wide-eyed picka-ninnies—that found their way into American culture by way of popular art and entertainment. Narrated by Esther Rolle. Directed and produced by Marion Riggs.

EYE OF THE STORM
1971, 29 minutes, color, video/film
Explores the nature of prejudice, and how it is learned and developed, by dividing a rural, all-white third-grade class into "blue eyes" and "brown eyes." Discrimination is practiced against each group on alternate days, and the academic performance of each group is related to whether they are "top dogs" or "underdogs." From the Human Relations series. Written, directed, and produced by William Peters for ABC. Blue Ribbon winner, American Film Festival. Also see A Class Divided, which examines the long-term effects of the experiment.

FACES OF CULTURE: 7—CULTURE AND PERSONALITY
1983, 30 minutes, color, video
Defines enculturation and describes Margaret Mead's studies of child rearing in several cultures to document the influence of culture on individual personality. Shows how anthropologists developed the concept of national character.

FACES OF CULTURE: 13—AGE, COMMON INTEREST, AND STRATIFICATION
1983, 30 minutes, color, video
Looks at three types of groupings common to all cultures: by age, by specialized interest, and by social-economic class. Describes practices that promote group unity.

FEAR OF FAT: DIETING AND EATING DISORDERS
1987, 26 minutes, color, video/film
Examines cultural preoccupation with being thin, placing the most severe eating disorders—anorexia nervosa, bulimia, and compulsive overeating—within a broad so-cial context. Looks at psychological causes, such as low self-esteem, and encourages viewers to accept their body type and eat to be healthy, not to be thin. Five young women in various stages of recovery discuss their eating disorders.

FEMALE ALCOHOLISM
1987, 19 minutes, color, video
Examines the stereotype of the female alcoholic and ana-lyzes case histories of recovered alcoholic women. Dis-cusses the dangers of drinking during pregnancy, the ef-fect of fetal alcohol syndrome on newborns, and the emotional effect on children raised by alcoholic mothers. Explains why women are reluctant to seek help and sug-gests ways to overcome it.

FIRE ON THE WATER
1982, 56 minutes, color, film
Documents prejudice and discrimination in the Galveston Bay area, where long-time residents have clashed with Vietnamese refugees over fishing rights. Focuses on Hung Nguyen, a young Vietnamese fisherman whose catch is the principal means of support for his family; James Stansfield, a boat mechanic who is the local leader of the Ku Klux Klan; and Jim Craig, a dock operator who har-bors the Vietnamese shrimp boats. Emotional confronta-tions reveal a common fear: that there isn't enough to go around anymore. Directed and produced by Robert Hillman. Blue Ribbon winner, American Film Festival.

FITNESS FOR LIFE: BODY COMPOSITION
1988, 29 minutes, color, video
Looks at the relationship between exercise and body com-position through discussion of weight control via diet and exercise, popular nutritional supplements, and weight-con-trol gimmicks. Features W. Larry Kenney, assistant profes-sor of applied psychology, and Susan Puhl, assistant pro-fessor of exercise and sport science at Penn State. Developed by Penn State's Department of Exercise and Sport Science and produced by Penn State Television/ WPSX-TV.

FITNESS FOR LIFE: EXERCISE— NATURE'S TRANQUILIZER
1988, 25 minutes, color, video
Examines the body's physiological response to stress, health problems associated with unmanaged stress, and techniques for managing stress. Emphasizes the beneficial role of exercise as a stress management technique. Fea-tures Dorothy V. Harris, professor of exercise and sport science at Penn State. Developed by Penn State's Depart-ment of Exercise and Sport Science and produced by Penn State Television/WPSX-TV.

FITNESS FOR LIFE: EXERCISE YOUR RIGHT
1988, 28 minutes, color, video
Provides guidelines for the safe implementation of an aero-bic exercise program, including means of determining frequency, duration, and intensity. Discusses goal-setting based on the results of fitness assessments and the calcu-lation of a target exercise heart-rate range. Features Patricia Kenney, instructor in exercise and sport science at Penn State. Developed by Penn State's Department of Exercise and Sport Science and produced by Penn State Television/WPSX-TV.

FITNESS FOR LIFE: FITNESS ASSESSMENT
1988, 29 minutes, color, video
Offers directions for the safe administration and correct interpretation of fitness tests to assess flexibility, body com-position, muscular strength, muscular endurance, and car-diorespiratory endurance. Features Susan Rankin, instruc-tor in exercise and sport science at Penn State. Developed by Penn State's Department of Exercise and Sport Science and produced by Penn State Television/WPSX-TV.

FITNESS FOR LIFE: OVERSTATED OR UNDERRATED?
1988, 29 minutes, color, video
Examines the state of fitness and wellness in our society and serves as an overview of the video series. Features Davies Bahr, instructor in exercise and sport science at Penn State. Developed by Penn State's Department of Exercise and Sport Science and produced by Penn State Television/WPSX-TV.

FITNESS FOR LIFE: PAY ATTENTION TO DETAILS
1988, 29 minutes, color, video
Makes the point that fitness programs often are curtailed because of exercise-related injuries. Presents methods of preventing injuries, first aid for common injuries, and re-habilitation techniques. Features William Buckley, assis-

tant professor of health education at Penn State. Developed by Penn State's Department of Exercise and Sport Science and produced by Penn State Television/WPSX-TV.

FOR A CHANGE: BREAKING OLD HABITS AND MAKING NEW ONES
1983, 27 minutes, color, film

Presents an active, systematic program for behavior change that can work for losing weight, quitting smoking, or building exercise into one's life. Explains how to increase motivation, keep records, and set objectives. Features several individuals who describe the concrete strategies they used for changing their habits.

THE FORGOTTEN AMERICAN
1968, 25 minutes, color, film

The story of the economic, social, and spiritual plight of American Indians. Points out that a shorter life span, higher infant mortality rate, and greater suicide rate indicate the disparity between Indians and white Americans. Discusses the problem of alienation, suggesting that Indians do not know who they are in the midst of the white middle-class values they are taught. Shows economic exploitation by the traditional trading posts as well as efforts being made to provide work for Indians by locating industries on reservations. Produced by CBS.

THE GROWING YEARS: 16—SOCIAL STEREOTYPING
1977, 30 minutes, color, video

Focuses on the development of sex-role stereotypes and examines the negative consequences of stereotypes and prejudice. Studies the nonstereotyped environment of the Pacific Oaks Preschool.

HERPES: THE EVASIVE INVADER
1983, 16 minutes, color, film

Examines the various types of herpes viruses and describes the clinical manifestations and lesion development of infection. Explains the body's defensive immune response to the herpes virus and discusses potential treatment, including antiviral therapy and immunotherapy. Employs computer graphics, time-lapse microcinematography, and animation. Directed and produced by Bob Settineri for Newport Pharmaceuticals International.

HISPANIC AMERICA
1980, 13 minutes, color, video/film

Presents an overview of Hispanic groups in the United States—Cubans, Mexicans, and Puerto Ricans—and their efforts to achieve a place and a voice in U.S. society. Points out that high immigration and birth rates make them the fastest growing minority in the country, and that their language and diverse traditions are not always welcomed by those Americans who see them as a denial of the melting pot ideal. Produced by CBS with Walter Cronkite.

THE HUMAN ANIMAL: LOVE AND SEX
1986, 52 minutes, color, video

Investigates human sexuality, looking at love, monogamy, heterosexuality, and homosexuality. Includes an odyssey to a male strip club, a gay rights march, a hospital birth, and a classroom where sexuality is being discussed. Host: Phil Donahue.

INDIAN MAINSTREAM
1971, 25 minutes, color, film

Describes a program sponsored by the Department of Labor that was designed to regenerate the Indian culture of the tribes in northern California—specifically the Hupa, Kerok, Tocowa, and Yurok tribes. Emphasizes the rediscovery of languages and rituals that have been suppressed over the last three generations and the need to pass on the Indian heritage to the young before it is forgotten. Thomas Parsons.

AN ISLAND IN AMERICA
1972, 28 minutes, color, film

Looks at Puerto Rican communities in the United States experiencing the problems of overcrowding, unemployment, delinquency, crime, and discrimination that have faced all immigrant groups in this country. Interviews prominent Puerto Ricans Joseph Monserrat, Senator Herman Badillo, and Ramon Arbonna, and presents a short history of Puerto Rico. Produced by the Anti-Defamation League B'nai Brith.

LETTER TO THE NEXT GENERATION
1990, 68 minutes, color, video
By Jim Klein
Distributor: New Day Films

"Set at Kent State, twenty years after four students were shot dead by National Guardsmen during an anti-war demonstration, the film uses that benchmark event to gauge the feelings of today's students about activism, success, racism, getting ahead, and having a good time. Nonjudgmental in tone, *Letter to the Next Generation* offers significant insight into the changes of the past two decades, and is a wonderful discussion starter" (*New Day Films Catalog*). (PBS Broadcast, P.O.V.)

LIVING WITH STRESS
1981, 16 minutes, color, film

Shows, through interviews with highly stressed people, some of the ways we can cope with stress on a long-term basis—and reject the harmful, temporary relief provided by drinking alcohol, smoking, overeating, and taking drugs.

MANAGING DIVERSITY
1990, 22 minutes, color, video

Taking into account demographics that show that white males, once the majority, now constitute a minority in the workplace, this program addresses the challenge of managing a diverse workforce. Vignettes of interactions among colleagues in a fictitious computer manufacturing firm illustrate that an individual's cultural background predisposes her/him to view such universal workplace issues as power, authority, and communications in certain ways. A CRM production.

MANAGING OUR MIRACLES: HEALTH CARE IN AMERICA—AIDS: IN SEARCH OF A MIRACLE
1986, 60 minutes, color, video

Professor Arthur Miller and panel examine some of the fears and vital questions raised by AIDS, the deadly disease that already has claimed thousands of victims. Produced by Columbia University Seminars on Media and Society, in association with WQED, Pittsburgh, and WNET.

MANAGING STRESS (Revised Edition)

1989, 26 minutes, color, video/film

Focuses on work-related stress: common sources such as overwork and time pressures, physiological and psychological effects, assessment of capacity to tolerate, and control techniques, including exercise, meditation, and biofeedback training. Also covered are the pioneering research by Dr. Hans Selye and "eustress"—moderate stress that promotes creativity and productivity. A CRM production.

MAN OH MAN

1987, 18 minutes, color, video

By J Clements

Distributor: New Day Films

"Man Oh Man takes a loving, curious look at the forces which mold young boys into men. Men from all walks of life speak with humor and sadness about what is expected of them. Explores personal definitions of masculinity, inter-gender communications, self-worth, gender stereotyping, and changing roles" (New Day Films Catalog). (Award: Silver Apple, National Educational Film & Video Festival)

MEDICAL EFFECTS OF ALCOHOL USE

1984, 12 minutes, color, film

Treats alcohol as a powerful drug that can do great damage to the body and mind. Shows how the body metabolizes one alcoholic beverage, then examines what happens to organs and tissues under habitual "social drinking," a common, but often unrecognized, form of alcohol abuse.

MEN AND DEPRESSION

1984, 27 minutes, color, film

Studies male stress and depression in terms of antisocial behavior, the problems men have in showing grief and sharing their feelings, and the myths of the male role and male stereotypes. Produced by Thames Television.

MEN'S LIVES

1974, 43 minutes, color, video

By Josh Hanig and Will Roberts

Distributor: New Day Films

"This definitive film captures the essence of the American male experience through a lively tapestry of scenes at schools, fraternity parties, marriage ceremonies, football games, in barber shops and the workplace. By shedding light on issues of intimacy, competition, violence, and love, the film helps women better understand men, and men better understand themselves" (New Day Films Catalog). (Awards: Gold Ducat, Mannheim International Film Festival; Blue Ribbon, American Film Festival)

MILES FROM THE BORDER

1988, 15 minutes, color, video

By Ellen Frankenstein

Distributor: New Day Films

"Twenty years after emigrating from a rural village in Zacatecas, Mexico to an ethnically divided community in southern California, the Aparicio family shares its experiences of dislocation and the difficulties of crossing cultures. Their timely story of claiming a place in the American mainstream poses critical questions about identity, adaptation, and survival in our multicultural society" (New

Day Films Catalog). (Awards: Special Jury Award, San Antonio Cine Fest; Nissan Focus Documentary Award)

THE MOSAIC WORKPLACE: 1—WHY VALUE DIVERSITY?

1990, 26 minutes, color, video

This ten-part series centers on the challenges for both managers and employees in the 1990s and beyond as a result of demographics that show that native-born whites whose first language is English constitute a minority in the workplace. The first program deals with the realities of a multiracial, multilingual work force in a society that continues to practice racism and sexism.

THE MOSAIC WORKPLACE: 2—UNDERSTANDING OUR BIASES AND ASSUMPTIONS

1990, 14 minutes, color, video

Considers the nature of biases and preconceptions, stressing the need to examine one's own thinking about "us" and "them." Discusses the roles of peer groups, community institutions, schools, and the media in determining what is "good" and what is "bad." Members of minority groups tell how bias affects their lives.

THE MOSAIC WORKPLACE: 3—MEN AND WOMEN WORKING TOGETHER

1990, 18 minutes, color, video

Investigates the issues raised by the increasing numbers and changing roles of women in the workplace, including legal aspects of discrimination based on sex as well as the behavioral problems of confusion, resentment, and lack of cooperation/support that often occur when men and women must work in close proximity.

THE MOSAIC WORKPLACE: 4—SEXUAL HARASSMENT

1990, 19 minutes, color, video

Points out how damaging and expensive a problem sexual harassment can be in the workplace, why it occurs and escalates, and what can be done about it. Reviews the excuses for ignoring harassment, provides suggestions for action when harassment is suspected, and highlights the cost of failing to take action.

THE MOSAIC WORKPLACE: 5—MANAGING A DIVERSE WORKPLACE: RECRUITING AND INTERVIEWING

1990, 18 minutes, color, video

Examines two theories prevalent in the workplace. There are not enough qualified employees and there are not enough minority employees who will "fit in" or possess the proper skills. Illustrates how sound recruitment efforts and nonbiased job interviews will result in locating and selecting the best employees.

THE MOSAIC WORKPLACE: 6—MANAGING A DIVERGE WORKPLACE: HELPING NEW EMPLOYEES FEEL VALUED

1990, 12 minutes, color, video

Designed to provide a sense of what it is like to be a new minority employee in a department or company by following a black professional woman on her first few days on the job and pointing out the behaviors that cause her to feel isolated, unimportant, unwanted, and unmotivated.

THE MOSAIC WORKPLACE: 7—MANAGING A DIVERSE WORKPLACE: UNDERSTANDING DIFFERENT CULTURAL VALUES AND STYLES

1990, 56 minutes, color, video

Refutes the melting-pot theory, explaining that employees do not, and should not be expected to, set aside their particular cultural values when they come to work. States that minorities expect no more than openmindedness in the workplace and that the most successful managers are those who understand diversity and seek to profit by it.

THE MOSAIC WORKPLACE: 8—MEETING THE DIVERSITY CHALLENGE

1990, 16 minutes, color, video

This program begins with a blurred image to help make the point that managers in an increasingly diverse workplace need to have a clear view of the situation. Identifies the six challenges managers face in developing unbiased attitudes and presents ways they can hone their techniques to achieve this goal.

THE MOSAIC WORKPLACE: 9—SUCCESS STRATEGIES FOR MINORITIES

1990, 21 minutes, color, video

A prominent black business consultant shares some practical techniques for minority success in corporate America and explains how to turn the anger that results from discrimination into a positive force. Shows managers how to make diversity a harmonious, rather than disruptive, fact of life in the workplace.

THE MOSAIC WORKPLACE: 10—THE FUTURE IS NOW: CELEBRATING DIVERSITY

1990, 26 minutes, color, video

Presents the ways in which the demands of a diverse work force can best be met: how schools can prepare students, how businesses can build bridges, and how all Americans can and must learn to value, respect, and benefit from diversity in society and in the workplace.

THE MULTICULTURAL WORKPLACE

1990, 30 minutes, color, video

Demonstrates the importance for managers to value cultural diversity, not to repress or avoid it. Shows the difficulties that usually result when people from differing cultural backgrounds interact in business and reveals how, because of misunderstanding and cultural assumptions, many employees are undervalued. Produced by Jay Anamia for WGBH.

NATION OF IMMIGRANTS

1976, 53 minutes, color, film

Children of older, European-based immigrant families discuss with children of newer black, Puerto Rican, and Oriental groups the similarities and differences in the immigration experience then and now. Focuses on how the older immigrants began to consider the newer ones a threat; shows extremist groups such as the Ku Klux Klan. From the *Destination America* series. Produced by Thames Television.

NATIONAL HEALTH TEST: 2—REPRODUCTION AND BIRTH

1967, 20 minutes, b&w, film

Presents questions and answers about abortion, reproduction, sex hygiene, venereal disease, and sexual relations.

THE NATURE OF DEPRESSION

1984, 27 minutes, color, film

Identifies behavior that masks depression, defines stress in terms of sensory input, and considers the reactions of the human body to stress-related depression. Also explores such stress-causing factors as improper diet, environmental pollution, and chemical malfunctions in the brain. Produced by Thames Television.

THE NINE NATIONS OF NORTH AMERICA: MEXAMERICA

1987, 60 minutes, color, video

Illustrates how the North American continent actually consists of nine separate "nations," one of which, "Mexamerica," stretches from Los Angeles to Houston and from Pueblo, Colorado, to San Luis Potosi, Mexico. Looks beyond the stereotypical views of Hispanics and the Southwest to the dynamism of the richest and most powerful of the nine nations. Based on the book by journalist Joel Garreau, who serves as program host.

NUTRITION FOR BETTER HEALTH

1984, 14 minutes, color, film

Illustrates how the consumption of too much sugar, salt, and saturated fats can hurt the body and how a diet of balanced nutrition can help avoid problems such as obesity, osteoporosis, hypertension, and heart disease. Emphasizes the dietary importance of vitamin D, calcium, and fiber.

ONE NATION UNDER STRESS

1988, 52 minutes, color, video

A comprehensive overview of stress in the United States and its causes. Looks at a broad range of ongoing research on its possible relationship to the immune system and disease, its effects on mood and personality, how to reduce it, how to manage it, and how stress may be learned in infancy. Points out that all the answers have not been found, and may not be for some time. Narrated by Merlin Olsen. Produced by Phyllis Ward.

120/80: ARE YOU IN CONTROL?

1988, 22 minutes, color, video

Conveys information about risk factors and nutrition concerns related to hypertension. Designed to be offered in a group setting where participants can examine and subsequently modify behaviors that increase susceptibility to high blood pressure. Answers to questions asked in the program's quiz format apply to a wide variety of eating situations. Print material included. Developed by the Penn State Nutrition Center and produced by Penn State Television/WPSX-TV.

ORAL COMMUNICATIONS : RESEARCHING A TOPIC

1969, 12 minutes, color, film

Outlines the steps involved in preparing a speech: selecting a topic, obtaining firsthand information, and compiling references and bibliography. Stresses the importance of thorough research and effective interview techniques. Illustrates an oral presentation using visual aids.

OUR IMMUNE SYSTEM

1988, 26 minutes, color, video/film

Explores the anatomy of the body's defense system and, by use of an electron microscope and advanced optical equipment, shows how enemies such as bacteria, viruses, and parasites attack the body. Also shows how the AIDS virus wrecks the immune system by attacking white blood cells. Photographed by Lennart Nilsson and produced by the National Geographic Society.

PHYSICAL FITNESS: IT CAN SAVE YOUR LIFE
1977, 23 minutes, color, video
Suggests ways to correct the vicious circle of inactivity, overeating, and poor physical health by offering a program of correct dietary habits and daily exercise. Produced by Alan P. Sloan.

PLEASURE DRUGS: THE GREAT AMERICAN HIGH
1982, 51 minutes, color, film
Edwin Newman reports on the use of pleasure drugs, focusing on cocaine use and abuse, which was estimated at the time the film was made to be a $30-billion annual business in the United States alone. Examines drug use in the military, in industry, and among professionals, and interviews authorities in the fields of prevention and detection as well as drug addicts themselves. Points out the inadequacies of laws that deal with use of drugs such as marijuana, quaaludes, and cocaine while operating a motor vehicle. Produced by Robert Rogers for the NBC White Paper series.

POCKETS OF HATE
1988, 26 minutes, color, video
Examines the increase in racial crimes, particularly those perpetrated against recent immigrants such as Asian Indians. Tries to determine where young people pick up their racial attitudes and why they are becoming more comfortable in acting out their prejudices. Host: Marlene Sanders. Directed by Tony Marshall and produced by Henry Singer.

PORTRAITS OF ANOREXIA
1985, 51 minutes, color, video/film
Reveals through in-depth interviews the emotional and physical effects of anorexia nervosa on its victims, mostly young women, and their families. Explores the tangled family relationships and feelings of worthlessness and guilt that can underlie this eating disorder, and describes the physical complications, including fatal heart attacks, that it can cause. Directed and produced by Wendy Zheutlin.

THE POWER OF THE WORD WITH BILL MOYERS: 3—ANCESTRAL VOICES
1989, 58 minutes, color, video
Features three poets with distinctive heritages that influence their work: Joy Harjo, a Native American of Creek and Cherokee-French background; Garrett Hongo, a U.S.-born Japanese-American; and Mary TallMountain, a Native American born in Alaska. Presented at Glassboro State College in New Jersey.

THE POWER OF THE WORD WITH BILL MOYERS: 4—VOICES OF MEMORY
1989, 58 minutes, color, video
Reading at Glassboro State College, Li-Young Lee, a Chinese-American, reflects upon his struggles with being bound to a heritage he has never lived, and Gerald Stern draws on his Jewish heritage that provides him with inspiration and direction.

PRAISE
1983, 60 minutes, color, video
Story of an Englishwoman and a priest who discover the raw intelligence of Praise, an impoverished black child living on the streets of Johannesburg. Nadine Gordimer's contemporary version of the Pygmalion story poignantly expresses the conflict between well-intentioned white adults' desires for a black child and the child's own needs for identification with his ethnic heritage. From the Nadine Gordimer's Stories from South Africa series.

PREJUDICE: CAUSES, CONSEQUENCES, AND CURES
1974, 23 minutes, color, video/film
Explores the nature of prejudice in its many forms—racial, sexual, economic, and educational. Offers examples of the problems of conformity, socialization, double standards, overgeneralized observations, severe and punitive upbringing, and territorial and economic group conflicts. From the Social Science series. Produced by Peter Jordan.

THE PRIMAL MIND
1984, 58 minutes, color, video
Explores the basic differences between Native American and European cultures, which perceive life and evolution from dramatically different perspectives. Discusses in detail the two cultures' contrasting views of nature, time, space, art, architecture, and dance, and identifies language as playing a crucial role in bringing about serious misunderstandings. Based on the book The Primal Mind: Vision and Reality in Indian America by Jamake Highwater, the program's writer and host. Produced by Alvin H. Perlmutter.

QUACK
1976, 24 minutes, color, film
An experimental film by Scott Guthrie and John Huckert about a young black woman who fantasizes about becoming a documentary filmmaker. The obstacles she encounters symbolize her oppression by a white, male-dominated world. Judge's Award, Penn State Student Film Festival, 1976.

RACISM 101
1988, 58 minutes, color, video
Tracks the trend of increased racism and violence at America's colleges and universities, focusing on the University of Massachusetts, the University of Michigan, and Dartmouth College. Reveals an apparent and unsettling return to the kind of racial prejudice that flared during the early days of the civil rights movement. Produced by David Fanning for PBS's Frontline series. Blue Ribbon winner, American Film Festival.

RACISM IN AMERICA
1985, 26 minutes, color, video
Examines the resurgence of racially motivated violence during the early and mid-1980s. Looks at the reasons why people vent anger against minorities, the social and economic implications of racist acts, and how one community successfully responded to its racial problems. Features Althea Simmons, chief lobbyist for the NAACP; Peter Salins of the Manhattan Institute for Policy Research; and Donald Tucker, chairman of the New Jersey Black Issues Convention. Host: Marty Goldensen. Directed by Bob Morris and produced by Jane Petroff.

THE RIGHT TO BE MOHAWK

1989, 17 minutes, color, video

By George Hornbein, Lorna Rasmussen, and Anne Stanaway

Distributor: New Day Films

"This film is a stereotype-breaking look at contemporary people deeply rooted in the past—traditionalist Mohawks of Akwesasne in New York State. The film documents their determination not only to survive, but to expand and solidify their nation, in spite of increasing pressure to assimilate" (*New Day Films Catalog*).

A SEASON IN HELL

1990, 59 minutes, color, video

By Walter Brock

Distributor: New Day Films

"This film is a compelling in-depth exploration of a young rural Kentucky woman and her family's struggle with anorexia and bulimia" (*New Day Films Catalog*). (Awards: Best of Festival, Charlotte Film & Video Festival; Silver Plaque, Chicago International Film Festival)

SEXUALLY TRANSMITTED DISEASE: INTRODUCTION

1986, 19 minutes, color, video

Provides a general introduction to sexually transmitted diseases, and discusses the causes, treatments, and prevention of AIDS, herpes, vaginitis, syphilis, gonorrhea and chlamydia, and sexually transmitted skin disease. Produced by Planned Parenthood of Ohio.

SMOKELESS TOBACCO: THE SEAN MARSEE STORY

1986, 16 minutes, color, film

This dramatization of the true story of Sean Marsee, a high school track star and habitual user of snuff, who died of oral cancer at age nineteen, serves as a springboard for a discussion about the dangers of smokeless tobacco. Dr. Jim Nethery, a mouth and throat specialist, describes the stages of oral cancer, and Johnny Johnson, defensive back for the Los Angeles Rams, points out snuff's addictive nature. Produced by Walt Disney Educational Media.

SMOKER'S LUCK

1980, 54 minutes, color, film

Explains the risks involved in tobacco smoking, including the dangers of carbon monoxide, the effect of smoking on an unborn child, and the danger of smoke to nonsmokers. Includes animated sequences. Produced by the BBC.

STEROIDS AND SPORTS

1987, 19 minutes, color, video

Intersperses scenes of athletes training and participating in sports with comments by athletes on the use of steroids. Host Michael Salort interviews Dr. Pascual Bidot, endocrinologist, and Dr. Joseph Diaco, general surgeon, on the pros and cons of steroid use as well as the use of growth hormones.

A STORM OF STRANGERS: JUNG SAI, CHINESE-AMERICAN

1977, 29 minutes, color, film

Follows the quest of a young Chinese-American journalist, Jung Sai, as she seeks out her ethnic origins in a journey throughout the western United States. Along the way, she interviews Chinese of all ages about early coolie labor immigrations, work on the transcontinental railway, labor in the mines, and formation of the great Chinatowns. Directed by Frieda Lee Mock and Terry Sanders.

THE STORY OF ENGLISH: 5—BLACK ON WHITE

1986, 60 minutes, color, video

Probes the roots and the flowering of black American English from its beginnings on Africa's west coast through its transformations in the rural South and urban North to its presence today in the street culture of rappers and breakers.

STRESS MANAGEMENT: 1—CAUSE AND EFFECTS

1988, 32 minutes, color, video

This four-part series deals with the recognition and management of stress through the presentation of information by six consultants and dramatizations of the concepts in business settings. The first program explains what is meant by excess stress, the type that is constant and unremitting and can cause physical and emotional disorders. Defines coping and shows how to recognize what stress feels like and what triggers it.

STRESS MANAGEMENT: 2—STRESS TRIGGERS

1988, 25 minutes, color, video

Describes how stress build-up can affect health, relationships, and job performance. Emphasizes the importance of examining one's typical coping style—behavior patterns that an individual develops to deal with stress.

STRESS MANAGEMENT: 3—RELAXATION TECHNIQUES

1988, 26 minutes, color, video

Concentrates on specific options and methods that an individual can use to manage internal reactions to stressful situations, including ways of handling thoughts and feelings and achieving deep physical relaxation.

STRESS MANAGEMENT: 4—COPING SKILLS

1988, 22 minutes, color, video

Focuses on options for changing stressful situations. Provides guidelines for applying problem-solving skills to stress management and offers rules of thumb for low-stress communicating. Also addresses the manager's role and responsibility for stress management in the workplace.

STUDY HINTS

1967, 30 minutes, b&w, film

Explains how good study habits are essential to academic success in college. From the College Bound series. Produced by NET.

SUMMER OF THE LOUCHEUX

1983, 27 minutes, color, video

By Graydon McCrea and Linda Rasmussen

Distributor: New Day Films

"This film is about values, self-esteem, and the critical importance of tradition. The remarkable beauty of the North and the rich mosaic of camp life blend with unique archival photos to create a film that documents the living heritage of a northern native people" (*New Day Films Catalog*). (Awards: Blue Ribbon, American Film Festival; Best Documentary Short, American Indian Film Festival; Editor's Choice, Booklist)

SYLVIA: SUMMER BEFORE COLLEGE
1983, 30 minutes, color, film
A glimpse into the life of a talented black teenager, during the busy summer before she enters college. Sylvia Hall takes time to reflect on her high school experiences and the people who have influenced her. The film reveals a young woman's personal assessment of her priorities and her realization that one can have a lot without needing to "have it all." Directed and produced by Grania Gurievitch. Blue Ribbon winner, American Film Festival.

TAKING CHARGE OF YOUR HEALTH
1984, 18 minutes, color, video
Stresses that individuals have the potential to enhance the quality of their lives by profiling five people who have been successful in making changes in the way they live. Points out that because such leading causes of death as heart disease, cancer, and stroke often are tied to smoking, lack of exercise, obesity, drug and alcohol abuse, and chronic stress, a change in habits or lifestyle can effect a change for the better in one's health. Produced by Penn State Television/WPSX-TV.

TELL THEM I'M A MERMAID
1983, 23 minutes, color, film
A musical theater performance that reveals the private world of seven extraordinary women with physical disabilities. Their stories, enhanced by humor, music, and unconventional choreography, convey the message that all people can move beyond the barriers and definitions set for them by others. Host: Jane Fonda. Directed by Victoria Hochberg. Produced by Constance Kaplan and Elizabeth Daley.

TONGUES UNTIED
1989, 55 minutes, color, video
A personal, subjective, advocacy film on behalf of acceptance of the black, gay, male lifestyle. Confronts the derogatory accusations, judgments, and jokes that abound, using poetry, personal testimony, rap, and drama to counter the homophobia and racism that attempt to split black gay men into opposing loyalties. Written, directed, and produced by Marlon T. Riggs. Blue Ribbon winner, American Film Festival.

UP IN SMOKE: HOW SMOKING AFFECTS YOUR HEALTH
1983, 35 minutes, color, video
Relates the origin and history of tobacco use and examines the economic, governmental, and scientific controversy surrounding its growth, sale, and consumption. Describes the immediate chemical and physical changes that occur when cigarette smoke is inhaled, as well as its long-range addictive nature and the physical diseases, such as cancer, emphysema, and heart disease, that may result. Enumerates ways to quit smoking.

VALIUM
1977, 17 minutes, color, film
A report on the extensive use and abuse of Valium, a widely used drug prescribed as a relaxant. Medical experts attest to its effectiveness but admit to its addictive potential and the severe withdrawal symptoms experienced by heavy users. Reveals how Valium, now listed as a controlled substance, has become the opiate of the middle class largely due to ease of access and how, when combined with methadone, it triggers a "kick" for heroin addicts. Produced by CBS for *60 Minutes*.

VALUING DIVERSITY: 1—MANAGING DIFFERENCES
1987, 30 minutes, color, video
Illustrates how assumptions, real differences, and organizational culture affect the performance of managers. Designed to enhance managers' sensitivity to possible racial, ethnic, and gender prejudices, and to encourage use of nondiscriminatory criteria in evaluating employees. Deposited by the Pennsylvania Department of Aging.

VALUING DIVERSITY: 3—COMMUNICATING ACROSS CULTURES
1987, 30 minutes, color, video
Shows how misunderstandings in the workplace result from different styles of communication; addresses the discomfort people feel when dealing with issues of race, gender, disabilities, and lifestyles; and suggests ways to communicate more effectively. Deposited by the Pennsylvania Department of Aging.

VD EPIDEMIC
1965, 27 minutes, b&w, film
Examines the epidemic proportions of venereal disease and its high cost to the nation. Emphasizes the need for early treatment and follow-up of contacts. Produced by ABC.

VD: NAME YOUR CONTACTS
1968, 22 minutes, color, film
Presents the case histories of seven young men and women who provide links in a chain of gonorrhea infection. After being informed by a doctor of the necessity of locating and examining all sexual contacts in order to curb infection, individuals display varying emotional reactions.

VD: PREVENT IT
1971, 11 minutes, color, film
Offers practical precautions to avoid venereal disease during and after sexual contact.

VD QUIZ: GETTING THE RIGHT ANSWERS
1977, 25 minutes, color, film
Designed to help young people understand the causes of venereal diseases and the importance of prompt treatment of symptoms. Covers gonorrhea, nongonococcal urethritis, trichomoniasis, herpes simplex virus type 2, syphilis, and cytomegalovirus, with special emphasis on symptom identification in both males and females of all six diseases. Also points out the consequences for those who do not seek early diagnosis and treatment.

VENEREAL DISEASES
1973, 17 minutes, color, film
Covers ignorance and superstition concerning venereal diseases, describes how the organisms that cause syphilis and gonorrhea are transmitted, and shows patients being examined and treated. Includes group discussion about protecting oneself from venereal disease, detecting symptoms, and seeking treatment. Due to explicit treatment and live-action photography, preview by the instructor is essential. From the Human Sexuality series. T.E. Pengelley and S. Kaplan.

WEIGHING THE CHOICES: POSITIVE APPROACHES TO NUTRITION
1981, 20 minutes, color, film

Discusses positive, practical menu choices for breakfast, lunch, and dinner, emphasizing not the elimination of certain foods but a conscious selection of some foods more often than others in order to be healthier. Bases nutrition guidelines on the relation of physical activity to calorie intake and on studies showing the risks of diets high in fats, calories, cholesterol, and sodium. Blue Ribbon winner, American Film Festival.

WHAT PRICE EQUALITY?
1987, 56 minutes, color, video

Focuses on Yonkers, New York, where the city and school district intentionally discriminated against minorities in housing and education. Under a 1986 federal order, the schools integrated, but the city council waited until the eleventh hour before deciding upon a plan to build low- and middle-income housing in the mostly white area of East Yonkers. Another segment takes place in San Francisco, where women sued for the right to join the city's all-male fire department. Host: Peter Jennings. Produced by Robert Epstein.

WHERE IS PREJUDICE?
1968, 60 minutes, b&w, film

Twelve college students of different races and faiths are shown candidly while participating in a week-long workshop to test their common denial that they are prejudiced. As frank discussion and questioning of one another continues, latent prejudices emerge, and students are unable to cope with this revelation. Produced by NET.

WHO KILLED VINCENT CHIN?
1988, 82 minutes, color, video

Documents the circumstances surrounding the murder of Vincent Chin, the trial of his European-American murderer, and the outcry of the Asian-American community over the outcome of the trial. Explores the cultural context of the event, the depth of bigotry and racism throughout the United States, and the charges that the judicial system fails to value equally every citizen's rights. Directed by Christine Choy and produced by Renee Tajima.

WHOSE AMERICA IS IT?
1985, 46 minutes, color, video

Correspondent Bill Moyers examines the problems created by immigrants, legal and illegal, that according to U.S. immigration officials are creating a national crisis. Looks at the effects of many immigrants' refusal to assimilate and of their acceptance of low-paying work. Considers the irony of a nation of immigrants debating what to do about the new strangers in its midst. Directed and produced by Elena Mannes for the CBS Reports series.

A WOMAN'S PLACE IS IN THE HOUSE
1975, 28 minutes, color, film

A profile of Massachusetts politician Elaine Noble. Young, vigorous, idealistic, and dedicated to her multiracial, economically diverse constituents, Elaine Noble is also homosexual and believes it is important to confront the issue with candor. Produced by Nancy Porter and Mickey Lemle. Blue Ribbon winner, American Film Festival.

WOMEN AND DEPRESSION
1982, 25 minutes, color, film

Questions the commonly held view that women are more vulnerable to depression than men. The conflicting demands placed upon women in society are identified in terms of how girls are brought up differently from boys, how women deal with the conflict between being feminine and attractive or clever and competitive, and how women respond to the sexual stereotypes used in the media. Produced by Thames Television.

WOMEN AND WEIGHT LOSS
1988, 28 minutes, color, video

Author Eda Le Shan discusses women's attitudes toward weight loss and distinguishes between the psychological and physiological problems of being overweight.

WOMEN IN THE WORKPLACE
1984, 18 minutes, color, film

Filmed lecture by Carole Keller explains the twelve basic behaviors of the troubled female employee, pointing out employee and employer barriers in discussions about problems. Emphasizes identification of alcohol and drug abuse indicators among working women and discusses the subtle differences between troubled male and female workers. Useful for professionals in the Employee Assistance Program.

WORKING WOMEN: THE CORPORATE GAME
1987, 21 minutes, color, video

Explores the unequal treatment of women senior executives resulting from the corporate clubhouse mentality of some male colleagues. Features one businesswoman who has been able to work successfully within the corporate system and two others who found an entirely different way to avoid workplace barriers: They started their own companies. From the *MacNeil-Lehrer News Hour* with Charlayne Hunter-Gault.

A WORLD OF IDEAS WITH BILL MOYERS: ANNE WORTHAM
1988, 57 minutes, color, video

Journalist Bill Moyers interviews outstanding individuals who have made notable contributions in their fields of endeavor and who are in a position to assess society as the end of the 20th century nears. In this first program, Anne Wortham criticizes the civil rights movement and its leaders for what she says is promotion of reverse racism and the welfare state. She points out that all blacks do not share one common experience.

A WORLD OF IDEAS WITH BILL MOYERS: ARTURO MADRID
1988, 29 minutes, color, video

Arturo Madrid, a teacher, talks about Hispanic stereotypes, issues and policies affecting the Latin community, and the controversy over bilingual education and the status of education for minorities.

A WORLD OF IDEAS WITH BILL MOYERS: AUGUST WILSON
1988, 29 minutes, color, video

Black American playwright August Wilson shares his insights on the influence of blues music on literature and how it has shaped his philosophy of life and drama. He also talks about finding the African-American cultural identity and the portrayal of black America on television.

A WORLD OF IDEAS WITH BILL MOYERS: CARLOS FUENTES
1988, 28 minutes, color, video
Author, teacher, and diplomat Carlos Fuentes, who specializes in the policies of North and South America, discusses current Latin American economics and the prospects for political independence of nations such as Nicaragua.

A WORLD OF IDEAS WITH BILL MOYERS: CHEN NING YANG
1988, 29 minutes, color, video
Chen Ning Yang, professor of physics and Nobel Prize winner, shares his views about science in the East and in the West and offers his opinions as to why Asians lead Americans in science education.

A WORLD OF IDEAS WITH BILL MOYERS: CHINUA ACHEBE
1988, 28 minutes, color, video
Nigerian writer Chinua Achebe, president of the town council in his village, discusses the impact of colonialism on his culture and relates how he began writing in reaction to certain stereotypes in Western literature.

A WORLD OF IDEAS WITH BILL MOYERS: DEREK WALCOTT
1988, 29 minutes, color, video
Derek Walcott, a British subject born on the Caribbean island of St. Lucia, presents a melting-pot perspective of the lives of the privileged and the disenfranchised. The poet/teacher talks about the impact of the English language on his oppressed homeland and the struggle of blacks in a world ruled by whites.

A WORLD OF IDEAS WITH BILL MOYERS: JOHN SEARLE
1988, 28 minutes, color, video
Professor of philosophy John Searle discusses the intellectual elitism of the Western world that emphasizes the classic writings of dead, white, European males, and argues that educators must accept equally significant works from other cultures.

A WORLD OF IDEAS WITH BILL MOYERS: LOUISE ERDRICH AND MICHAEL DORRIS
1988, 29 minutes, color, video
Louise Erdrich and Michael Dorris, a Native-American wife-husband team who write novels based on their heritage, discuss the values and difficulties of modern Native Americans, the concept of "ironic survival humor," and the Native American's ability to live on the land in harmony with nature.

A WORLD OF IDEAS WITH BILL MOYERS: WILLIAM JULIUS WILSON
1988, 27 minutes, color, video
Writer and sociologist William Julius Wilson offers his thoughts on the origins of poverty: Inner-city blacks stay poor because they live in the wasteland of the inner city, not simply because they are black.

THE WRONG IDEA
1988, 20 minutes, color, video
The use of a culturally diverse cast in nine vignettes portraying campus sexual harassment incidents is designed to stimulate discussions of differing perceptions about each incident. Attempts to sensitize U.S. and international students, faculty, and staff to the cultural and gender issues surrounding sexual harassment, and informs them of their legal rights and responsibilities. Training manual available. Developed and produced at the University of Minnesota.

YOU ARE THE GAME: SEXUAL HARASSMENT ON CAMPUS
1985, 60 minutes, color, video
A discussion among two women and a counselor, interwoven with dramatized flashbacks, provides insight into the difficulty college students have in dealing with sexual harassment and the impact it has on their lives. A panel discussion follows, focusing on why sexual harassment occurs, how it affects the educational climate, and what can be done about it. Moderator: Connie Dyer, director of the Indiana University Office for Women's Affairs. Directed and produced by Chris Lamar.

YOU'RE IN CHARGE: MANAGING YOUR MEDICATIONS
1985, color, film
Focuses on older adults as a high-risk population relative to drug and alcohol abuse. Covers medication misuse, common problems, individual responsibility for health management, and communication with the physician. Developed by Family and Youth Programs of Norristown. Deposited by the Pennsylvania Department of Aging. Consists of two audiocassettes, two sets of slides, and print material.

Transparency Masters

Chapter 5 ►   **11**   *Précis Writing*
Comments: Précis writing can be very useful. You may wish to highlight the instructions in the text (*YCE*, p. 89) by using the short form in TM 11 as reinforcement and as a vehicle for answering student questions.

                   12   *Required Reading*
Comments: Use TM 12 in class to help students understand the nature of the assigned reading for their various courses. Use the results to lead a class discussion.

Chapter 6 ►   **13**   *Lecture System*
Comments: Review the mind map from p. 97 of *YCE*. Then work with the class to create a new mind map, perhaps based on the material from the mini-lecture used for TM 10. One way to do this is to show the completed notes from TM 10 and ask students to translate this into a mind map that could serve as a useful study aid for an exam.

                   14   *Principles for Taking Essay Exams*
Comments: TM 14 summarizes techniques for successfully answering essay questions.

                   15   *Tips on Memory*
Comments: TM 15 offers memorization techniques.

Chapter 8 ►   **16**   *Outline*
Comments: TM 16 shows the outline (from p. 131 of *YCE*) students should follow for their oral presentation of the information they have gathered at the library. It also serves as a way to test as they go the relevancy to their topic of the information they have gathered.

                   17   *Major Library Sources*
Comments: TM 17 outlines six major sources of information found in the library.

Chapter 10 ►   **18**   *Ideal Career*
Comments: A person's *ideal* career is where the five circles shown in TM 18 intersect; however, in the real world, one must usually accept something less.

                   19   *School Alternatives*
Comments: TM 19 offers ten types of schools from which students might choose when considering a transfer.

Chapter 11 ►   **20**   *Successful Interpersonal Communication*
Comments: TM 20 is a handy checklist on how to ensure successful interpersonal communication.

                   21   *Formula for Assertiveness*
Comments: Use the formula shown in TM 21 as a springboard for a class discussion of assertiveness.

Chapter 12 ►   **22**   *STD Risk Factors*
Comments: Seeing these risk factors (from p. 216 of the text) on an overhead should drive this information home more forcefully than simply reading it in the text would. The seriousness of the information warrants the possibility of overkill (no pun intended!).

                   23   *Sex – Yes = Rape*
Comments: This simple message should speak for itself; however, it is not possible to overemphasize for students that NO means NO and that rape does not occur only between strangers; often victims know their assailants.

SETTING SHORT-TERM GOALS

1. SELECT A GOAL.

2. ASK WHETHER THE GOAL IS ACHIEVABLE.

3. BE SURE YOU <u>GENUINELY</u> WANT TO ACHIEVE THIS GOAL.

4. IDENTIFY WHY THIS GOAL IS WORTHWHILE.

5. ANTICIPATE AND IDENTIFY DIFFICULTIES YOU MIGHT ENCOUNTER.

6. DEVISE STRATEGIES TO ACHIEVE THE GOAL.

SMART ALTERNATIVE PROCESS FOR GOAL SETTING

1. SPECIFIC

2. MEASURABLE

3. ACTION STEPS

4. REALISTIC

5. TIME-FRAMED

RETURNING STUDENTS

1. DON'T DOUBT YOURSELF.

2. TEACHERS VALUE YOUR LIFE EXPERIENCES.

3. ENROLL PART-TIME IF YOU'RE OVERLOADED.

4. GET THE SUPPORT OF PEOPLE IN YOUR LIFE.

5. FIND FACULTY AND STAFF SUPPORT ON CAMPUS.

6. GET TO KNOW OTHER STUDENTS.

7. TAKE REVIEW OR "HOW TO STUDY" COURSES.

8. BE REALISTIC.

MINORITY STUDENTS

1. KEEP A POSITIVE ATTITUDE.

2. SHOOT FOR AN A.

3. JOIN OR FORM A STUDY GROUP.

4. SEE INSTRUCTORS OUTSIDE OF CLASS.

5. TAKE ADVANTAGE OF SUPPORT SERVICES.

6. TAKE PART IN CO-CURRICULAR ACTIVITIES.

7. ATTEND COLLEGE FULL-TIME IF YOU CAN.

8. DON'T BE INTIMIDATED BY MATH AND SCIENCE FIELDS.

9. PRACTICE FOR STANDARDIZED TESTS, ESPECIALLY IF YOU'RE INTERESTED IN GRADUATE SCHOOL.

10. CHOOSE A CAREER WITH LONG-TERM PAYOFFS. BE SURE YOUR COURSEWORK MATCHES YOUR GOAL.

11. BE PROUD OF YOUR HERITAGE AND CULTURE.

BEAT PROCRASTINATION

1. SAY TO YOURSELF, "I'M A CAPABLE, RESPONSIBLE SELF-STARTER."

2. ON 3 × 5 NOTECARD MAKE A LIST OF WHAT YOU NEED TO DO. CHECK OFF ITEMS AS YOU DO THEM.

3. BREAK BIG JOBS INTO SMALLER STEPS.

4. APPLY THE GOAL-SETTING TECHNIQUE.

5. PROMISE YOURSELF A SUITABLE REWARD WHEN YOU FINISH A DIFFICULT PROJECT.

6. TAKE CONTROL OF YOUR STUDY ENVIRONMENT.

5 (Chapter 2)

TIMETABLE

	Su	M	Tu	W	Th	F	Sa
6:00							
7:00							
8:00							
9:00							
10:00							
11:00							
12:00							
1:00							
2:00							
3:00							
4:00							
5:00							
6:00							
7:00							
8:00							
9:00							
10:00							
11:00							
12:00							

PERSONALITY PREFERENCES /
THE MYERS-BRIGGS TYPE INDICATOR

EI **(EXTROVERSION/ INTROVERSION)**

Focus your attention on the outer or inner world.

SN **(SENSING/ INTUITION)**

Acquire information through facts versus intuition.

TF **(THOUGHT/ FEELING)**

Make decisions by analysis versus feelings.

JP **(JUDGING/ PERCEPTION)**

Relate to outer world in a planned, orderly way versus in a spontaneous way.

PERSONALITY TYPES

	Strengths	Weaknesses
Introvert		
Extrovert		
Intuitor		
Sensor		

8a (Chapter 3)

PERSONALITY TYPES (cont.)

	Strengths	Weaknesses
Feeler		
Thinker		
Perceiver		
Judger		

8b (Chapter 3)

TEACHING AND LEARNING

TEACHERS

SF: Supporters   ST: Information Givers

NT: Inquirers   NF: Originators

LEARNERS

SF: Friendly   ST: Practical

NT: Intellectual   NF: Curious

NOTE-TAKING

PRÉCIS WRITING

1. **READ THE ARTICLE**

2. **ANALYZE THE ARTICLE**

3. **SELECT AND CONDENSE**

4. **DRAFT**

5. **REWRITE**

REQUIRED READING

Class/Subject	Type of Reading Required	Ideal Time	Ideal Location	Why?

12 (Chapter 5)

LECTURE SYSTEM

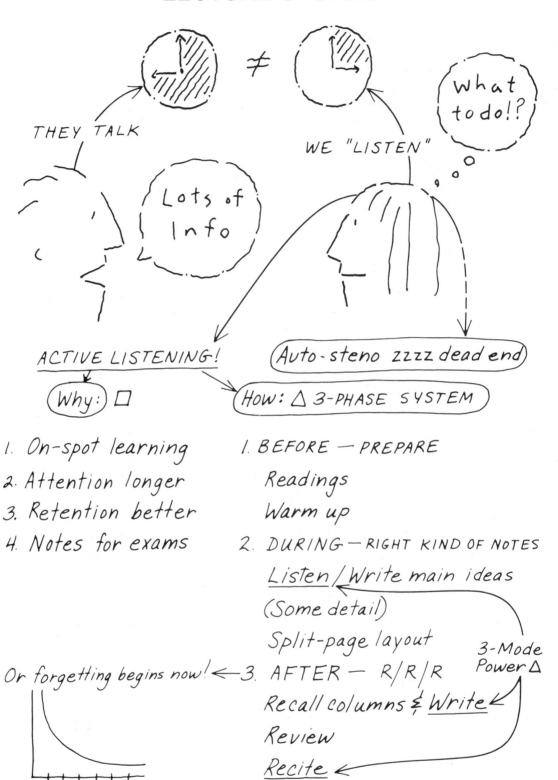

THEY TALK

WE "LISTEN"

what to do!?

Lots of Info

ACTIVE LISTENING!

Auto-steno zzzz dead end

Why: □

How: △ 3-PHASE SYSTEM

1. On-spot learning
2. Attention longer
3. Retention better
4. Notes for exams

1. BEFORE — PREPARE
   Readings
   Warm up
2. DURING — RIGHT KIND OF NOTES
   Listen / Write main ideas
   (Some detail)
   Split-page layout

Or forgetting begins now! ← 3. AFTER — R/R/R
   Recall columns & Write
   Review
   Recite

3-Mode Power △

Time

PRINCIPLES FOR TAKING ESSAY EXAMS

1. READ THE ENTIRE QUESTION CAREFULLY.

2. READ IT AGAIN. UNDERLINE KEY WORDS.

3. BRAINSTORM. WRITE DOWN ALL IDEAS YOU CAN THINK OF; INCORPORATE MOST IMPORTANT POINTS IN YOUR ANSWERS.

4. USE UNDERLINED WORDS (FROM THE QUESTION AND YOUR BRAINSTORMING) TO CONSTRUCT BRIEF OUTLINE.

5. BEGIN ANSWER BY REWRITING THE QUESTION TO REINFORCE YOUR FOCUS.

6. WRITE THE REST OF THE ANSWER ACCORDING TO YOUR OUTLINE.

7. BEGIN ANSWER WITH AN INTRODUCTION AND END IT WITH A CONCLUSION.

TIPS ON MEMORY

1. USE MNEMONICS—CREATE RHYMES, JINGLES, SAYINGS, OR PHRASES THAT REPEAT OR CODIFY INFORMATION.

2. ASSOCIATE—RELATE AN IDEA TO SOMETHING YOU ALREADY KNOW.

3. PEG—VISUALIZE IN ORDER A NUMBER OF LOCATIONS OR OBJECTS, AND ASSOCIATE EACH ONE WITH AN ITEM THAT YOU NEED TO REMEMBER.

4. VISUALIZE—MAKE YOURSELF SEE WHAT YOU WANT TO REMEMBER.

5. OVERLEARN—GO OVER THE MATERIAL AGAIN AND AGAIN.

6. USE FLASHCARDS—WRITE THE WORD/ INFORMATION TO BE LEARNED ON ONE SIDE AND THE DEFINITION ON THE OTHER.

7. CATEGORIZE—LOOK FOR AN ORDER IN THE INFORMATION TO BE MEMORIZED.

8. DRAW A MIND MAP—VISUALIZE RELATIONSHIPS.

15 (Chapter 6)

OUTLINE

A. <u>DEFINITION</u>: What is this topic about? What does it mean?

B. <u>IMPORTANCE</u>: Why is topic important? How important is topic? What would happen if problem were not addressed or if no one knew about problem?

C. <u>EFFECT</u>: How does this influence my thinking? Does my research tell me something I did not know? Have I changed my mind as the result of reading this? What is there about this information that contributes to my understanding the topic?

D. <u>REACTION</u>: What do I want to say? What insight do I wish to report? What is important enough that I want to tell others? How does this information make me feel?

MAJOR LIBRARY SOURCES

1. GENERAL ENCYCLOPEDIAS
    (*ENCYCLOPEDIA AMERICANA*)

2. SUBJECT ENCYCLOPEDIAS
    (*ENCYCLOPEDIA OF SCIENCE &
    TECHNOLOGY*)

3. PERIODICAL INDEXES, GENERAL
    (*READERS' GUIDE*)

4. PERIODICAL INDEXES, SUBJECT
    (*SOCIAL SCIENCE INDEX*)

5. BOOKS (ORGANIZED BY SUBJECT,
    TITLE, AUTHOR)

6. OPINIONS AND POINTS OF VIEW
    (NEWSPAPER EDITORIALS ON FILE)

IDEAL CAREER

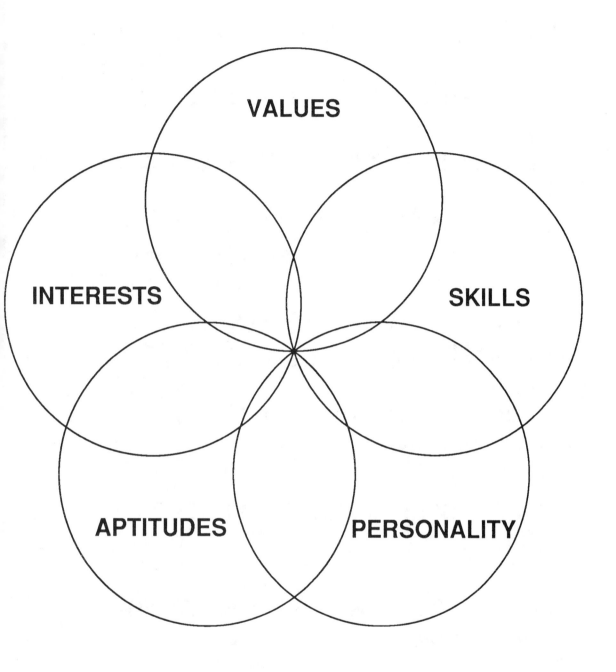

VALUES

INTERESTS

SKILLS

APTITUDES

PERSONALITY

SCHOOL ALTERNATIVES

- TWO-YEAR VERSUS FOUR-YEAR SCHOOL

- SMALLER VERSUS LARGER SCHOOL

- LESS URBAN VERSUS LESS RURAL SCHOOL

- LIBERAL ARTS VERSUS VOCATIONAL-TECHNICAL TRAINING SCHOOL

- SCHOOL THAT FITS PERSONAL ACADEMIC LEVEL

- SCHOOL WITH SPECIAL PROGRAMS (E.G., FINE ARTS)

- RELIGIOUSLY AFFILIATED VERSUS UNAFFILIATED SCHOOL

- SCHOOL CLOSER VERSUS FARTHER FROM HOME

- MORE AFFORDABLE SCHOOL

- MORE "SOCIALLY FITTING" SCHOOL

SUCCESSFUL INTERPERSONAL COMMUNICATION

1. PRACTICE SELF-DISCLOSURE.

2. SHOW MUTUAL RESPECT.

3. FIND A COMMON FRAME OF REFERENCE.

4. LISTEN ACTIVELY AND CHECK THE
    MEANING OF COMMUNICATION.

5. EXPRESS FEELINGS APPROPRIATELY.

6. EMPATHIZE.

7. ACKNOWLEDGE LEGITIMACY OF
    ANOTHER'S FEELINGS.

8. ACCEPT CONFLICT.

FORMULA FOR ASSERTIVENESS

R ——>   (RESPECT FOR OTHER PERSON)
R <——   (RESPECT FOR YOURSELF)
+ S   (SPECIFICITY)*
——————— ————————————————————————
A   (ASSERTIVENESS)

* THE CLARIFICATION OF VIEWS, FEELINGS, AND WANTS FOR ONESELF AND FOR OTHERS.

STD RISK FACTORS

1. BEING 15 TO 24 YEARS OLD

2. HAVING MULTIPLE SEX PARTNERS

3. NOT USING A CONDOM

SEX – YES = RAPE

23 (Chapter 12)